Klaus Weinhauer, Anthony McElligott, Kirsten Heinsohn (eds.)
Germany 1916-23

Histoire | Volume 60

Klaus Weinhauer, Anthony McElligott, Kirsten Heinsohn (eds.)
Germany 1916-23
A Revolution in Context

[transcript]

The book was kindly funded by the Fritz Thyssen Foundation.

Bibliographic Information published by the Deutsche Nationalbibliothek
The Deutsche Nationalbibliothek lists this publication in the Deutsche Nationalbibliografie; detailed bibliographic data are available in the Internet at http://dnb.d-nb.de

© 2015 transcript Verlag, Bielefeld

All rights reserved. No part of this book may be reprinted or reproduced or utilized in any form or by any electronic, mechanical, or other means, now known or hereafter invented, including photocopying and recording, or in any information storage or retrieval system, without permission in writing from the publisher.

Cover concept: Kordula Röckenhaus, Bielefeld
Printed and bound in Great Britain by
Marston Book Services Limited, Oxfordshire

Print-ISBN 978-3-8376-2734-3
PDF-ISBN 978-3-8394-2734-7

Content

Introduction
In Search of the German Revolution
Klaus Weinhauer/Anthony McElligott/Kirsten Heinsohn | 7

VIOLENCE, STATE AND ORDER

The Crowd in the German November Revolution 1918
Mark Jones | 37

"Incapable of Securing Order?"
The Prussian Police and the German Revolution 1918/19
Nadine Rossol | 59

Labour Conflict and Everyday Violence as "Revolution"?
Barcelona, 1919-23
Florian Grafl | 83

COMMUNICATION AND IMAGINARIES

Gender and the Imaginary of Revolution in Germany
Kathleen Canning | 103

Fear of Revolution
Germany 1918/19 and the US-Palmer Raids
Norma Lisa Flores | 127

German Defeat in World War I, Influenza and Postwar Memory
Oliver Haller | 151

SUBJECTIVITIES AND SOCIAL MOVEMENTS

Activist Subjectivities and the Charisma of World Revolution
Soviet Communists Encounter Revolutionary Germany, 1918/19
Gleb J. Albert | 181

'Moral Power' and Cultural Revolution
Räte geistiger Arbeiter in Central Europe, 1918/19
Ian Grimmer | 205

Simultaneity of the Un-simultaneous
German Social Revolution and Polish National Revolution
in the Prussian East, 1918/19
Jens Boysen | 229

Commentary
Stefan Berger | 251

Commentary
Dirk Schumann | 257

About the Authors | 263

Introduction
In Search of the German Revolution

KLAUS WEINHAUER/ANTHONY MCELLIGOTT/KIRSTEN HEINSOHN

The extent and meaning of the German revolution in 1918 was at the time and has been ever since, contested. On the one hand, in early November 1918, the editors of the Social Democratic *Schleswig-Holsteinische Volks-Zeitung* declared 'the revolution is on the march'. That was on 5th November. A few days later, General Groener reported to the Kaiser at Spa in Belgium, how he had 'encountered the revolution' in Berlin and that his majesty should abdicate in order to avert Russian conditions, alluding to the revolution that toppled the Romanov dynasty the previous February. At the same time, the Social Democrat Philip Scheidemann told the chancellor Prince Max von Baden that Wilhelm had to go in order to secure the October reforms and save the country from bolshevism. After the Kaiser's flight to neutral Holland (less in fear of the crowds and more likely to avert the grasp of the victors), Gustav Noske, at that point, like Scheidemann, still the darling of the masses and 'crowned people's admiral' of Kiel by the mutinous sailors, announced the following Monday (11 November) that the revolution had been achieved; it could thus pass into history together with the dethroned Kaiser. The transfer of political power and its broadening through an expanded franchise that would validate reform through the mechanism of orderly legal institutions, as intimated by Scheidemann's concern for the safeguarding of the October constitutional reforms, constituted for these actors the revolutionary act.[1]

On the other hand, there were voices claiming that the revolution had not gone far enough and so it was far from over. Within a week of Noske's an-

---

1 Anthony McElligott, Rethinking the Weimar Republic: Authority and Authoritarianism 1916-1936, London 2014, 15-28.

nouncement, Rosa Luxemburg published an article in *Die Rote Fahne* under the heading: 'The Beginning' in which she called for the broadening and deepening of the revolution. 'The revolution has begun', she wrote, 'Not jubilation for that achieved; not triumph over the defeated enemy are appropriate [at this time], but the toughest self-criticism and iron discipline over the energy needed to continue the work started.'[2] There were other radical voices, not least those of the Independent Socialist Emil Barth and Richard Müller, the leader of the revolutionary Greater Berlin Workers' and Soldiers' Council. These radicals had a fundamentally different vision for Germany than that of the Social Democrats and their liberal allies. They sought a thorough-going transformation of Germany's political and economic institutions that would spell the end of the capitalist era and the inauguration of the 'dictatorship of the proletariat'.

That a revolution of sorts had occurred was nonetheless acknowledged by contemporaries. Hermann Müller, who would twice serve as chancellor at the head of coalition governments, recounted in his memoirs published little more than a dozen years later, how on 5 November when Admiral Souchon gave up command of Kiel, a sailor's mutiny transformed into a revolution.[3] Ernst Troeltsch noted that 'revolution hung in the air' already since the winter of 1917. He was unambiguous in his verdict that in November 'the long feared and expected revolution had broken out'. But he also noted that it was over as soon as it had taken place. Writing barely three weeks after the 9 November, Troeltsch used the past tense: 'Germany had its victorious revolution as once England, America and France had'; but unlike these revolutions, Germany's had been a quiet affair, with hardly any bloodshed spilled.[4] His well-known contemporary, Harry Graf Kessler, the 'red count', also noted the brevity and muteness of the revolution.[5] By mid-November, Kessler observed what he believed to be the *unrevolutionary* character of the revolution: 'The first Sunday *after* the revolution. Late in the afternoon large crowds of walkers crossed [Unten den] Linden to the Marstall to look at the marks on the buildings left by gunfire. All were very peaceful in their petty-bourgeois curiosity [...].'[6] And when he returned from Poland in mid-

---

2 Rosa Luxemburg, 'Der Anfang', Die Rote Fahne, 18 Nov. 1918, reprinted in: Karl-Egon Lönne (ed.), Die Weimarer Republik 1918-1933, Darmstadt 2002, 79.
3 Hermann Müller, Die November Revolution. Erinnerungen, Berlin 1931, 16, 24.
4 Ernst Troeltsch, Spektator-Briefe. Aufsätze über die deutsche Revolution und die Weltpolitik 1918/22, edited by H. Baron, Tübingen 1924 (reprint Aalen 1966), 13, 19.
5 Harry Graf Kessler, Tagebücher 1918-1937, Politik, Kunst und Gesellschaft der zwanziger Jahre, edited by Wolfgang Pfeiffer-Belli, Frankfurt am Main 1961, (4th printing 1979), 10 November 1918, 26-27.
6 Kessler, 17 November 1918, 35. Emphasis added.

December, there was no sign of the revolution at all! Looking back half a century, Carl Zuckmayer, who at the time was a 22 year old lieutenant, there was not a revolution at all, merely a collapse which had fleeting transitory revolutionary moments, nothing more.[7] Nevertheless, for eleven year old Sebastian Haffner, the revolution was real and at the same time full of contradiction and confusion. 'It was never clear what exactly it was all about. One could not be enthusiastic. One could not even understand.'[8]

Haffner's memory of the revolution was partly conditioned by his bourgeois socialisation and partly by the fact that as a young boy he had a childish excitement for war and what he imagined as Germany's invincibility. And although Haffner was a child at the time, his memory expresses the sentiment of many from his class background.[9] The revolution was the Janus-face of an imagined good world: it brought disorder and was disorientating. Such perceptions ran through parts of German society, even though many contemporary accounts, such as those found in the diaries of Thomas Mann, Käthe Kollwitz and Victor Klemperer, as well as Kessler and Troeltsch, while capturing the heady atmosphere of 'revolutionary days' at the same time caution against over-stating revolution *á la russe*.

INTERPRETING THE GERMAN REVOLUTION

Not only are revolutions always contested, their histories too. In the case of the German revolution its history was challenged from the outset, and with the notable exception of Arthur Rosenberg's two-volume work on the revolution and republic,[10] remained largely forgotten or ignored after 1945.[11] In the decades

---

7 Carl Zuckmayer, Als wär's ein Stück von mir. Horen der Freundschaft, Frankfurt am Main 2006 (orig. 1966), 305. Nevertheless, the description that follows in his autobiography conveys the turmoil and élan of these revolutionary days.
8 Sebastian Haffner, Geschichte eines Deutschen. Die Erinnerungen 1914-1933, Munich 2000, 33.
9 See the autobiographical sketches collected in Rudolf Pörtner (ed.), Alltag in der Weimarer Republik. Erinnerungen an eine unruhige Zeit, Düsseldorf etc. 1990.
10 See Arthur Rosenberg, Die Entstehung der deutschen Republik 1871-1918, Berlin 1928; id., Geschichte der Deutschen Republik, Karlsbad 1935.
11 For a succinct summary of the current state of research see Eberhard Kolb/Dirk Schumann, Die Weimarer Republik, Munich 2013, especially 166-178; also Nils Freytag: Steckengeblieben - Vernachlässigt - Vergessen. Neuerscheinungen zur Revolution 1918/19 (Rezension), in: sehepunkte 13 (2013), Nr. 3 [15.03.2013], URL:

following the war, the revolution remained obscured by international politics where historical interpretation played a role. In these years research on revolution was never a widely discussed topic among West German historians. For example, at the biannual meeting of the German historians in 1964, the panel on 'The Problem of the Councils in the Creation of the Weimar Republic' attracted much less controversy than the panel 'German War Aims in the First World War' where Fritz Fischer defended his provocative theses on the German responsibility for the outbreak of World War I.[12] The dominant interpretation of the revolution of 1918/19 was that of a successful struggle against bolshevism; Walter Tormin's balanced study of the role of the council movement was clearly a minority position.[13]

Nonetheless, a swathe of studies based on archival research by a rising generation of historians and political scientists emerged from the late 1950s. This generation, which included Erich Matthias, Peter von Oertzen, Eberhard Kolb, and later Reinhard Rürup, Ulrich Kluge, while critically engaging with the interpretative model put forward by authors from the German Democratic Republic, promoted the idea of the revolution as a 'missed opportunity'. Their studies set the scene until the late 1980s in which competing paradigms of 'two opportunities' prevailed: a conservative republic based on an alliance between social democrats, free trade unions and old powers of military and economy versus social democracy based on the council movement. Little original research was produced while the embers of the revolution of 1918/19 were raked over.[14] The

---

http://www.sehepunkte.de/2013/03/21766.html (20.10.2014); Karl Christian Führer et al. (eds.), Revolution und Arbeiterbewegung in Deutschland 1918-1920, Essen 2013; for a well-balanced summary of interpretations see Andreas Wirsching, Die paradoxe Revolution 1918/19, in: Aus Politik und Zeitgeschichte 58 (2008), H. 50/51, 6-12.

12 See Bericht über die 26. Versammlung deutscher Historiker in Berlin. 7. bis 11. Oktober 1964, Stuttgart 1965, 42-51 and 63-72.

13 See Walter Tormin, Zwischen Rätediktatur und sozialer Demokratie: Die Geschichte der Rätebewegung in der deutschen Revolution, Düsseldorf 1954; see for the following Wolfgang Niess, Die Revolution von 1918/19 in der deutschen Geschichtsschreibung. Deutungen von der Weimarer Republik bis ins 21. Jahrhundert, Berlin/Boston 2013, 552-573.

14 Ulrich Kluge, Die deutsche Revolution 1918/1919. Staat, Politik und Gesellschaft zwischen Weltkrieg und Kapp-Putsch, Frankfurt am Main 1985 still stands out as the best book-length summary of the main interpretations and research results up to this point. As a short summary see also Volker Ullrich, Die Revolution von 1918/19, Munich 2009. In the early 1990s some senior researchers like Reinhard Rürup (1993) and

ensuing historical debates that focused on the binary poles of 'councils bolshevism' versus parliamentary democracy, recalled the very same positions adopted prior, during and after the revolution of 1918/19 itself.[15] Looking back on the debates up to the 1980s, Wolfgang Niess probably captures a kernel of truth when he states 'research on the revolution clearly is becoming increasingly politically suspect.'[16]

Part of the problem with interpretation, at least until the late 1980s, had to do with the ebb and flow of the revolution itself. Curiously, most historians were agreed on the three phases that broadly made up the revolutionary period. The first phase roughly covering the months November/December 1918, when the political consolidation of new republic as a parliamentary system gained the upper hand over council based democracy; the second phase stretching from December 1918 until spring 1919, which saw the growing radicalization of the rank and file (mostly workers), who were disappointed because they had expected more democratic impulses from the revolution. This phase saw a "turn towards civil war" (Wende zum Bürgerkrieg),[17] when military forces (supported by the new political leaders) constituted a privatized internal state monopoly of physical violence thus eroding the compromise between the working-classes and military administration. At the end of this phase stood the violent suppression of the Munich Council Republic (Münchener Räterepublik) in May 1919. The third phase from April/May 1919 until May 1920, and which for some authors does not belong to the revolution proper, was discovered fairly late and is probably the least studied period. This phase was marked by a double bind process of the actions of radicalized social protest movements and the "purifying" and "cleansing" actions of the Free Corps, culminating in the smashing of the March Revolution (Märzrevolution) in the Ruhr area.

There is a case to be made for approaching the German revolution from both narrow and broader perspectives. As the cold war lost intensity the old certainties about <u>the</u> (one and only) revolution became even more obvious, and interpretations of the (periodization of the) German revolution more flexible. Already

---

Eberhard Kolb (1993) published some comments on the interpretative aspects of the revolution, see the literature listed in: Niess. See also the source based case study Peter Brandt/Reinhard Rürup (eds.), Volksbewegung und demokratische Neuordnung in Baden 1918/19. Zur Vorgeschichte und Geschichte der Revolution, Sigmaringen 1991.

15 See Niess, 281, 563; Peter Lösche, Der Bolschewismus im Urteil der deutschen Sozialdemokratie, Berlin 1967.
16 Niess, 565.
17 Kluge, 83.

in 1983, Peter von Oertzen put forward a broader time frame for periodization, which stretched from October 1918 until October 1923, but his proposal went more or less unheard.[18] Recent research on the war years now allows us to move in the other direction chronologically and to seek the origins of the revolution in the mid-years of the war itself. The justification for this is not only the presence of the growing social protest movement but the existence of an ideologically-delineated political movement that provided a revolutionary language to social unrest, at the same time articulating this in its program for power. Moreover, changes in historians' approaches to the period, especially with the cultural-turn, necessitate a rethinking of the revolution.[19]

This new interest in the revolution is long overdue. The various methodological impulses that fed into the historiography over the past three decades broadening and enriching our understanding of the past, largely by-passed scholarship on the revolution. Notably the 'history of everyday' (Alltagsgeschichte) has been conspicuous by its absence in the main studies on the revolution 1918/19. Similarly, the turn from the history of the labor movement (Arbeiterbewegungsgeschichte) to Labor History (Arbeitergeschichte) also missed the historiography of the revolution.[20] This omission was not only on the side of the researchers of the

---

18 Peter von Oertzen, Arbeiterbewegung, Arbeiterräte und Arbeiterbewußtsein in der Deutschen Revolution 1918/19, in: Helga Grebing (ed.), Die deutsche Revolution 1918/19. Eine Analyse, Berlin 2008, 68–102 (Orig. 1983). See also the periodization elaborated by Klaus Tenfelde, Massenbewegungen und Revolution in Deutschland 1917-1923, in: Helmut Konrad/Karin Maria Schmidlechner (eds.), Revolutionäres Potential in Europa am Ende des Ersten Weltkrieges. Die Rolle von Strukturen, Konjunkturen und Massenbewegungen, Vienna 1991, 9–15; see also Boris Barth, Dolchstosslegenden und politische Desintegration. Das Trauma der deutschen Niederlage im Ersten Weltkrieg 1914-1933, Düsseldorf 2003, 202-212; still important is Pierre Broué, The German Revolution 1917-1923, Chicago 2006 (orig. 1971).

19 Alexander Gallus (ed.), Die vergessene Revolution von 1918/19, Göttingen 2010. See also his Revolutions (Germany), in: Ute Daniel et al. (eds.), 1914-1918 online. International Encyclopedia of the First World War, Berlin 2014-10-08.

20 Franz-Josef Brüggemeier, Leben vor Ort. Ruhrbergleute und Ruhrbergbau 1889-1919, Munich 1983; Michael Grüttner, Arbeitswelt an der Wasserkante. Sozialgeschichte der Hamburger Hafenarbeiter 1886-1914, Göttingen 1984; Karin Hartewig, Das unberechenbare Jahrzehnt. Bergarbeiter und ihre Familien im Ruhrgebiet 1914-1924, Munich 1993; Thomas Welskopp, Arbeit und Macht im Hüttenwerk. Arbeits- und industrielle Beziehungen in der deutschen und amerikanischen Eisen- und Stahlindustrie von den 1860er bis zu den 1930er Jahren, Bonn 1994; Klaus Weinhauer, Alltag und

revolution. The problem was also that most of these studies, which had much to say on every day history (at the shop floor and in the neighborhood) and on collective action, did not explicitly address the revolution, unlike those studies of the Russian revolution.[21] Few historians took up the challenge of Wolfgang Mommsen to study the importance of the "social protest movement of high intensity and considerable extent" which shaped the revolution.[22] With few exceptions (notably, Erhard Lucas[23]), the social and ideological currents and subjectivities that fed into these local protests were ignored and instead approached vaguely as mass movements (Massenbewegungen).[24]

Arbeitskampf im Hamburger Hafen. Sozialgeschichte der Hamburger Hafenarbeiter 1914-1933, Paderborn etc. 1994.

21 Stephen A. Smith, Red Petrograd. Revolution in the factories, Cambridge etc. 1986; Diane Koenker/ William Rosenberg, Strikes and Revolution in Russia, 1917, Princeton 1989; see also Leopold Haimson/Charles Tilly (eds.), Strikes, Wars, and Revolutions in an International Perspective. Strike waves in the late nineteenth and early twentieth centuries, Cambridge 1989.

22 Wolfgang J. Mommsen, Die deutsche Revolution 1918-1920. Politische Revolution und soziale Protestbewegung, in: Geschichte und Gesellschaft 4 (1978), 362–391, here 390.

23 Erhard Lucas, Arbeiterradikalismus. Zwei Formen von Radikalismus in der deutschen Arbeiterbewegung, Frankfurt a.M. 1976. His three volume study Märzrevolution (Frankfurt 1970-1978), however, is nearly unreadable, as the author does not formulate guiding theses while he more and more gets lost in his sources where he tries to find a 'real' reality. Among the numerous local studies still important are Peter Kuckuk, Bremer Linksradikale bzw. Kommunisten in der Militärrevolte im November 1918 bis zum Kapp-Putsch im März 1920, PhD Hamburg 1970; id. (ed.), Die Revolution 1918/19 in Bremen. Aufsätze und Dokumente, Bremen 2010; Volker Ullrich, Die Hamburger Arbeiterbewegung vom Vorabend des Ersten Weltkriegs bis zur Revolution 1918/19 Hamburg 1976; Dieter Schott, Die Konstanzer Gesellschaft 1918-1924. Der Kampf um Hegemonie zwischen Novemberrevolution und Inflation, Konstanz 1989.

24 The main study is Gerald D. Feldman et al., Die Massenbewegungen der Arbeiterschaft in Deutschland am Ende des Ersten Weltkrieges (1917-1920), in: Politische Vierteljahresschrift 13 (1972), 84–105; see also Gerald D. Feldman, Socio-economic Structures in the Industrial Sector and Revolutionary Potentialities, 1917-1922, in: Charles L. Bertrand (ed.), Revolutionary Situations in Europe, 1917-1922: Germany, Italy, Austria-Hungary, Montreál 1977, 159-169; and Friedhelm Boll, Massenbewegungen in Niedersachsen 1906-1920. Eine sozialgeschichtliche Untersuchung zu den unterschiedlichen Entwicklungstypen Braunschweig und Hannover, Bonn 1981; see

Finally, missing from the German debates on the revolution 1918/19 was its wider international context. Apart from reference to events in Russia a year earlier, upheavals taking place in other European regions were seldom included, let alone the revolutionary upheavals occurring globally; where a comparative approach was adopted, it was mainly by scholars working outside Germany.[25] As the foregoing discussion shows, most research in Germany was focused on the early months of the revolution until the spring 1919. Few efforts were made to intellectually connect this research to wider historical trends, for instance to the phase of worldwide turbulent upheavals between roughly 1916 and 1923; or to the erosion of colonial empires; or to the early phase of the Weimar Republic from1918/19 to the stabilization of the German currency in late 1923.[26]

Interpreting the period under consideration (1916-23) as an important period not only in European but in global history integrates three recent historiographical trends. First, we can agree with John Darwin that these years were explicitly a turbulent and decisive "great phase of upheaval".[27] Second, these years of

---

also Tenfelde, Massenbewegungen, in: Konrad/Schmidlechner (eds.), Potential, 9–15. See as pioneering studies Peter von Oertzen, Die großen Streiks der Ruhrbergarbeiterschaft im Frühjahr 1919, in: Vierteljahrshefte für Zeitgeschichte 6 (1958), 231–262; Erhard Lucas, Ursachen und Verlauf der Bergarbeiterbewegung in Hamborn und im westlichen Ruhrgebiet 1918/19, in: Duisburger Forschungen 15 (1971), 1–119; see also the early comparative study by Hans Bötcher, Zur revolutionären Gewerkschaftsbewegung in Amerika, Deutschland und England, Jena 1922.

25 See Bertrand; Francis L. Carsten, Revolution in Central Europe, 1918-1919, London 1972; Charles S. Maier, Recasting Bourgeois Europe. Stabilization in France, Germany, and Italy in the Decade after World War I, Princeton, N.J. 1975; Barrington Moore, Injustice. The Social Basis of Obedience and Revolt, White Plains 1978; James E. Cronin/Carmen Sirianni (eds.), Work, Community, and Power. The Experience of Labor in Europe and America, 1900-1925, Philadelphia 1983; Hans A. Schmitt (ed.); Neutral Europe between War and Revolution 1917-23, Virginia1988; Helmut Konrad/Karin M. Schmidlechner (eds.); Chris Wrigley (ed.), Challenges of Labour. Central and Western Europe, 1917-1920, London etc. 1993.

26 Klaus Tenfelde in his brief 1991 summary Massenbewegungen und Revolution in Deutschland 1917-1923 mentions the inflation as an important problem which influenced the course of revolution. Due to the lack of explicit research he did not find a way to integrate the inflation explicitly into the history of the revolution in Germany. See now Martin Geyer, Verkehrte Welt. Revolution, Inflation und Moderne: München 1914-1924, Göttingen 1998.

27 John Darwin, After Tamerlane. The rise and fall of global empires, London etc. 2008, 402.

upheaval must be embedded into a broader time frame in order to make sense of them. They come at the end of an unique epoch of *relative* peace in Europe stretching from circa 1814 to 1914 while "the big excesses of violence" happened mainly outside Europe: in the colonies, in the US, China, Mexico; this is not to understate the intense waves of strikes and their bloody repression in these years.[28] Third, while interstate affairs in Europe where relatively non-violent, on a global scale the intra-state relations were quite turbulent, sometimes even massively violent. As Jürgen Osterhammel has put it, the long 19th century from 1765 until the years immediately following World War I was a time of revolution.[29] In this period he identifies three revolutionary phases: 1765-1830, 1847-1865, and the Eurasian revolutions stretching from c. 1905 (Russia, Iran, Turkey) until 1917 (Russia).[30] Historical sociologist Michael Mann in his analysis of proletarian revolutions also takes 1917 as a decisive year because of the impact of the Russian revolution. In this wave of revolutions in most countries except Russia (where there was a successful revolution) workers were the "leading (though again not the sole) actors in reforming capitalism and deepening democracy, generating not revolution but ... social citizenship".[31] This phase of turbulence in which different models of citizenship were being put forward and contested, ends in 1923.

*

There is no denying, that the revolution as a political, social and cultural event altered things. In the short term, it seemed to cast the country adrift of old certainties, which could both frighten and excite. Zuckmayer's memoir is full of the latter emotion expressed through artistic experimentalism and expressionism, especially in the years up to 1924, before yielding to the cold rationalism of *Neue Sachlichkeit* as the spirit of the age. Meanwhile, the shifting landscape of interlocking and competing political practices during the eight years between

---

28 Jürgen Osterhammel, Die Verwandlung der Welt. Eine Geschichte des 19. Jahrhunderts , Munich 2009, 193. See for Latin America Stefan Rinke, Lateinamerika und der Erste Weltkrieg. Ein Drama der gesamten Menschheit, forthcoming Frankfurt/New York 2015 (Campus); id., Labour Movements, Trade Unions and Strikes (Latin America), in: Ute Daniel et al. (eds.), 1914-1918 online. International Encyclopedia of the First World War, Berlin 2014-10-05.
29 Osterhammel, 705 and 736.
30 Ibid., 777.
31 Michael Mann, The Sources of Social Power. Volume 4: Globalizations, 1945-2011, Cambridge 2013, 248.

1916 and 1923 configured the era that followed before eventually disappearing into the Moloch of the Nazi terror system. For the political right the revolution provided a discourse revolving around the twin-paradigms of the 'stab-in-the-back' and the 'November criminals'. For the radical left, the revolution had been betrayed and therefore remained to be completed; for the mass it awoke the promise of a better life to come. What was left for the next four years were the 'birth pangs' of the republic (Zuckmayer).

This sense of a new era, understood as both the beginning of something new as well as a rupture with familiar patterns, and the impact of all that, are the focus of this volume. As we have already mentioned, our concern is not with the familiar political history of the revolution, but rather with new cultural-historical questions – questions that were already intimated in the memories of the likes of the young Haffner and Zuckmayer. Both, the child and the young man, in their descriptions of war, imperial collapse and revolution expose the existential aspect that is too often missed in conventional political historical accounts of the revolution. But what about the fantasies regarding revolution and a Republican radical future, i.e. the "dreamland" of those who wished to implement and achieve lasting political and social changes?[32] What role did the experiences of disorder and insecurity play for people's perceptions of events from November 1918 on and for the course those events took?

These are the questions that underpin the contributions to this volume. And while the volume aims at presenting cultural historical perspectives on the German revolution, this does not necessarily mean a rejection of the political historical historiography of this revolution. Quite the contrary – most of the contributors to the volume take this older historiography as their starting point for formulating new questions. Ever since the international impact of the 'cultural turn' in history since the 1980s, subjectivity as an historical agent has come more prominently to the foreground; thus the time has come to study the history of the revolution with this in mind. Our aim is not only to revive the German revolution as a relevant scholarly field but also to revise its labels, not least that of 'thwarted' (steckengeglieben) or 'incomplete' (unvollständig).

This volume, therefore, is an attempt to resituate the German Revolution into a broader context of recent methodological trends, particularly those of cultural history and transnational and global studies. As we have seen above, hitherto in

---

32 The term "Traumland" (dreamland) was coined by Troeltsch, Spektator-Briefe. For the evaluation of expectations about the future and for coping with war defeat see Michael Geyer, Zwischen Krieg und Nachkrieg – die deutsche Revolution 1918/19 im Zeichen blockierter Transnationalität, in: Gallus, Revolution, 187-222. See also the contribution of Kathleen Canning in this volume.

Germany research on the revolution of 1918/19 was heavily overridden by competing political positions, which, in some respects, were not far removed from those of 1916/23. As Ulrich Kluge put it "during the 1970s referring to one source base two substantially different images of the revolutionary and the council movement emerged".[33] These highly politicized interpretations were about the potential outcomes of the revolution 1918/19. Thus it can hardly come as a surprise that research was mainly focused on state institutions, political parties and the council movement. The overwhelming majority of the studies followed political historical and less social historical perspectives, not to speak of cultural approaches to the revolution. Moreover, research on the revolution was strongly embedded in the cold war climate of the time and, in Germany at least, shaped by the antagonism towards Soviet-led communism. Taken together, this research was less a study of complex processes of revolutionary transition and a close reading of local interaction than a study of the end of the *Kaiserreich*, of the prehistory the Weimar Republic, of the Third Reich and of the West and East German State. The revolution as an object of study in its own right remained largely missing.

SOME TERMS OF REFERENCE

Before continuing, it might be useful to assert some clarity in the use of our terms of reference. The first point for clarification is that of 'revolution'; the second relates to the 'revolutionary situation'. The two are of course linked: the latter usually provides context for the former; but a revolutionary situation should not be confused for revolution.

Until the mid-1980s, few historians engaged in a thoroughgoing discussion of the key characteristics defining the German revolution. This changed in 1985 when Ulrich Kluge put forward a working definition. In his view a revolution is characterized by four elements: (i) A rupture in or discontinuity of the political system; (ii) social conflicts that were carried out violently; (iii) changes in traditional positions of power (economic, political and administrative elites); (iv) an intended and sometimes realized creation of a new political and social order.[34] With these criteria Kluge more or less echoed the dominant state of international research on revolution at that time, which was strongly biased towards structures and national patterns – human agency and culture were not at the forefront. In particular, these studies were strongly influenced by US-American sociology and

---

33 Kluge, 20.
34 See ibid., 13.

political science. Particularly influential for the study of European revolutions and social upheaval were Theda Skocpol and Louise and Charles Tilly.[35] Skocpol's 1979 book on modern revolutions in France, China and Russia located their origins structurally between geopolitical pressures, state regimes, social classes and insurgent movements. In a similar vein and more recently, Michael Mann in his impressive overview "The Sources of Social Power" defined a revolution as "a popular insurgent movement that overthrows a ruling regime and then transforms substantially at least three of the four sources of social power - ideological, economic, military and political".[36]

Echoing the earlier studies in a collection of essays edited by Charles Bertrand, Charles Tilly has recently restated that full revolutions have to combine two elements: a revolutionary situation and a revolutionary outcome. In a revolutionary situation there are "at least two centers of power" which not only claim to have command over a "significant coercive force" but also claim "exclusive control over the state". A revolutionary outcome is characterized by a) a transfer of power over the state in which is now ruled b) a "largely new group of people".[37] In some respects, these approaches of the late twentieth century were already anticipated by Zuckmayer who failed (at least in his memoir) to recognise a revolution in the events of November 1918, because for him there was neither a mass movement, nor an organised revolt, nor a victorious revolutionary party. While the historical record challenges his first observation, he was probably right about the latter two key ingredients.

These approaches, conditioned by social and political structural analysis can be useful to the historian of the German Revolution, but they have their limitations once the social and political terrain is left behind for cultural territory. After all, was not the revolution also a 'media event,' a historical event that in part had been created, even manufactured, by means of reports and news items as they were generated?[38]

A look at perceptions and experiences on the one hand, and media and public processes of communication on the other hand, opens a window onto a better understanding of the field of emotions and the imaginary that determined peo-

---

35 Louise and Charles Tilly, The Rebellious Century. 1830-1930, Cambridge, Mass. 1975; Theda Skocpol, States and Social Revolutions. A comparative analysis of France, Russia, and China, Cambridge/New York 1979.
36 Mann, Vol 4, 246.
37 Charles Tilly, Contentious Performances, Cambridge etc. 2008, 126; for Bertrand see footnote 24.
38 This question is also raised by Axel Schildt, Der lange November – zur Historisierung einer deutschen Revolution, in: Gallus, Revolution, 223-244, here 235.

ple's actions; anxiety and fear, hope and idealism, as well as mistaken interpretations due to lack of experience and knowledge, all counted towards crystallizing not only individual subjectivity but the collective subjectivity of the revolution itself. Nearly all diarists and memoirists from that period suggest the importance of their subjective interpretations of historical events as factors shaping the readiness – or not – to become politically active and involved. As Peter Fritzsche has emphasized, the months October to December 1918 were a crucial time when many, even conservatives, harbored the hope that the collapse of the old order could lead onward and upward to something new and positive.[39] But as history would show, for a generation of Germans looking back on November 1918, the defining moment was an armistice that soon transformed into unconditional capitulation. Looking back on these events, their experiences became over laden by a memory tainted by the shock of defeat, and for them, this defeat and the revolution became inextricably linked.[40]

These hopes burned brightly among supporters of the revolution, and historians have sometimes underestimated their driving force for energizing social movements. Moreover, the power of the imaginary, of hope or of anxiety, was also significantly manifest in the perceptions in other countries in Europe and overseas as events unfolded in Germany. From this broader perspective, the revolution also had an impact far beyond German domestic policy – not just in terms of foreign policy, as a partial process bound up with the German military defeat in the war,[41] but also culturally: as a kind of 'dreamland' for revolutionaries; or as a time of mounting insecurity for those who had no explicit political ambitions; or even as a kind of spectral monstrous nightmare instilling fear in conservatives and monarchists across the world.

Today there are an increasing number of culturally sensitive international studies on revolutions, on collective action (social movements, strikes, social protest, food riots), on state building and on (political) violence. Any discussion of revolution cannot avert dealing with the state and its institutions. If we look for other innovative scholarly fields which can give research on the revolution 1918/19 a more culturally informed direction we find interesting impulses in newer studies on state power and in recent research on urban violence. As the

---

39 Peter Fritzsche, Breakdown or Breakthrough? Conservatives and the November Revolution, in: Larry Eugene Jones/James Retallack (eds.), Between Reform, Reaction and Resistance. Studies in the History of German Conservatism from 1789 to 1945, Oxford 1993, 299–328.
40 See Wolfgang Schivelbusch, Die Kultur der Niederlage. Der amerikanische Süden 1865, Frankreich 1871, Deutschland 1918, Berlin 2001.
41 Geyer, Krieg.

state plays an important role in revolution it must be mentioned here that a state is neither a fixed entity, nor is it a reality in itself – it is a construction, in which social and cultural perceptions play a highly important role, which have often been neglected. As Wolfgang Reinhard reminds us quite simply, "nobody has ever seen the state". There are only the activities of its institutions or state symbols which can be perceived and interpreted.[42]

Partly influenced by the seminal studies by Edward P. Thompson, Eric Hobsbawm, and George Rudé,[43] many of these newer studies follow an understanding of culture as a set of shared beliefs, meanings attitudes, values and symbols. Thus authors like Lynn Hunt, Arlette Farge, Eric Selbin and Francesa Polletta place a strong emphasis on culture, patterns of communication and on perceptions. They remind us that "revolutions are fundamentally about people." While Hunt investigates the new political culture of the French revolution, Farge focuses on the important role of rumors, Selbin and Polletta pay attention to stories people tell during and about revolutions and how [revolutionary] subjectivities are shaped. These stories provide access to symbolic politics, collective memory and the social and cultural context of politics - on a local as well as on a global level, which otherwise might remain hidden to the cursory eye.[44]

Scholarly approaches to the German Revolution can learn a lot from such studies, as indeed Roger Chickering's great book on Freiburg, but also the work of Ute Daniel and Belinda Davis in their studies of women in war-time protests demonstrate.[45] Approaches to 'revolutionary' violence (more of which below)

---

42 Wolfgang Reinhard, Geschichte der Staatsgewalt. Eine vergleichende Verfassungsgeschichte Europas von den Anfängen bis zur Gegenwart, Munich 1999, 18.

43 Edward P. Thompson, The Making of the English Working Class, London 1963; Eric Hobsbawm, Primitive Rebels. Studies in Archaic Forms of Social Movement in the 19th and 20th Centuries, Manchester 1959; George Rudé, The Crowd in the French Revolution, Oxford 1959.

44 Eric Selbin, Stories of Revolution in the Periphery, in: John Foran et al. (eds.), Revolution in the Making of the Modern World. Social Identities, Globalization, and Modernity, Milton Park, Abingdon etc. 2008, 130–147, 130 (quote) and 144; Eric Selbin, Revolutions in the Real World. Bringing Agency Back in, in: John Foran (ed.), Theorizing Revolutions, London/New York 1997, 123–136, here 132, Francesca Polletta et al., The Sociology of Storytelling, in: Annual Review of Sociology 37 (2011), 109-131; Lynn Hunt, Politics, Culture, and Class in the French Revolution, Berkeley 1984.

45 Roger Chickering, The Great War and Urban Life. Freiburg 1914-1918, Cambridge 2007; Ute Daniel, Arbeiterfrauen in der Kriegsgesellschaft. Beruf, Familie und Politik im Ersten Weltkrieg, Göttingen, 1989, translated as The War from Within, German Working-Class Women in the First World War, Oxford/New York, 1997; Belinda

can take much from recent innovative studies on physical violence that interpret it as a pattern of communication that was frequently determined by communal and spatial factors. This approach does not interpret space as a mere container in which violence occurs. Rather, following Henri Lefèbvre in particular, space is understood as a relational concept which shapes and is shaped by human actions. Space integrates urban practices (lived), perceptions/concepts (perceived), and symbolically constructed (conceived) elements. With these culturally informed insights in mind in what follows we focus on three key aspects of revolutions: violence, state and order (1); communication and imaginaries[46] (2); subjectivities and social movements (3).[47]

Our starting point appears as an obvious assumption, namely: revolutions are locally based collective confrontations in which social movements and crowds are centrally involved. These local collective conflicts are transnationally influenced and in turn have their own transnational, transregional and translocal repercussions. They are enacted in several gendered arenas stretching from formal political institutions (parliament) to streets and public places. Revolutions sometimes can turn violent. Revolutions are shaped by overlapping gendered conflicts about the state, about local as well as nation-wide order, about subjectivities, about related gendered imaginaries (fear, anxiety, security) and about social practices. Obviously, revolutions are also about re-ordering time, space and the future. The interpretative framework of this volume starts from the assumption that 1916 was a tipping point for the intensification of protests, riots, uprisings and even revolutions.[48] In 1916 violent actions shook the Ottoman Empire in Arabia, in Greece but also in Ireland and the Americas, where militants committed many violent attacks. From 1916 the perceptions of the war changed. While its prosecution totalized societies, elites drew up plans for the

---

Davis, Home Fires Burning: Food, Politics, and Everyday Life in World War I, Berlin/New York 2000.

46 We prefer the term "imaginary" to the term "imagination". Imaginaries focus much more on the socio-cultural context than on individual feelings etc.

47 See Klaus Weinhauer/Dagmar Ellerbrock, Perspektiven auf Gewalt in europäischen Städten seit dem 19. Jahrhundert, in: Informationen zur modernen Stadtgeschichte 2/2013, 5–20; Katharina Inhetveen, Gewalt in ihren Deutungen. Anmerkungen zu Kulturalität und Kulturalisierung, in: Österreichische Zeitschrift für Soziologie 30 (2005), 28–50; also as an early study Edward P. Thompson, The moral economy of the English crowd in the eighteenth century, in: Past & Present 50 (1971), 76–136.

48 Donald Bloxham et al., Europe in the World. Systems and cultures of violence, in: Donald Bloxham/Robert Gerwarth (eds.), Political violence in twentieth-century Europe, Cambridge 2011, 11–39.

creation of a post war reordering of the national landscape. On the home front in national states and in empires food protests intensified,[49] and the dissatisfaction with a state grew as, on the one hand, it became more and more centralized and involved in organizing the war effort, while on the other hand it became obvious that in many countries the state was unable to deliver the goods for the nutrition of wide segments of the populace. In Germany already in 1916 a wish for peace overlapped with protests against state-military repression. These trends intensified in 1917 when news about the revolution in Russia and the important role industrial workers had played.[50] Thus the unity of the home front slowly began to erode. Most authors agree that this 'era of unrest' triggered by social movements comes to an end around 1923.[51] What then followed in the decade from the later 1920s can be interpreted as an 'era of authoritarian assertion' as states everywhere expanded and tightened their grip on society.

VIOLENCE, STATE AND ORDER

Revolutions were/are not *per se* violent. Violence is/was a matter of contingency.[52] But: political violence[53] is meanwhile seen as a signifier for Weimar's

---

49 Jörn Leonhard, Die Büchse der Pandora. Geschichte des Ersten Weltkriegs, Munich 2014, 525-612.

50 See as an early study Jürgen Kocka, Klassengesellschaft im Krieg. Deutsche Sozialgeschichte 1914-1918, second, revised print, Göttingen 1978 (orig. 1973), 47f.; see also the summary by Richard Bessel, Revolution, in: Jay Winter et al. (eds.), The Cambridge History of the First World War, Vol 2: The State, Cambridge etc. 2014, 126-144; id., Germany after the First World War, Oxford 1993.

51 See as an overview Darwin. Some still important local studies which focus on revolutionary syndicalism sketch the importance of this phase (c. 1916-1923): see Ulrich Klan/Dieter Nelles, "Es lebt noch eine Flamme". Rheinische Anarcho-Syndikalisteninnen in der Weimarer Republik und im Faschismus, Grafenau-Döffingen 1986; Hartmut Rübner, Freiheit und Brot. Die Freie Arbeiter-Union Deutschlands: eine Studie zur Geschichte des Anarchosyndikalismus, Berlin 1994; see also Marcel van der Linden/Wayne Thorpe (ed.), Revolutionary Syndicalism. An international perspective, Aldershot 1990.

52 Martin Conway/Robert Gerwarth, Revolution and Counterrevolution, in: Donald Bloxham/Robert Gerwarth (eds.), Political Violence, 140-175.

53 Under the term political violence we summarize all, mostly collectively enacted forms of physical violence which were aimed at political enemies (groups, the state etc.) and/or which were in a process of communication labeled as being political.

political culture.⁵⁴ This paradox makes it worthwhile to ask when/why violence began to shape the German revolution and which forms of violence were practiced. This is a hitherto neglected field of research. These questions bring not only the groups into focus which practice violence but also the institutions of the state's monopoly of physical violence, like the police or the military.

The outbreak of revolution since 1918/19 cannot fully be explained by war weariness, longing for peace and defeat. It is highly important to add the fact that at the end of the war in the eyes of the populace of many countries the state (its personnel, its bureaucratic organization) had lost much of its former credibility and respect.⁵⁵ What in earlier studies has often been forgotten is that Germany had not only lost the war but also its colonies. This double loss affected the perception as well as the practice of state power (including the military and its leaders).⁵⁶ But even this erosion of trust in the state does not automatically lead to mass violence. Rather, as recent studies on violence have convincingly demonstrated, violence is only a very last resort people turn to; many barriers must be overcome to act violently.⁵⁷ We thus start from the double assumption that also in revolutions people do not employ violence light heartedly and that violence is never senseless. This has to be mentioned since many earlier studies on revolutions were influenced by mass psychologist thinking that 'crowd' action inevitably leads to destruction and thus to massive physical violence.

Mark Jones in his chapter to this volume interprets the revolution of 1918/19 as a 'spatial revolution', where space was not only physically occupied but also used for symbolic interactions. As he points out, in its initial stage the revolution occurred 'without the explosions of violence that so often characterize clashes between rulers and ruled'. He focuses on crowds in the naval port of Kiel where

---

54 See Dirk Schumann, Political Violence in the Weimar Republic, 1918-1933. Fight for the Streets and Fear of Civil War, New York etc. 2009 (Orig. German 2001); Benjamin Ziemann, Gewalt im Ersten Weltkrieg. Töten, Überleben, Verweigern, Essen 2013; Andreas Wirsching, Vom Weltkrieg zum Bürgerkrieg? Politischer Extremismus in Deutschland und Frankreich 1918-1933/39, Munich 1999; Bernd Weisbrod, Gewalt in der Politik. Zur politischen Kultur in Deutschland zwischen den beiden Weltkriegen, in: Geschichte in Wissenschaft und Unterricht 43 (1992), 391-404; see also the contributions in: Journal of Modern European History 1 (2003).
55 Still important for these insights is Kocka, 132-136.
56 See as overview Robert Gerwarth/Erez Manela (eds.), Empires at War, 1911-1923, Oxford 2014.
57 See Randall Collins, Entering and Leaving the Tunnel of Violence: Microsociological Dynamics of Emotional Entrainment in Violent Interactions, in: Current Sociology 61 (2012), 132–151; Inhetveen.

the revolution ignited and then moves on to analyze crowd actions in Berlin. In the tradition of Thompson, Rudé and Hobsbawm, Jones shows how crowds employed symbolic street politics to move peacefully, sometimes in a carnivalesque fashion, from the periphery of cities to their centers. Victory parades were staged during which protestors carried red flags, pointed their rifles to the ground, and in highly symbolic acts some of the revolutionaries removed officers' cockades and swords. Arguing against undifferentiated mass psychological interpretation, he works out a pattern of five different ideal types of crowds; the crowd in formation or dispersal (1); the assembly (2); the procession (3); the curious crowd (4). Only from members of the fifth ideal type "the confrontational crowd" could it be expected that when they were confronted with armed forces they might employ physical violence. Moreover Jones argues that over the course of the winter of 1918/19 the state, mainly inspired by a fear of a fusion of bolshevism and crowd action, resorted to military force in an effort to restore its control over urban spaces. Thus, as he puts it, a Republic that was "brought into existence by revolutionary crowds occupying urban spaces" sanctioned violence "against similar crowds in the same spaces in 1919 and 1920. In the end, it was the dangerous image of dirt and revolt from below that came to define how the revolution's crowds were remembered for the remainder of the Weimar era."[58]

To put it briefly: The winter months of 1918/19 marked the turning point of an up to then quite peaceful revolution. This militant military-based reoccupation of (urban) space supported the motivation to employ physical violence in collective street actions. This use of military force in domestic affairs has to be explained – was there no police to handle these tasks?

Interestingly, the history of the police and of policing in the revolution as well as during the Weimar Republic has been researched only very inadequately.[59] During the revolution the uniformed police had disappeared from the

---

58 The question of an unavoidable escalation of violence in the post-war years is studied in the dissertation project of Niels Ungruhe (Bielefeld University): Gewaltkulturen im Ruhrgebiet 1916-1923.

59 See the overview by Nadine Rossol, Beyond law and order? Police History in Twentieth-century Europe and the Search for New Perspectives, in: Contemporary European History 22 (2013), 319-330; as a monograph still important is Peter Lessmann-Faust, Die preußische Schutzpolizei in der Weimarer Republik. Streifendienst und Straßenkampf, Frankfurt am Main 2012; as a case study see Klaus Weinhauer, Protest, kollektive Gewalt und Polizei in Hamburg zwischen Versammlungsdemokratie und staatlicher Sicherheit c. 1890-1933, in: Friedrich Lenger (ed.), Gewalt in europäischen Großstädten im ersten Drittel des 20. Jahrhunderts, Munich 2013, 69-103; see for the

streets. The soldiers and workers councils established a number of improvised security organizations, often called "Sicherheitswehren" or "Volkswehren". Later dominantly middle-class based "Einwohnerwehren" were also established. Since late 1918/early 1919 the state sponsored paramilitary free corps – more information on them is given below – and employed them against workers and against their collective actions. These free corps often acted very brutally. In summer 1919 a strongly militarized Security Police (Sicherheitspolizei) was established which, instead of the old uniformed police, should fight 'bolshevist' uprisings which were deemed to be lurking everywhere, while the 'normal' police should only take care of order issues. After the intervention of the *Military Inter-Allied Commission of Control* (Interalliierte Militär-Kontrollkommission, IMKK) the Security Police had to be dissolved. In Prussia its personnel however was transferred into the newly built-up uniformed police: the Schutzpolizei.

Nadine Rossol analyzes the reform discussions on and the actions of the uniformed Prussian police in the revolution and in the early years of the Weimar Republic. There were two reasons why the police propagated reforms. On the one hand it was thought that the police had to adjust to the new political and social order. On the other hand there was a fear that through the installation of the militarized Security Police in summer 1919 the police might lose its influence on domestic security issues in the new state. This double tension supported the drive to expand police trade unions, which sometimes clashed with the state's quest for authority. Overall these early years were characterized by tensions between a state that was trying to strengthen its authority through a tough policing of strikes and upheavals and the actions of some police reformers who aimed at building a new democratic police, a new more democratic *Volkspolizei*. Her main argument is that building a reformed police aimed at having a strong institutional influence on shaping the architecture of Germany's security organizations, including cultivating a trade union culture, failed due to the state's strong quest for authority.

As we have already mentioned, in Europe, the years immediately following World War I saw many very violent actions of paramilitary forces, not only, but especially in its eastern regions. Recent research lists four factors that contributed to these conflicts.[60] (1) The legacy of the First World War: not the experience

---

broader context of gun culture Dagmar Ellerbrock, Waffenkultur in Deutschland, in: Aus Politik und Zeitgeschichte 35-37 (2014), 40-46.

60 See for the following Robert Gerwarth/ John Horne, Vectors of Violence: Paramilitarism in Europe after the Great War, 1917-1923, in: Journal of Modern History 83 (2011), 489–513; see as case studies Christine Hikel, (Un)Sicherheit. Terror, Angst

of fighting a war brutalized postwar societies, but the 'mobilizing power of defeat'.[61] (2) The direct or indirect impacts of the revolution in Russia, mainly through the perceived menace of bolshevism. Parallel to this the Russian revolution and its inherent threats led to a counterrevolutionary mobilization that bred 'a new political culture of the armed group' which promised to offer an opportunity 'to live a romanticized warrior existence' of living and fighting together in 'explosive subcultures of ultramilitant masculinity', often fueled by a rough mixture of right-wing nationalism, anti-bolshevism and anti-semitism.[62] (3) The collapse of empires and the disintegration of nation state proved to be sources for efforts to create ethnically homogenous nation states, which often initiated violent campaigns of purification and civil wars. (4) In countries which had lost the war, and where the monopoly of physical violence had been eroded and the cohesion of the state had deteriorated, the experience of defeat accelerated domestic violence.

In Germany the Free Corps can be seen as a good expression of these processes. This institution consisted of mentally tightly-knit collectives of young men who mostly had not fought in the war. The free-corps members did not accept the state's monopoly of physical violence. Rather, in a kind of militant "Selbsthilfe" (self-help) they took it into their own hands. Paramilitary violence was group based, uncontrolled and uncontrollable from above. Their actions often followed a logic of extermination and cleansing. Although paramilitary violence recently gained massive scholarly attention, until today there are no new integrative case studies on Germany which analyze the concrete interaction between these free corps and other paramilitary units and their opponents.[63]

---

und Männlichkeit in den Anfangsjahren der Weimarer Republik, in: id./Sylvia Schraut (ed.), Terrorismus und Geschlecht. Politische Gewalt in Europa seit dem 19. Jahrhundert, Frankfurt/New York 2012, 169-190; Martin Sabrow, Der Rathenaumord. Rekonstruktion einer Verschwörung gegen die Republik von Weimar, Munich 1994; id., Die verdrängte Verschwörung. Der Rathenaumord und die deutsche Gegenrevolution, Frankfurt am Main 1999; Klaus Gietinger, Der Konterrevolutionär. Waldemar Pabst – eine deutsche Karriere, Hamburg 2009.

61 Ibid., 491; see also footnote 54.
62 See for the quotes Gerwarth/Horne, Vectors, 498; for the broader context Robert Gerwarth/John Horne (eds.), War in Peace. Paramilitary violence in Europe after the Great War, Oxford 2013.
63 See the case studies in Gerwarth/Horne (eds.), War; and as a summary see Barth, 229-254. There also is a dissertation project of Jan-Philipp Pomplun (Berlin) on Freecorps in Germany http://www.walther-rathenau-kolleg.de/kollegiatinnen/jan-philipp-pomplun (8 August 2014).

There were European countries where physical violence was endemic although these countries had not participated in the war. As *Florian Grafl* vividly demonstrates, although Spain remained neutral during World War I, Barcelona, one of its most important industrial and port cities, gives an example how after the First World War a climate of fierce violence developed. Grafl stresses that in the imaginary repertoire of its politicians Barcelona always was on the verge of revolution. This assumption rested on four factors: Intensified Catalan regionalism challenged the unity (and thus the power) of the Spanish Central state (all the more as in the war some 40,000 Catalans had fought on the sides of the allies); anarchism threatened the conservative political system and violent interactions shaped the conflicts between employers and workers – not only at the shop floor but also in public. Moreover, the inefficient, undermanned, disorganized, corrupt und ill-paid police (*Guardia Civil*) was not able to maintain law and order. What Grafl also underlines is that employers and the political elites had themselves strongly contributed to these violent confrontations with their efforts to form private security forces, with their inability to reform the corrupt and ineffective police and also with their stubborn resistance towards corporate regulation of industrial relations and social political measures. Already in these years in Barcelona there was both a lack of compromise and a quest for purification which later shaped the mass killings of the Franco era.[64]

Grafl's contribution demonstrates that the First World War also affected the authority of nation states which had not directly participated in the fighting, especially when seen against the background of a crumbling colonial empire. Even there the impulses towards self-determination, the crisis of food supply and distribution during the war and workers' post-war efforts to increase their wages and to expand democracy to the shop-floor contributed to an erosion of trust in the state. These negative perceptions were reinforced when it became obvious that also in Spain the state was not able to put its monopoly of physical violence effectively into practice. Among the middle classes and the political elites this multifold threat was intensified by an acute fear of Bolshevik (in Spain: anarchist)-influenced revolution.

---

64 Helen Graham et al., Review Forum on the book written by Paul Preston, The Spanish Holocaust. Inquisition and extermination in twentieth-century Spain, London 2012, in: Journal of Genocide Research 16 (2014), 139–168.

COMMUNICATION AND IMAGINARIES

As we intimated earlier in this introduction, revolutions are shaped by intensified processes of communication. Not only media reports but also orally transmitted stories and rumors spread the news of a coming change. With the news came hopes and positive expectations about the future but also complex fears and anxieties.

In the dominant research on the German revolution these processes of communication, the related emotions and imaginaries are only mentioned in passing. As one recent study of rumors and patterns of communication, however, underlines, revolutions are strongly influenced by them.[65] In early November 1918, the military unsuccessfully tried to shield Berlin from incoming news by blocking access to railway stations and by cutting private telephone and telegraph communications. This in turn stimulated the production and distribution of leaflets and other informally printed materials and intensified the spread of rumors, which in turn grew steadily more dramatic. All these processes contributed to a further erosion of the authority of the state. This was the hour of informal meetings and discussion groups eager to collect all available information. As one author has put it: "(T)his demonstrative curiosity proved to be something like an unintended plebiscite against the existing order as it questioned the continuance of the latter".[66] Such patterns of informal communication were not the sole preserve of those who welcomed the revolution. In the winter of 1918/19 fear of bolshevism was widespread among the ruling elites as well as among social democrats.[67] Moreover, among soldiers and free-corps members rumors existed about planned anti-military insurrections of the left, about a clandestine, omnipresent and well-equipped red army or about the coming of a second revolution.[68]

---

65 Florian Altenhöner, Kommunikation und Kontrolle. Gerüchte und städtische Öffentlichkeiten in Berlin und London 1914/18, Munich 2008, 291-301; more general is Jörg Requate, Medien und Öffentlichkeitsstrukturen in revolutionären Umbrüchen. Konstanten und Veränderungen zwischen der Französischen Revolution und dem Umbruch von 1989, in: Kurt Imhof et al. (eds.), Kommunikation und Revolution, Zurich 1998, 17-34. For the broader context see Thomas Mergel, Propaganda in der Kultur des Schauens. Visuelle Politik in der Weimarer Republik, in: Wolfgang Hardtwig (ed.), Ordnungen in der Krise. Zur politischen Kulturgeschichte Deutschlands 1918-1933, Munich 2007, 531-559.

66 Altenhöner, 297. See also Weinhauer, Protest.

67 See Lösche.

68 Barth, 287-290.

While there as some fine studies on female activities during the First World War,[69] we still miss gendered studies on the revolution. This is not to argue that we should only focus on women since gender is a relational concept that has to include masculinities, an aspect already broached by Klaus Theweleit in his path-breaking psycho-analytical study of the Free Corps.[70] *Kathleen Canning* in her chapter focuses on the experience, imaginary, and emotions of the 'prolonged revolutionary moment of 1918-19' in which Germany's war, defeat and revolution became inextricably entwined. Her key argument is that the revolution was a gendered 'social imaginary' which started a process of imagining the future of Germany – be it a longing for or a fear of change. Thus revolutionary circumstances led individuals and groups to dream of new opportunities and a very different social order. New actors entered the stage of politics in 1918, especially women, who gained the right to vote through the revolution, after the women's movement had fought for it since the end of the 19th century. Moreover, war and revolution influenced and changed also the traditional gender-order or, at least, many contemporaries were afraid of such a change. Canning presents material from personal sources (ego-documents) as well as art works which clearly indicate a more or less open debate on the future of gender and social order in Germany. There was, however, an absence of women in the leading institutions of the revolution, such as the 'Räte'. Canning suggests we look closer at those places and institutions where women took part actively to develop a 'new form of political subjectivity'. To become a citizen of a Republic – or to reject this offer - meant different things for men and women after 1918. A gendered perspective on the revolution and the following years is therefore necessary to understand the new gendering of politics and nationhood after the war.

The fears and anxieties of revolution after the First World War did not only affect European countries, but also US-American society. In her comparative study *Norma Lisa Flores* addresses how the images of bolshevist revolutions and uprisings in Europe influenced domestic policy in the United States. For many US-Americans, Germany was seen as a modern advanced society, if such a nation should succumb to bolshevism, it also had the potential to overrun the USA. Flores argues that both in Germany and in the United States the responses to the threat of bolshevism were fundamentally similar. Her contribution demonstrates the importance of imaginaries of threat in three aspects. First, the fear of bolshevism and of the revolution it might breed was a transnational phenomenon. Second, in the US, similar to other post-World War I societies, the fear of revolution was not only a fear of bolshevism, it was class-based. It was the fear

---

69 Daniel, Arbeiterfrauen; Davis.
70 Klaus Theweleit, Männerphantasien (2 vols), Frankfurt am Main 1977/78.

of a radical working class, its unions and strikes. Third, in the years immediately following the First World War, the tendency to purge communities of any unwanted foreigners, could not only be found in Europe, similar imaginaries and practices characterized US-society. What becomes obvious from Flores study as with Jones, is that urban settings are the main terrain where these conflicts occurred.[71]

Oliver Haller's chapter indicates the meaning of communication and perception from a very different perspective. His investigation is located in a classical field of history, namely the military history of World War I. But he re-reads the story of the German defeat in 1918 as caused by illness and misperception, in which the outcomes of the influenza pandemic played the main role. Because thousands of German soldiers suffered from a severe form of influenza in 1918, but were diagnosed only as afflicted with a common cold, it spread on the war fronts in spring and summer 1918 causing acute 'manpower difficulties' during the German offensives in the West. Nonetheless, German military leaders were not prepared to 'see' what the influenza 'really' meant to their plans, argues Haller. This misperception was led by the 'iron will' of the military leadership to start an offensive on the one hand, and by missing knowledge of the disease at that time on the other hand. Both, the will and the misperceptions, led to fatal military decisions. As Haller clearly argues, it was only after the non-successful offensive in summer 1918, conducted by sick, tired and weak men, that 'German soldiers began to surrender in large numbers' and morale declined rapidly. Hence, the German revolution had its origins probably also in so-called environmental factors, which had a transnational character.[72]

SUBJECTIVITIES AND SOCIAL MOVEMENTS

The third part of this volume focuses on a highly important collective actor in revolutions: on social movements and on subjectivities therein. Definitions of

---

71 The importance of local (mostly urban) settings in this revolution is also stressed by Weinhauer, Protest; Pierre Purseigle, Beyond and Below the Nations. Towards a comparative history of local communities at war, in: Jenny McLeod/Pierre Purseigle (eds.), Uncovered Fields. Perspectives in First World War studies, Leiden/Boston 2004, 98-123; Stefan Goebel, Cities, in: Jay Winter et al. (eds.), The Cambridge History of the First World War, Vol. 2: The State, Cambridge etc. 2014, 358-381.

72 See for an innovative discussion of the influence of ecological factors on colonial warfare John Robert McNeill, Mosquito Empires. Ecology and War in the Greater Caribbean, 1620-1914, Cambridge 2010.

social movements mainly focus on social change, on collective actors and on their networks. These studies also pay attention to patterns of communication among the members of these movements and between movements and the state.[73] The actors of social movements are often excluded from formally organized institutions (like political parties). Movement research, which mainly is conducted by social/political scientists and thus lacks explicit historical perspectives, was often influenced by structural approaches where the activists and their concrete actions only played a minor role.[74] As a consequence, knowledge about the members of social movements and about their subjectivities still is rare.[75] The contributions to this section focus on such often neglected cultural aspects of social movements.

Following a transnational perspective *Gleb Albert's* case-study looks at how the German Revolution was perceived by regional and local communist activists in the early Soviet-Union. These activists played a highly important role in the establishment of the Soviet state and in its defense against opposing forces. Active solidarity towards revolutionary movements stood at the centre of their subjectivisation[76] as "true" Bolsheviks. As the author points out, the German Revolution had an enormous importance for these activists. They were united by

---

73 See Jürgen Mittag/Helke Stadtland, Soziale Bewegungsforschung im Spannungsfeld von Theorie und Empirie, in: id. (eds.), Theoretische Ansätze und Konzepte der Forschung über soziale Bewegungen in der Geschichtswissenschaft, Essen 2014, 13-60, here 14f.; Roland Roth/Dieter Rucht, Einleitung, in: id. (eds.), Soziale Bewegungen in Deutschland seit 1945. Ein Handbuch, Frankfurt/New York 2008, 10-36; Donatella della Porta/Mario Dini, Social Movements. An introduction, Malden MA 2006; Charles Tilly/Lesley. J. Wood, Social Movements, 1768-2004, Boulder 2009. As an innovative case study still important is Ingrid Gilcher-Holtey, "Die Phantasie an die Macht". Mai 68 in Frankreich, Frankfurt am Main 1995.

74 See the critique put forward by Andreas Pettenkofer, Radikaler Protest. Zur soziologischen Theorie politischer Bewegungen, Frankfurt am Main 2010.

75 See as innovative contributions about the relationship between left intellectuals and left-wing radical social movements the publications of Detlef Siegfried: Revolution und Sozialforschung – linke Sozialwissenschaftler am Kieler Institut für Weltwirtschaft, in: Gallus, Revolution, 140-159; Das radikale Milieu. Kieler Novemberrevolution, Sozialwissenschaft und Linksradikalismus, Wiesbaden 2004; Der Fliegerblick. Intellektuelle, Radikalismus und Flugzeugproduktion bei Junkers 1914-1934, Bonn 2001.

76 In Albert's contribution subjectivisation is understood as an active and perpetual process in which a social identity is assumed that is intelligible both for him-/herself and for others.

a self-perception of "dedicated revolutionaries" for whom "world revolution" became a "charismatic idea". Their identification with revolution abroad could help bridge the manifold patterns of social isolation these party activists had to face at the local level. The revolution in Germany sparked an intense response from below: A vast number of solidarity telegrams were sent, the local press discussed the events in Germany and many activists planned to join the revolutionary struggle in Germany. The German revolution was the first significant revolution abroad after 1917. Moreover, the German working-class seemed to be a strong ally in the world-wide revolutionary struggle. This was all the more important as Germany was not any far-away country.

On a general level Gleb Albert's chapter teaches us two facts. As the Soviet and US-American case demonstrates, the German Revolution fueled imaginaries (fears and hopes) nearly on a global scale. Moreover, the social movement in the early Soviet state was not the product of centralist orders but a lively locally rooted social entity where activists' subjectivities and imaginaries were fueled by a local translation of transnationally entangled flows of ideas.[77]

Meanwhile *Ian Grimmer* goes back to the events in Germany itself. Although much research was done on the councils during the 1970s, it is surprising that one section of this social movement was neglected until recently. Grimmer presents a survey of the development of several councils of 'intellectual workers', mostly writers and publishers, in Germany in 1918/19. Leading figures, such as Kurt Hiller, searched for a cultural revolution besides a political one (as did Carl Zuckmayer who we cited above). Hiller and his followers believed they had the moral authority to accompany and lead a cultural revival of Germany after the war. Their aim was to educate the 'new people', seen as important for the stability of the new republican order. Based on Pierre Bourdieu's writings on modern intellectuals and extensive research on the council movement, Grimmer demonstrates the peculiarities of these 'intellectual' councils. On the one hand, the activists were well-known personalities with a strong self-awareness; on the other hand, they failed to unite their efforts on the national level. Very different political ideas were discussed between Berlin, Munich and Vienna, but all council members felt united in their belief of having moral authority. Similar to the social imaginary of women in the revolution studied by Canning, Grimmer states that the councils played an important role in creating 'an institutional space in

---

77 See on the often underestimated interaction of local and transnational factors the special issue of the journal Historische Anthropologie 21:1 (2013), Felix Brahm/ Angelika Epple (eds.), Lokalität und transnationale Veflechtungen, especially the article by Angelika Epple, Lokalität und die Dimensionen des Globalen. Eine Frage der Relationen, 4-25.

which men and women of letters could advance cultural reforms outside the parameters of the traditional labor movement and its parties.' Therefore the councils of intellectual workers searched for a way to act as political subjects but with the notion of intellectualism. They tried to establish an autonomous political group alongside parties and unions. It was this peculiar situation that gave the councils their 'moral power' and simultaneously fixed their political marginalization.

By the end of the war the map of Europe had changed dramatically. The old empires of Ottoman Turkey, Austria-Hungary and Russia had collapsed and were now divided into a multitude of successor states. The German empire had gone too and was under pressure from ethnic-national calls for its own 'amputations'. One of the old/new states was Poland, which [re]gained independence in 1918/1919. *Jens Boysen* demonstrates in his chapter the impact the German revolution had on this development. He investigates how the Polish national movement in the eastern parts of Prussia acted during the autumn 1918, especially in West Prussia and Posen. Boysen notes how 'the drawn-out war and the accompanying political changes created a situation in the Prussian east by which a long-term, but rather inactive tension between the ethnic Polish population and the German-Prussian state was gradually heated up and turned into a sort of postwar 'front'.' The revolutionary events in Berlin and elsewhere thus provided the community of Prussian Poles with a specific new opportunity as a power vacuum opened, and which enabled the Polish-national movement to gain more influence. Boysen, as other authors in this volume, points also to the change in perceptions: During the heyday of Prussian authoritarianism Poles and Social Democrats were both seen as enemies of the state; they perceived each other as fellows or comrades. When the Social Democrats became the leading force in German politics during the revolution, they didn't change attitudes towards the Polish national movement. Boysen states this was a misperception that created a blind spot. As a result, tensions between 'Germans' and 'Poles' rose in East Prussia as a national conflict emerged that poisoned daily life and led to violence.

CONCLUSION: THE GERMAN REVOLUTION MISSING AND FOUND

The contributions to this volume offer fresh insights into the nature of the German revolution, without claiming to have the final say on its historiography. Indeed, each of the authors would agree that many of the issues raised in this volume remain understudied and thus require further and more intensive attention. Nevertheless, we can agree on a number of points in our search for new patterns of interpretation of the German Revolution. The first point concerns the revolution's periodization: its origins broadly can be dated to 1916. The waves of social protest from 1916, created a 'revolutionary situation' or atmosphere that went unrequited by the limits of the political 'compromise' of 1918/19. This was then articulated through violent confrontation between state agencies and the crowds comprising the politicised social movements. The mobilisation of a 'revolutionary moment' in October/November, created the cultural-imaginary moment that was formed by and formed (the revolutionary) subjectivities that lasted beyond 1923.

The second and related point we hope this volume demonstrates, is the importance of cultural aspects such as perception and imaginaries. On the one hand the fear of bolshevism – however diffuse the understandings of it might have been, was strongly present in these years. Its menace did not only grow out of its potential as a political idea but was also – perhaps even mainly – related to its social movement potentialities. On the other hand, the German revolution for many 'progressive' internationalists served as a powerful beacon of hope. These hopes were not only focused on political changes, for not least among the aspirations and results of the revolution were newly-created gendered imaginaries about citizenship, about new social and cultural orders and institutions.

The third point demonstrated by this volume, is that the shape and direction of the German revolution (as any other) was strongly influenced by the collective actions of 'the crowd'. As crowds and social movements took to public spaces (streets, market places etc.) as their field of action, the police or the military as important actors inevitably were challenged. This in turn, raises questions about the perceptions and practices of the state, especially its monopoly and use of physical violence. If violence is understood as a communicative act this enables us to rethink the meaning of the evolving often violent confrontations between the crowd, social movements and the state.[78] Finally, it should be clear that studying the German revolution cannot continue without taking into account its transnational context. Revolution does not necessarily follow the strictures of political borders, but is often transgressive, as between 1916-23. Indeed, the period from the Mexican Revolution (1910), to the Irish Easter Rising (1916), to the Russian Revolution (1917) through to the Central European revolutions (1917/1920), through to the waning of revolutionary impulses in Europe by 1923/24, must be regarded as an era of transnational upheaval.

---

78 This is not to assume that there is an inevitability for collective action to lead to violence.

As the German revolution approaches its centenary, the above points (and they are not exclusive by any means) may offer some fresh impetus and possible avenues in researching its history. In this context only, we argue, is it possible to search, find and understand the German revolution. Finally, given the greater intellectual awareness today among historians of global history, newer studies of the German revolution might self-consciously leave national borders behind and employ translocal, transregional and transnational gendered and space related perspectives. This volume is only a beginning of exploring these dimensions.

This book is based on papers given at a conference the editors convened in March 2013. The meeting was generously financed by the Fritz Thyssen Foundation and by the German Research Foundation (DFG). We also received financial assistance from the Forschungsstelle für Zeitgeschichte in Hamburg (FZH) and from the Universität der Bundeswehr München. Prof. Axel Schildt and Prof. Doro Wierling also gave some very helpful comments on an early draft of the conference proposal. The publication of the volume was made possible by an important financial support from the Fritz Thyssen Foundation. The conference took place at the wonderful Cologne conference center of the Fritz Thyssen Foundation and was opened with a very friendly welcome by its director, Dr. Frank Suder. We also received organizational support from Carmen Ludwig. The many challenges of transforming the contributions into a book manuscript were professionally mastered by Trond Kuster. We are also very thankful to Christine Jüchter, Birgit Kloepfer, Annika Linnemann, and Kai Reinhardt at *transcript* for their excellent support. We cordially thank all these institutions and persons; without their support this project would have been impossible to realize!

The Crowd in the German November Revolution 1918

MARK JONES

1. INTRODUCTION

The November Revolution was a spatial revolution. As an increasingly influential body of scholarship has shown, by the end of the nineteenth century, the newly built urban world contained a richly textured set of ideas about national history, as well as regional, religious, class and gender identities.[1] In capital cities and regional centers, but also in small towns and villages, the energy invested in the creation of meaning through construction ensured that urban spaces became increasingly sensitive political stages, places were buildings, monuments, urban planning, as well as legal and cultural codes of behavior all communicated ideas that either reinforced or challenged existing hierarchies of power.[2] At the start of November 1918, this often subtle processes of political negotiation was swept away by a tidal wave of urban politics: in a short period of time, less than two to three days in most cases, large pro-revolutionary crowds formed in the symbolic centers of towns and inner cities across Germany; they

---

1 My approach to the concept of urban space is influenced by Henri Lefebvre, The production of space, trans. Donald Nicholson-Smith, Oxford 1991; Judith R. Walkowitz, City of dreadful delight. Narratives of sexual danger in late-Victorian London, London 1992; Jon Lawrence, Public space, political space, in: Jay Winter/Jean-Louis Robert (eds.), Capital Cities at War. Paris, London, Berlin, 1914-1919. Volume 2: A Cultural History, Cambridge 2007, 280-312; Matthias Reiss (ed.), The street as stage. Protest marches and public rallies since the nineteenth century, Oxford 2007; Leif Jerram, Streetlife. How cities made modern Europe, Oxford 2011.
2 Lawrence, 280-281.

assembled, marched, and paraded under the red flag, calling out for peace and a new political order. By the end of their week of protest, the crowds' presence made the streets Germany's most important political forum, the space which, more than any other, determined the decision-making of political and military elites, leading to the abdication of the monarchies and the proclamation of a Republic on 9 November; and to the signing of the Armistice at Compiègne two days later. The latter achievement was especially important: since the beginning of diplomatic exchanges between President Wilson and the German government at the start of October, many influential German decision makers had called for the rejection of Wilson's terms in favor of continued warfare; the revolutionary crowds in the streets demanding peace took that possibility away from them.[3]

Remarkably, despite the tremendous potential for things to have gone badly wrong, the spatial revolution occurred without the explosions of violence that so often characterize clashes between rulers and ruled.[4] Compared to the war that preceded it, and to the thousands of lives lost in the crescendos of violence that followed in 1919 and 1920, the November Revolution had an unexpectedly low body count. In Kiel, from 3-5 November 23 people died as a result of the revolution, while in Hamburg, the revolution cost at least another five lives.[5] In Munich, the body count was zero.[6] And in Berlin, only 15 people lost their lives – 8 of whom were buried in revolutionary funerals on 20 November 1918.[7] All in

---

3 On plans for continued warfare see Michael Geyer, Insurrectionary Warfare. The German Debate about a Levée en Masse in October 1918, in: Journal of Modern History 73 (2001), 459-527.

4 On military planning for operations against revolution in the homeland see Ernst-Heinrich Schmidt, Heimatheer und Revolution 1918: die militärischen Gewalten im Heimatgebiet zwischen Oktoberreform und Novemberrevolution, Stuttgart 1981.

5 Dirk Dähnhardt, Revolution in Kiel. Der Übergang vom Kaiserreich zur Weimarer Republik 1918/19, Neumünster 1984, 66; Kieler Zeitung, 11 Nov. 1918 Evening edition; Schleswig-Holsteinische Volks-Zeitung, 9 Nov. 1918; Schleswig-Holsteinische Volks-Zeitung, 11 Nov. 1918; Neue Hamburger Zeitung, 12 Nov. 1918 Evening edition; Neue Hamburger Zeitung, 13 Nov. 1918 Morning edition; Hamburger Nachrichten, 13 Nov. 1918 Morning edition.

6 Alan Mitchell, Revolution in Bavaria 1918-1919. The Eisner Regime and the Soviet Republic, Princeton 1965.

7 Tägliche Rundschau, 15 Nov. 1918, Bundesarchiv Berlin (BArch Berlin) R901/555724 Bl.51; Berliner Tageblatt, 21 Nov. 1918 Morning edition, BArch Berlin R901/555724 Bl.44.

all, in November 1918, *the furies* were conspicuous by their absence.[8] As the first issue of the Independent Socialist's newly founded *Freiheit* newspaper put it on 15 November 1918, 'the Empire collapsed like a skeleton lifted out of a crypt after many years of rest. A breath of air was enough. It hardly needed to be touched.'[9]

Even though the German Empire had a long history of contested street politics and the patterns of crowd behavior during the first half of November 1918 were not entirely new, the scale and speed of the transformation of political spaces was what made this successful transformation possible. In Germany up to 1914, the on-going politicization of urban space may have occasionally threatened the Imperial order, increasing fears of revolutionary violence and adding to elite disgust at the untrained politics of the *lumpenproletariat* – as manifested in the extraordinary success of Herman Poppert's novel *Helmut Harringa* – but they never fully defined it. At no point in the pre-1914 era did local, regional or imperial rulers cede power to the representatives of protesting crowds in the streets.[10] At no point in the pre-1914 world were protestors able to entirely redefine the meanings attributed to sacred national or local sites of power such as Hamburg's town hall, Munich's Wittelsbach palace or Berlin's Unter den Linden. All of this, however, is exactly what happened during the week between 4 and 9 November. It is one of the most important reasons for viewing November 1918 as a historical moment that was both *revolutionary* in terms of its historical originality and its political and cultural outcomes.

And yet, for all that the crowds that made this transition possible were a fundamental part of the revolution's history, they have never been central to its historiography. That omission is all the more striking when we recall that the 1960s and 70s, key decades in the evolution of the German Revolution's historiography, also marked the high point of the first wave of internationally influential studies of crowds in history – one of the formative subjects of social histo-

---

8   Arno Mayer, The furies. Violence and terror in the French and Russian Revolutions, Princeton 2000.
9   Freiheit, 15 Nov. 1918, BArch-Berlin R901/55625 Bl.42.
10 Richard Evans, "Red Wednesday" in Hamburg. Social Democrats, Police and Lumpenproletariat in the Suffrage Disturbances of 17 January 1906, in: Social History 4 (1979), 203-224; Thomas Lindenberger, Straßenpolitik. Zur Sozialgeschichte der öffentlichen Ordnung in Berlin 1900 bis 1914, Bonn 1995. See also Dieter Groh, Negative Integration und revolutionärer Attentismus. Die deutsche Sozialdemokratie am Vorabend des Ersten Weltkrieges, Frankfurt 1973, 135ff.

ry.[11] Although Germany did not remain immune to these international trends, a German edition of George Rudé's classic, *The Crowd in the French Revolution* was published in 1961, the concerns of the emerging field of German social history soon lay elsewhere and the work of scholars like Rudé, Eric Hobsbawn, George Lefebvre, or even E.P. Thompson never had the kind of imprint upon the revolution's historiography that might have otherwise occurred.[12] The lacuna becomes more remarkable when we think across the field of German history from 1914 to 1933: in the recent past, thanks to the work of scholars like Jeffrey Verhey and Belinda Davis, we have learnt more about the crowds that accompanied Germany's entry to the war, and about the pre-revolutionary protests that grew as hunger inspired new waves of wartime street politics, than we have about the revolutionary crowds that brought an end to the war and led to the proclamation of the Republic in Berlin on 9 November.[13] This essay is a first attempt to challenge this lacuna: it starts with one of the revolution's key crowd scenes.

2. CROWDS AND THE SPATIAL REVOLUTION IN KIEL

On 2 November 1918, in woods to the north of Kiel, trickles of sailors, sometimes as many as 30 strong, disembarked from trams before continuing on foot to an exercise field. The first 100 men to arrive included two police spies who were convincingly disguised as sailors.[14] Like the rebel sailors, they had been

---

11 For a brief introduction see: Jeffrey Verhey, The Spirit of 1914. Militarism, Myth and Mobilization in Germany, Cambridge 2000, 22-26.

12 George Rudé, Die Massen in der Französischen Revolution, trans. Angela Hillmayr and Rudolf Bischoff, Munich 1961. On German social history see Bettina Hitzer and Thomas Welskopp (eds.), Die Bielefelder Sozialgeschichte. Klassische Texte zu einem geschichtswissenschaftlichen Programm und seinen Kontroversen, Bielefeld 2010.

13 Verhey; Belinda Davis, Home Fires Burning. Food, Politics and Everyday Life in World War I Berlin, Chapel Hill 2000. See further: Roger Chickering, The Great War and Urban Life in Germany. Freiburg, 1914-1918, Cambridge 2007; Klaus Weinhauer, Protest, kollektive Gewalt und Polizei in Hamburg zwischen Versammlungsdemokratie und staatlicher Sicherheit ca. 1890-1933 in: Friedrich Lenger (ed.), Kollektive Gewalt in der Stadt. Europa 1890-1939, Munich 2013, 69-102, here 74-75.

14 Kriminal-Kommissariat 5. Betrifft heimliche Versammlung von Marinemannschaften am 2. November 1918, Kiel, 3 Nov. 1918 Bundesarchiv Militärarchiv (BA-MA) RM31/2373 Bl.11-14. On events in Kiel see further: Karl Artelt/Lothar Popp, Ur-

brought there by word of mouth. Outside the trade union building in central Kiel, a group of unnamed men told them that it was their duty to attend the meeting. Not to do so, they said, was to abandon their comrades arrested during the recent naval mutiny that had prevented the German surface fleet from crossing the north sea, where its commanders hoped that its heroism would inspire Germans to continue fighting. The location for the meeting was chosen at the last minute. The previous day, 1 November, a group of conspirators had agreed to meet inside the trade union building. However, when that location was closed to them, they tried to move to a large *local*. Its owner refused them entry and the organizers put out word that they would meet in the woods.[15]

Later that day the police spies wrote reports that captured the events that followed: while 12 men kept watch for uninvited guests from the police or army; another 100 or so stood around waiting as the trickles continued. Out of the tens of thousands of sailors and workers in Kiel who could have attended, it was eventually decided to start the meeting when the assembled crowd reached between 600 and 700. This figure was insufficient to cover the entire exercise field and when the first speaker addressed the crowd he began by lamenting that so few sailors had turned up – alone of the arrested men's comrades in the III Flotilla there were more than 5,000 sailors in Kiel who could have done so.[16] The speakers that followed, whose names are sadly not recorded, called upon the men to show solidarity with their arrested comrades. They openly debated why so few men had joined with their side and they made repeated promises that it was time to bring an end to the war and to Germany's class system. One speaker explained that many men had stayed away because of a false rumor that a Bavarian officer was present in the crowd. Others spoke up about how they could win over the crews of other ships and submarines to join in their struggle.[17] Typical of the language used at the meeting, the police agents recorded that one of the speakers told the men: 'There are still many members of the propertied classes around, and they want to continue the war. If they want to, they can take your places, continue fighting, and let themselves be shot.'[18] The final speaker concluded with the promise that they would meet again at the same place the following day and, revealing his own awareness of the importance of street politics, he

---

sprung und Entwicklung der November-Revolution 1918, Kiel, 1919; Bernhard Rausch, Am Springquelle der Revolution. Die Kieler Matrosenerhebung, Kiel 1918.
15 BA-MA RM31/2373 Bl.11.
16 Ibid. Bl.11RS; Dähnhardt, 54-55.
17 BA-MA RM31/2373 Bl.13.
18 Ibid. here Bl.12.

announced that the time had come for them to come out of hiding and show themselves in Kiel city centre.[19]

The crowd that formed on the same spot the following day, 3 November 1918, was at least 5 times larger. Estimates of its size range from 4,000 to 8,000 strong. It consisted of sailors as well as an unknown number of women and civilian males.[20] Although the composition and size of the crowd was different, the speeches were not dissimilar from the previous day. However, when the assembly ended the mood had changed: militant voices called out that it was time to march into central Kiel to free sailors held in a small prison in the Feldstraße. Others spoke out against such a drastic course of action. They warned that danger was in the air and that it was best to abandon the demonstration and make away to safety. Alarmed by what they saw and heard, the police agents did their job: they rushed a message to the military command, which in turn sent an armed patrol to protect the prison in the Feldstraße.[21] Its commander was Reserve Lieutenant Steinhäuser, an injured veteran.[22] When the police agents returned to the crowd, they then watched in horror as part of the crowd set off in the direction of the city centre – raiding the first barracks they encountered along the way.[23]

Steinhäuser's patrol of 30 to 40 soldiers cut off the protestors' path outside of the Kaisercafé, at a junction in central Kiel.[24] When the soldiers arrived at the junction, they took up a position about twenty steps behind a line of police.[25] Soon after, the soldiers heard the noise of the crowd before it came into sight under the gaslights of the old-town. At this point the police fled. Conforming to the pre-war guidelines for confrontations between the army and civilian crowds, Steinhäuser called upon the protestors to disperse before ordering his soldiers to open fire.[26] They fired their first salvo over the heads of the encroaching crowd before directing a second into the protestors' bodies: 7 protestors were killed

---

19 Ibid. Bl.14.
20 Abschrift, Kiel. 4 Nov. 1919 BA-MA RM31/2373 Bl.18-19; Kriminal-Kommissariat, Kiel, 4 Nov. 1918, Kriminal-Kommissariat BA-MA RM31/2373 Bl.20-21.
21 BA-MA RM31/2373 Bl.20-21.
22 On his injuries see Dähnhardt, 66 here footnote 299.
23 BA-MA RM31/2373 Bl.20-21.
24 BA-MA RM31/2373 Bl.21.
25 Dähnhardt, 65.
26 Vorschrift über den Waffengebrauch des Militärs und seine Mitwirkung zur Unterdrückung innerer Unruhen. 19. März 1914, Geheimes Staatsarchiv Preußischer Kulturbesitz (GStAPK) Rep.84a Nr. 2245 Rechte und Pflichten der Militärwachen usw. bei Verhaftungen und dergleichen (Gebrauch der Waffen usw.) Bd.III 1845-1918 Bl.337.

instantly, 2 more died later and another 29 were injured.[27] Steinhäuser did not escape unharmed. During the commotion that followed he was struck upon the head and shot at least once – he collapsed and was rescued by another officer and a policeman who brought him to safety in a nearby *local*.[28] But the firing was sufficient to disperse the crowd and soon after, reluctantly aided by the fire brigade, order had been restored to the city.[29] In one of the first newspaper reports about the incident, the correspondent of a local newspaper wrote that 'only some pools of blood on the road surface and several smashed show-windows in the nearby shops testify, that something sad had happened here.'[30]

The next day, 4 November 1918, the woods to the north of Kiel were quiet: no one returned to mark the spot where the previous days' demonstrations had taken place. Instead, the space of protest had moved from the periphery to the centre. That morning small groups of men moved from barracks to barracks in central Kiel where they called upon men to join their protest against the previous night's violence, before at lunchtime, sailors stationed in the naval complex at Wik, announced en masse that they no longer accepted the authority of officers.[31] The explosion of opposition from below surprised the naval commander in Kiel, Admiral Souchon, who had spent most of the war serving as commander in chief of the Ottoman Navy. Faced with increasingly obvious signs that trouble was brewing in the naval-garrison, during the previous days, his command had increased police surveillance over likely trouble spots, such as the trade union building, and it had placed extra units of armed men in visible positions in the town centre.[32] After the gunfire of 3 November, extra patrols could even be heard singing patriotic songs as they marched through the streets of central Kiel.[33] But by the afternoon of 4 November, it was clear that this public projection of military power would not suffice. Unwilling to risk the test of whether he had sufficient men willing to open fire upon the protestors, at this point, Souchon effectively surrendered. He called for representatives of the men to meet with him and agreed to release a small number of sailors from the prison later that afternoon. When they got out, the released men took centre stage in a victory

---

27 Dähnhardt, 65.
28 Steinhäuser Statement 20 Jan. 1919 BA-MA RM31/2373 Bl.23.
29 Dähnhardt, 66.
30 Kieler Neueste Nachrichten, 5 Nov. 1918.
31 Dähnhardt, 68-73.
32 Fernschreiben an Marineamt Berlin, Kiel 3 Nov. 1918 BA-MA RM31/2373 Bl.16.
33 Auszug aus dem Tagebuch einer 18-jährigen Kielerin. Abschrift von Unterlagen im Kieler Stadtarchiv durch Klaus Kuhl, (Juni 2008); Kieler Stadtarchiv in der Akte "1c.1 Geschichte Kiel, Revolution 1918." Veröffentlicht auf www.kurkuhl.de.

procession that included sailors carrying red flags and singing as they paraded through the streets of central Kiel.[34] Their power secured by the crowds in the streets, a delegation presented 14 demands to the naval commanders.[35] Later that night Souchon was replaced by Gustav Noske, the Social Democratic spokesman on military affairs, who along with state secretary Conrad Haußmann had been rushed to Kiel from Berlin that morning in order to calm the city and report back to the government. Soon after their arrival, Noske was 'crowned' *Ziviladmiral* by a large crowd of revolutionary sailors who interrupted his first public speech with loud cheering and calls for a German Republic.[36]

Of course, Kiel, the birthplace of the revolution, has a special place in its history. But the events that took place there from 2 – 5 November were not entirely unique: as the protest spread across Germany from 5 – 9 November, crowd behavior followed a similar pattern – with the exception of a handful of contested Polish-German cities in the east. When the first protests occurred, they took place either on the outskirts of towns or cities or in spaces that were traditionally associated with socialist politics, such as trade union buildings. However, once the number of revolutionary protestors increased dramatically, the spaces where they held their protest changed: repeating steps first taken in Kiel, the revolutionary crowds moved from the periphery to the centre, staging victory parades during which protestors carried red flags and soldiers and sailors pointed their rifles to the ground. In further acts of revolutionary symbolism, the revolutionaries removed officers' cockades and swords.[37] Often all of this occurred in highly symbolic public spaces that had been created to celebrate the political and cultural order that the revolution had just overthrown. For example, on 10 November 1918, the Bismarck memorial in central Berlin was the location for a demonstration that celebrated the end of the Empire that Bismarck had helped to create.[38]

The sense that actions such as these inverted the spatial order of politics was enhanced by the micro-dynamics of the previous week. Like Souchon, before the outbreak of revolution in a town or city, military commanders tried to 'tame' potential revolutionary spaces by sending out extra patrols and erecting new military checkpoints. In turn, once the revolutionaries took control over the same

---

34 Dähnhardt, 75.
35 Popp/Artelt, 21-22; Wilhelm Deist (ed.), Militär und Innenpolitik im Weltkrieg 1914-1918, 2 Vols., Düsseldorf 1970, Vol.2 Nr.503, 1363-1371.
36 Anthony McElligott, Rethinking the Weimar Republic. Authority and Authoritarianism, 1916-1936, London 2013, 36; Hamburger Nachrichten, 5 Nov. 1918 Evening edition.
37 Rote Fahne, 9 Nov. 1918; Neue Hamburger Zeitung, 10 Nov. 1918 Morning edition.
38 Frankfurter Zeitung, 11 Nov. 1918 Morning edition.

urban centers, their sudden disappearance made the victorious revolutionaries presence in the same places all the more conspicuous.

3. THE REVOLUTIONARY TRANSFORMATION OF POLITICAL SPACE

Diary entries provide us with important examples of how contemporaries experienced this sudden transformation of political spaces. During the morning of 9 November 1918, only hours before a series of key revolutionary events took place in Berlin, including the announcement of the Kaiser's abdication and the proclamation of the Republic, aristocratic count Harry Kessler was able to pass through the streets of central Berlin without any trouble. As he made his way to the bank opposite the state library on Unter den Linden, he nevertheless paid considerable attention to the mood in the streets, noting the increased presence of military checkpoints. In front of Potsdam station, he paused to watch a soldier 'haranguing a crowd.' Later he described a machine-gun company in front of the station as 'ready for action.' Between half past ten and eleven a.m., nevertheless, he thought that the area of Friedrichstrasse and Unter den Linden was quiet.[39] Like Kessler, at approximately the same time, Theodor Wolff, chief editor of Berlin's most important liberal newspaper, the *Berliner Tageblatt*, was equally struck by the presence of extra machine-guns in German capital. Capturing the mood of the people that morning, he noted that his barber told him that the area around the Reichsmarineamt was protected by soldiers with machine-guns. Fearful for the fate of children in a nearby school, Wolff remarked that this was 'very unpleasant news.' Later, as he made his way on foot to the newspaper's editorial offices, he thought that the streets looked 'pretty normal,' except for the presence of military checkpoints on many street corners. When he arrived in the office his colleagues told him that they had seen similar sights across the city.[40]

In turn, when the revolutionary crowds arrived in central Berlin, the same spaces that had previously been defined by projections of imperial power now became key sites of revolutionary politics.[41] Wolff and Kessler were both struck

---

39 Harry Kessler, The Diaries of a Cosmopolitan 1918 – 1937, Count Harry Kessler trans. and edited by Charles Kessler, London 1999, 9 Nov. 1918, 6.
40 Theodor Wolff, Tagebücher 1914-1919. Der Erste Weltkrieg und die Entstehung der Weimarer Republik in Tagebüchern, Leitartikeln und Briefen des Chefredakteurs am "Berliner Tageblatt" und Mitbegründers der "Deutschen Demokratischen Partei," introduced and edited by Bernd Sösemann 2 Vols., Boppard am Rhein 1984, 9 Nov. 1918, 647.
41 Frankfurter Zeitung, 10 Nov. 1918 First morning edition.

by the new streets scenes that they witnessed.[42] At lunchtime, Wolff watched from the windows of the *Berliner Tageblatt*'s editorial offices where 'large masses of people processed forwards in groups with red flags.' They were going to Berlin's most important street, Unter den Linden, the street that linked the Imperial city palace with the Brandenburg Gate and had been at the heart of the symbolic rituals of Imperial politics for decades. Wolff learnt from word of mouth that the red flag was now flying from the Social Democrat's *Vorwärts* newspaper building and that the Kaiser Alexander and other regiments in Berlin had gone over to the side of the revolution. Word also circulated that the military defense had collapsed entirely. Karl Liebknecht, the leader of the pro-Bolshevist Spartacist group, they were told, was speaking to the crowd from the balcony of the city palace while Social Democrat Philipp Scheidemann addressed another crowd from a window in the Reichstag.[43] Wolff did not witness all of these dramatic scenes but he continued to learn about them from his colleagues. Notably, his summary of what the revolution meant in Berlin on 9 November 1918 emphasized acts of street politics: 'everywhere officers had their cockades torn off them. *Schutzleute* are nowhere to be found; with one blow the city has been changed entirely, the trams are no longer running, the Wolff telegraph bureau has been occupied by revolutionaries, the red flag flies over the Brandenburg Gate.'[44]

On 9 November 1918, the same transformation gripped the mind of the aristocratic princess, Evelyn Blücher, the English wife of Count Blücher. Sufficiently privileged to live in the vicinity of the Brandenburg Gate, she spent most of the day gazing down upon the street from her window. That morning she described how numerous cars of sailors and soldiers passed along Unter den Linden with 'nothing much to do' while people stood 'about in groups talking and gesticulating excitedly.' Her servants told her that the people in the streets had not said that they intend to riot, but rather – quoting her servants' words – "as the Government could not put an end to the war, they meant to show them how to do it."'[45] Over the course of the morning, she continued to gaze onto the street, hoping that the armistice would soon be announced, 'expecting' the conditions 'every-hour' and wishing for news which would 'quiet the growing agitation of

---

42 Kessler, 9 Nov. 1918, 7-9.
43 Wolff, 9 Nov. 1918, 647.
44 Wolff, 9 Nov. 1918, 647.
45 Evelyn Princess Blücher, An English Wife in Berlin. A private memoir of events, politics, and daily life in Germany throughout the war and the social revolution, New York 1920, 9 Nov. (1st entry) 278/79. 9 November 2 entry 280.

the people.'[46] It was not just a disinterested observation: since mid-October the princess had become increasingly pre-occupied by the thought that the revolution would turn violent and that her home was in danger. Amongst other dark fears, she believed in a rumor that the revolutionaries possessed 'black-lists' of people whose houses were to be raided once the revolution broke-out.[47]

At about 2 p.m. on 9 November 1918, her diary captures how the view from her window was entirely transformed by the revolution. In her words, a 'perfect avalanche of humanity began to stream by our windows, walking quietly enough, many of them carrying red flags.' The presence of women and girls in the crowds was especially intriguing to her: 'I noticed the pale gold of young girls' uncovered heads, as they passed by with only a shawl over their shoulders. It seemed so feminine and incongruous, under the folds of those gruesome red banners flying over them.'[48] Watching from her windows as the crowds passed along Unter den Linden, in her view, it was obvious that no one 'sorrowed at the loss of an emperor.'

"There could hardly have been a greater air of rejoicing had Germany gained a great victory. More and more people came hurrying by, thousands of them densely packed together – men, women, soldiers, sailors, and strangely enough, a never-ceasing fringe of children playing on the edges of this dangerous maelstrom, and enjoying it seemingly very much, as if it had been some public fête-day."[49]

In an important illustration of how the transformation of spaces was captured in generational terms, including the feeling that teenagers had subverted the pre-revolutionary political and cultural order, her diary entry continued:

"A characteristic feature of the mob was the motors packed with youths in field grey uniform or in civil clothes, carrying loaded rifles adorned with a tiny red flag, constantly springing off their seats and forcing the soldiers and officers to tear off their insignia, or doing it for them if they refused. They were mostly boys of from 16 – 18 years of age, who looked as if they were enjoying their sudden power immensely, and sat grinning on the steps of the grey motors like schoolboys out on an escapade."[50]

---

46 Blücher, 9 Nov. 1918 first entry 279.
47 Blücher, 8 Nov. 1918, 277. More generally see her diary entries for October and November 1918.
48 Blücher, 9 Nov. 1918 second entry 280.
49 Blücher, 9 Nov. 1918, 281.
50 Blücher, 9 Nov. 1918, 281.

She thought that about '200 of these big lorries must have passed by our windows in two hours, and every moment the feeling of so many elementary forces being suddenly let loose grew more alarming. We, of course, had all our iron blinds pulled down and the doors of the house locked, and only kept one window open to be able to see what was going on.'[51]

The primacy of street politics is equally evident in the case of the elite of the Social Democratic Party. On 9 November 1918, when a Social Democratic delegation confronted Prince Max von Baden in the Chancellery building, leading to his resignation and the appointment of Friedrich Ebert as Chancellor, the discussion revolved around the politics of the streets. When Prince Max von Baden queried if the Social Democrats could still control the situation, Philipp Scheidemann promised his critics that if any member of the existing government wanted evidence of their support, they only needed to join a member of the Social Democrats for a drive around the city.[52]

It was this transformation of political spaces that left many contemporaries dumbfounded by events. Once again, Theodor Wolff provides us with an important example. As the first paragraph of his editorial in the *Berliner Tageblatt* – published on 10 November 1918 – makes clear, the crowds' transformation of political spaces was foremost among his reasons for conceptualizing the events of 9 November 1918 as *revolutionary*:

"One can call it the greatest of all revolutions because never before has such an attempt taken such a firmly built Bastille surrounded by solid walls. A week ago a military and civil administrative organization still existed, that was so complex, so interwoven into each other, so deeply rooted, that it seemed that its regime was ensured to last the course of time. The grey cars of the officers raced through the streets of Berlin like monuments to power; *Schutzleute* were standing on the squares, an enormous military organisation seemed to surround everything, in the offices and Ministries an apparently undefeatable bureaucracy sat on its crown. Early yesterday morning, in Berlin at least, all of that was still there. Yesterday afternoon none of it existed anymore."[53]

---

51 Blücher, 9 Nov. 1918, 282. On the changing role of women and teenagers in Germany during and after the First World War, see Richard Bessel's seminal study: Richard Bessel, Germany after the First World War, Oxford 1993.

52 Erich Matthias (ed.), Die Regierung der Volksbeauftragten 1918/1919 2 Vols., Düsseldorf 1969, Vol.1: 'Aufzeichnung über die Vorgänge in der Reichskanzlei,' 3-4.

53 'Der Erfolg der Revolution,' TW, Berliner Tageblatt Nr. 576, 10 Nov. 1918, in Wolff, 814ff.

It was not just liberals like Wolff. The anti-revolutionary *Tägliche Rundschau* echoed the liberal editor of the *Berliner Tageblatt* in an editorial on 15 November 1918:

"The victory of the revolution in Germany happened so quickly and without a struggle, that it had the effect that it felt as if it was something that was impossible to avoid, something that could not be stopped, like an elemental force. The most permanently rebated state structure in Europe collapsed like a house of cards. The new powers only needed to touch it with their fingers to cause it to cave in."[54]

The pan-Germans' *Deutsche Zeitung*, another representative of the ultra-nationalist press, was equally enthralled by the transformation of urban spaces. It believed that the revolutionary movement was controlled by a single central command – it was not sure if that command was in the hands of the Spartacists, or an even more radical group.[55]

4. A Typology of Revolutionary Crowds

Only 6 days separates the meeting in the woods at Kiel, from the triumphal processions of revolutionaries through central Berlin. In these circumstances, revolutionary crowds were understood as single homogenous entities: streams of men and women who marched through town centers under the red flag. A closer examination of the dynamics of crowd behavior during the first half of November 1918, however, reveals that there was no single 'revolutionary crowd' and that the transformation of political spaces was defined by the interaction of at least five different ideal types, each of which may be organized according to forms of crowd behavior.[56] These ideal types are: 1.) the crowd in formation or dispersal 2.) the assembly 3.) the procession 4.) the curious crowd 5.) the confrontational crowd. To come to a better understanding of the politics of the streets in the November Revolution, the next section will examine each ideal type in turn.

---

54 Tägliche Rundschau, 18 Nov. 1918 Morning edition, BArch Berlin R901/55625 Bl.31.
55 Deutsche Zeitung, 9 Nov. 1918 Evening edition.
56 Verhey, 22-97. For an outstanding example of a historical typology see Sven Reichardt, Faschistische Kampfbünde. Gewalt und Gemeinschaft im italienischen Squadrismus und in der deutschen SA, Cologne 2002, 100-133.

The first ideal type, the crowd in formation or dispersal, was defined solely by movement. It was the transient moving crowd which occurred before and after a main 'crowd' assembled or dispersed. It is best defined as the movement of sufficient numbers of people on their way to or away from an assembly or procession, or simply sufficient numbers of curious individuals making their way to watch revolutionary events. The trickles of sailors who made their way to the woods in Kiel formed one such crowd – an unusual group of individuals that passed across a street changing the dynamics of what was a normal 'street scene.'

Transient crowds announced that something special was taking place. They were also potent sources of fear: watching men and women on their way to an illegal assembly or worrying about what would follow when demonstrators began to make their way home was an exceptionally threatening experience. In his diary entry of 8 November 1918, the day when Bavarians woke up to discover that radical Independent Socialist Kurt Eisner had proclaimed Bavaria a Republic, no less a figure than Thomas Mann, the famed author of *Buddenbrooks* and future nobel prize winner, was concerned by the threat posed by crowd dispersion. In the words of his diary, '"processions" of course mean discipline, but after they disperse in the dark the 'fun [*Spaß*]' will start once again [...].'[57] At its most dramatic the transient crowd form takes on the characteristic of the crowd in flight – as occurred when large numbers of protestors suddenly sprinted for safety following the sound of a gunshot, or because of rumours of the imminent arrival of anti-revolutionary forces. Such scenes served as potent reminders as to just how threatening the streets could become.[58]

The second crowd type may be defined as the assembly – the gathered, static crowd. In contrast to the transient nature of the crowd in formation or dispersal, assemblies were defined by their static nature: they were important occasions when crowds that had already formed paused to listen, support, and decide upon the course of their challenge to the state. In the early phases of the revolution, assemblies often took place in trade union buildings, as occurred in Kiel or Hamburg. However as the size of the movement increased, assemblies moved to outdoor locations, some of which were well known sites of political protest. The largest outdoor assemblies include the meetings at Heiligengeistfeld (40,000) in

---

57 Jens Inge/Peter de Mendelson (eds.), Thomas Mann Tagebücher 1918-1921, Frankfurt 2003, 8 Nov. 1918, 62. Thomas Mann also described them as 'festive' crowds – although he was not prepared to accept the idea that the revolutionary crowds amounted to 'replacement for fasching [Faschings-ersatz],' Mann, 7 Nov. 1918, 59.

58 See further: Mark Jones, Violence and Politics in the German Revolution 1918-19, PhD thesis, Florence 2011, 13-64.

Hamburg on 6 November 1918, and the Theresienwiese (100,000 to 150,000) in Munich a day later.[59]

Assemblies were defined by competing attempts upon the part of aspiring revolutionary leaders to position themselves at the head of the movement. In Kiel, Hamburg, and Munich, assembled crowds stood and listened as speakers addressed them and called upon the crowd to support their leadership. In these moments, the interplay between top-down and bottom-up models of political leadership was most apparent. Unlike more static forms of political exchange, during this fluid moment of history, if an aspiring crowd leader's message was unpopular that message was often ignored. This was especially the case during the intial assemblies that took place in Kiel: as the police records discussed at the start of this essay make clear, anyone present could speak and aspire to lead the course of future events. In Munich, at the assembly upon the Theresienweise, participants also faced a choice between the radical message of Independent Socialist Kurt Eisner, or the more conservative message of Bavarian Social Democratic Party leader, Erhard Auer.[60]

When assemblies were of a sufficient size they were preceded and followed by the third ideal type of crowd: the procession – the point when the static assembly became mobile as the crowd marched through urban spaces announcing its power and ownership of the streets. Once they began processions either reformed as assemblies or dispersed. Processions took place both before and after the military authorities ceded power. Examples of the former include the march into Kiel city centre during the evening of 3 November and the march from the Heiligengeistfeld towards the Generalkommando in Hamburg on 6 November. The later include the parades of freed sailors in Kiel during the late afternoon of 4 November 1918, as well as the famous parades in Berlin during the afternoon of 9 November when crowds streamed into the city centre after midday to celebrate the abdication of the Kaiser, perhaps the most festive moment of the entire November Revolution.[61]

---

59 On Hamburg see: Volker Ullrich, Die Hamburger Arbeiterbewegung vom Vorabend des Ersten Weltkrieges bis zur Revolution 1918-19, 2 Vols., Hamburg 1976; on Munich see: Felix Fechenbach, Der Revolutionär Kurt Eisner. Aus persönlichen Erlebnissen, Berlin 1929, 38-40; Münchener Post 8 Nov. 1918; Coburger Zeitung 10 Nov. 1918; Mitchell, 95.
60 Fechenbach, 40; Mitchell, 95.
61 Heinrich August Winkler, Von der Revolution zur Stabilisierung. Arbeiter und Arbeiterbewegung in der Weimarer Republik 1918 bis 1924, Bonn 1984, 45-58; Peter Fritzsche, Germans into Nazis, Cambridge MA 1998, 85-92; Wolfgang Schivelbusch, Die

Processions could be dangerous, as the example from Kiel on 3 November makes clear (when soldiers opened fire upon the protestors), but more often than not, during the November Revolution, processions were more passive than aggressive: they sought to demonstrate the crowd's power but not to actively confront authority, as was the case with Auer's Social Democratic led procession through Munich on 7 November, which had a far larger number of participants than the revolutionary crowd that followed Kurt Eisner.[62]

Assemblies and processions were organized: they relied upon stewards and well developed patterns of organized protest behaviour. When it wrote about the processions in Hamburg on 6 November, the bourgois *Neue Hamburger Zeitung* described stewards directing the crowds, shouting at children, telling them to go home and avoid mischief – the children had been given the day off school because disorder was expected.[63] Similarly, at around 7 p.m. on 9 November, Theodor Wolff watched on as stewards directed crowds in the vicinity of the Potsdamer Platz.[64] The next day, another journalist, the Berlin correspondent of the *Neue Hamburger Zeitung* was equally amazed to discover stewards working at the main junctions. As he made his way towards the city centre, he also watched on as trams were stopped so that passengers could be searched for weapons or ammunition.[65]

Wolff described one of the crowds that he saw at the Potsdamer Platz as a *schaulustige Menge*, thereby introducing us to the fourth kind of crowd: the curious crowd. Like the same groups in July and August 1914, the November Revolution's curious crowds formed as people gathered in public spaces in search of information or simply to pause and watch as revolutionary parades passed through the streets.[66] For example, on 9 November newspaper accounts referred to the numbers of curious observers in central Berlin.[67] From early morning the following day, large numbers of Berliners went to the city centre to view the second day of the revolution. Despite what he described to his diary as 'all of the adventures' of the previous night, Theodor Wolff was among them. He brought his wife and children with him to the centre of Berlin. His family, he confided to his diary 'definitely want to see revolution.' He added that on their

---

Kultur der Niederlage. Der amerikanische Süden 1865, Frankreich 1871, Deutschland 1918, Frankfurt 2007.

62 Mitchell, 95-97.
63 Neue Hamburger Zeitung, 6 Nov. 1918 Evening edition.
64 Wolff, 9 Nov. 1918, 648.
65 Neue Hamburger Zeitung, 10 Nov. 1918 Morning edition.
66 Verhey, esp. 26-33, 72-82.
67 Neue Hamburger Zeitung, 10 Nov. 1918 Morning edition.

way to central Berlin they encountered many cars and trucks with soldiers, red flags and machine-guns with lots of people 'watching.' In Wolff's opinion the observers were mostly nervous and the mood was 'downbeat.' He added that: 'It is not known [how many] thousands of inquisitive people are on Unter den Linden, watching the battles at a distance.'[68] Harry Kessler was also again out in the streets of central Berlin on November 10. He commented that overall the 'attitude of the people, despite the shootings has during the first two days of the revolution been admirable: disciplined, calm, orderly, trying to be fair, and in practically every instance scrupulously well behaved. A counterpart to the readiness for self-sacrifice in August 1914.'[69] As these illustrations show, curious participants added considerably to the numbers of people who gathered in the streets. The revolution, in this way, was a great act of urban political theatre.

Measured in terms of the numbers of participants, each of these four crowd types was considerably larger than the fifth kind of crowd: the aggressively confrontational crowd. Yet, despite its small size, by aggressively challenging authority, the actively confrontational crowd decisively defined the street politics of the German revolution. Already, we have seen how confrontational demonstrators led the procession from the Waldwiese to central Kiel on 3 November. Another example is provided by events at the *Maikäfer* barracks in northern Berlin on 9 November 1918. There, as protestors made their way south from the Schwarzkopf works towards the city centre, they encountered a hastily erected barrier at the entrance to the barracks. The barrier was manned by a group of officers who wanted to prevent soldiers from joining the revolutionary procession. When the crowd encroached upon the barriers, shots were fired. Three men were killed and one was injured. However, the officers soon surrendered – it was never fully established who was responsible for the firing.[70] News of the confrontation soon raced across Berlin and it was central to media representations of the revolution in the capital. Thus, what was a minor action that only involved a tiny fraction of the total number of protestors in the streets, was nevertheless symbolically central to the representation of events.[71]

---

68 Wolff, 10 Nov. 1918, 649; see also Gottfried Niedhart (ed.), Gustav Mayer. Als deutsche-jüdischer Historiker in Krieg und Revolution 1914-1920, Tagebücher, Aufzeichnungen, Briefe, Munich 2009, 9 Nov. 1918, 184.
69 Kessler, 10 Nov. 9-10.
70 The confrontation is described in: Rote Fahne, 9 Nov. 1918; Frankfurter Zeitung 10 Nov. 1918 Morning edition; Neue Hamburger Zeitung 10 Nov. 1918 Morning edition; Die Post 10 Nov. 1918; Frankfurter Zeitung, 11 Nov. 1918 Morning edition.
71 Soon after, according to one report, some of the soldiers left the barracks to join the protesting crowd, while others chose to stay, and a third group took the opportunity to

5. FEAR OF THE CROWD

There were key political and cultural consequences. In an age when social and political thought about crowds was defined by the now long discredited theories of crowd psychology contained in Gustave Le Bon's widely read *Psychologies des foules* (1895); a book that included the warning that the hypnotising effect of joining a crowd may even turn 'cultured' individuals into 'brutal barbarians', even though only a small number of violent confrontations took place, they were sufficient to ensure that many contemporaries vastly overestimated the dangers facing Germany in the aftermath of revolution and armistice.[72] Hence, even though his government derived its power from the presence of such crowds, Friedrich Ebert's proclamations on 9 November begged protestors to 'clear the streets, and to create order and peace.' He warned that failure to do so could worsen Germany's food supplies and see increases in plundering, robbery and general misery. Like so many others, he feared that Germany could soon be defined by 'Russian conditions' – the two words that had taken the place of the term Armageddon in contemporary Germans' cultural lexicon over the course of 1918.[73] At a time when the revolution's success demanded a founding discourse legitimizing the protestors and justifying their demands; while simultaneously rejecting the accusations of conservatives and nationalists who viewed the revolution as a crime without parallels in the history of the world, the language of the revolution's most important political leader was defined by dread.[74] Ebert imagined the future using terms such as anarchy, starvation, terrible misery, plunder and thievery. His only hope against such desperation was to call upon Germans

---

go home: Wolff's Telegraphisches Büro Nr. 3148, 10 Nov. 1918, BArch Berlin R901/55724 Bl.54.

72 For an English translation see: Gustave Le Bon, The Crowd. A Study of the Popular Mind, Kitchener, Ont. 2001. On Le Bon see: Susanna Barrows, Distorting Mirrors. Visions of the Crowd in Late Nineteenth-Century France, New Haven etc. 1981; on his importance to German counter-revolutionaries see Robert Gerwarth, The Central European Counter-Revolution. Paramilitary Violence in Germany, Austria and Hungary after the Great War, in: Past & Present 200 (2008) 175-209, 190-91.

73 Robert Gerwarth/John Horne, Bolshevism as Fantasy. Fear of Revolution and Counter-Revolutionary Violence, 1917-1923, in: Robert Gerwarth/John Horne (eds.), War in Peace. Paramilitary Violence in Europe after the Great War, Oxford 2012, 40-52.

74 Deutsche Tageszeitung Nr.572, 9 Nov. 1918 Evening edition, BArch Berlin R901/55561 Bl.11; 'Ein Stoß ins Herz,' Reichsbote Nr.569, 9 Nov. 1918 Evening edition.

to redeem their nation's future through hard work and selflessness.[75] It was hardly a roaring endorsement of the revolution that had brought the Social Democrats to power. For Ebert, the revolution was hopefully over as soon as it began.[76]

Liberal supporters of the revolution welcomed Ebert's words. With the revolutionary *Straßenbild* foremost in his mind, rather than give legitimacy to the crowds and their achievements, in the *Berliner Tageblatt*, Theodor Wolff praised the new Chancellor for wanting to put an end to the chaos. 'Everyone, who recognizes the dangers of the hour – and who could deny them?' Wolff wrote, 'will lend their full support to this government. Everything that Ebert said in his Appeal to the people is wise and true.' In Wolff's view, rather than call for vengeance, or even to dismiss those responsible for Germany's many wartime failures, Ebert was correct in recognizing that the revolution 'which wants to remain flawless must treat its defeated enemy with care and humanity.'[77] He added that the 'new men' faced unprecedented challenges. Among those challenges, Wolff argued that 'elements' would try to use the 'excitement' of the revolution to get closer to 'honest workers and soldiers' and cause their 'instincts' to run wild – he was referring to the threat posed by Karl Liebknecht and the pro-Bolshevist Spartacist group although he did not mention them by name.[78]

Outside of the Spartacist's *Rote Fahne*, which called upon the revolutionary crowds to stay in the streets, there was little criticism of Ebert's proclamations and the crowds that occupied the streets between 4 and 11 November soon receded back to where they had come from.[79] It was not until the turmoil of mid to late December that the Social Democrats called upon their supporters to take to the streets to show their support. This paradox had important political consequences during the weeks that immediately followed the 9 November: by calling upon the crowds that brought it into existence to leave the streets, the new revolutionary order deprived itself of one of its most important sources of political

---

75 Ebert's appeals were widely circulated. I have used the text found in the pan-German Deutsche Zeitung: 'Aufruf an die Beamtenschaft,' 'Aufruf zur Ordnung,' Deutsche Zeitung, 10 Nov. 1918 Morning edition.

76 See further: Walter Mühlhausen, Friedrich Ebert 1871-1925. Reichspräsident der Weimarer Republik, Bonn 2006; Ralf Krumpholz, Wahrnehmung und Politik: die Bedeutung des Ordnungsdenkens für das politische Handeln am Beispiel der deutschen Revolution von 1918-1920, Münster 1998, 171-207.

77 'Der Erfolg der Revolution,' Berliner Tageblatt, Nr. 576 10 Nov. 1918, in Wolff, Tagebücher, p.814ff.

78 Ibid.

79 In mid-November 1918, the media reflected the changed street scenes by bringing reports that the streets were calm.

legitimacy. Instead, by removing the crowds from the streets for the remainder of November, the revolutionary order weakened its own right to rule, while simultaneously strengthening the cultural spaces that allowed for conservative opponents of the revolution to spread discourses denying its legitimacy.[80]

6. CONCLUSION: VIOLENCE, STATE, AND ORDER

The German Revolution of 1918-19 did not have a sustained counter-revolution: there was no serious attempt to reverse the revolutionary changes of November and restore Wilhelm II as German Emperor. But when we define the revolution as a transformation in spatial politics, it is clear that over the course of the winter of 1918-19, there was a strong effort to restore the state's control over urban spaces. At its most violent, the restoration of spatial hierarchies saw towns and inner cities locked down by government approved military occupations, thus reversing the localized processes that had seen crowds control the same spaces during the November Revolution.[81] For example, in 1919, units of *Freikorps*, who wore military uniform and steel helmets, and were armed with machine guns and barbed wire, used excessive force to reoccupy spaces in central Hamburg that had previously belonged to revolutionary crowds.[82] Within this broader process, the wrong kind of political crowd became a legitimate target for physical violence and as a consequence, the new Republic did something at its birth that the old Empire could not do at its death: it deployed overwhelming military force to control the political uses of urban spaces. To accompany the increased physical violence, the men who carried it out and the audiences who cheered them on, repeatedly emphasized that the mob was the *Menge* – a dishonest feminized mess that was deserving of disciplining through hard military force.[83] The long-term consequences were profound: a Republic that was brought into existence by revolutionary crowds occupying urban spaces developed a political culture that sanctioned violence against similar crowds in the same spaces in 1919 and 1920. Despite efforts to reclaim political ownership of November's crowds in 1919 – see for example the front page of the *Vorwärts* newspaper on 9

---

80 On future attempts to provide the Republic with cultural authority see McElligott, Rethinking the Weimar Republic, 129-156.
81 Boris Barth, Dolchstoßlegenden und politische Destintegration. Das Trauma der deutschen Niederlage im Ersten Weltkrieg 1914-1933, Düsseldorf 2003.
82 Weinhauer, Protest, kollektive Gewalt und Polizei in Hamburg zwischen Versammlungsdemokratie und staatlicher Sicherheit ca. 1890-1933, 84-87.
83 Klaus Theweleit, Male Fantasies, II Vols. trans. Stephen Conway, Minnesota 1987.

November 1919 – in the end, it was the dangerous image of dirt and revolt from below that came to define how the revolution's crowds were remembered for the remainder of the Weimar era.[84]

---

84 Vorwärts, 9 Nov. 1919.

"Incapable of Securing Order?"
The Prussian Police and the German Revolution 1918/19

NADINE ROSSOL

1. INTRODUCTION

Writing in early December 1918, the West Prussian city of Marienburg asked the national authorities for financial help regarding the damages caused by revolutionary unrest in the previous month. The city council stated: "We and our police have repeatedly asked for military protection, but it was refuted time and time again. At first, our police managed to suppress the initially harmless uprisings and prevented others…" But in the end plundering, especially carried out by soldiers, could not be stopped anymore by a diminished police of only six men.[1] Turning to a much bigger city, Cologne's mayor Konrad Adenauer called the police protection of his city "completely inadequate" in mid-December 1918.[2] These are familiar descriptions for a number of German towns and cities in the winter of 1918. The revolution had hit the police by surprise and had created uncertainty for policemen throughout Germany. Furthermore, state ministries, including the Prussian Ministry of the Interior and the Reich Ministry of Defense, openly questioned the force's usefulness and capability to manage the

---

I would like to thank the Alexander von Humboldt Foundation for a fellowship in 2011/12 that allowed me to carry out the research of this article. I would like to thank the editors and Moritz Föllmer for their very helpful suggestions on my piece.

1 Bundesarchiv Berlin (herafter BArch Berlin), R43I/2695, 8-13, city of Marienburg to Ebert and Haase, 4.12.1918.
2 Landesarchiv NRW (Düsseldorf), BR 1001, Nr. 7626, mayor Konrad Adenauer to police president of Cologne, 17.12.1918.

difficult security situation that emerged from 1919 onwards.[3] This had not so much to do with a failure of state authority. Anthony McElligott reminds us that the collapse of the monarchy did not mean the end of state authority – quite the contrary.[4] But the crumbling of the state's monopoly on violence required filling a power vacuum with numerous short-lived security organizations which took over some police duties. In most cases, these improvised organizations had more weapons at their disposal than the police and championed a rather militaristic appearance.[5]

However, not all cities mirrored the difficult situation of Hamburg, Cologne or Berlin and policemen did not wait passively for changes announced by others. Writing in early December 1918, Ernst Schrader, the head of the numerically strong police association organizing Prussian *Schutzmänner*, called for the creation of a national police union.[6] Quickly police associations, civil servant unions and other representative bodies were founded to give a voice to policemen on local and national level. Demands calling for re-forming and re-structuring the police dominated police debates from November 1918 to early 1920. Demilitarizing the force's external appearance and internal structures, creating police training schools and allowing policemen to engage in politics were only some of these suggestions. Discussions on whether the police should be completely controlled by municipal authorities or by the state illustrate the openness of the situation. For a brief time period from November 1918 to early 1920, police associations tried to redefine the basis of an institution that had limited experience in changing from below. At a time of insecurity, unpredictability and danger, police forces were thinking, with a sense of urgency, about their role(s) in this *new* German state and how they could *contribute* to shaping its future. To be sure, difficulties of maintaining order and security informed these contemporary debates within the police, but they were not necessarily at its centre. What was

---

3 This point became particularly clear when the creation of a *Sicherheitspolizei* (security police) – a heavily militarised police force – was debated.
4 Anthony McElligott, Rethinking the Weimar Republic. Authority and Authoritarianism 1916-1936, London etc. 2014, here 10-11, generally chapter 2.
5 See Klaus Weinhauer's piece for the example of Hamburg: Klaus Weinhauer, Protest, kollektive Gewalt und Polizei in Hamburg zwischen Versammlungsdemokratie und staatlicher Sicherheit 1890-1933, in: Friedrich Legner (ed.), Kollektive Gewalt in der Stadt. Europa 1890-1933, Munich 2013, 69-102, here 75-78.
6 Preußische Schutzmanns-Zeitung, 49, 7.12.1928, 432, Aufruf zur Gründung eines Bundes Deutscher Polizeibeamter.

decisive was a feeling that a new time had started with the revolution and that this should mean changes for the better.[7]

Police historians have examined the re-organization and institutional changes of the German, mainly Prussian, police in the republic's early years.[8] But "the forgotten revolution" (A. Gallus) and a focus on the military and on paramilitary security organizations have left ordinary police forces neglected in more general studies. This is unfortunate as the police can serve to illustrate the mixture of challenges and opportunities state organizations faced in the aftermath of the revolution. For police forces in Germany, the revolution in 1918 meant a combination of feelings that included a painful loss of power, control and authority as well as – partly disappointed – hopes for a newly reformed police.

I want to examine the expectations police forces expressed and the actions they took in a time period that promised *and* required change. The proclamation of a *neuzeitliche* police for new times was not just based on hopes that reforms delayed in Imperial Germany could now finally be seen through, but also inspired by fears of being sidelined if the police did not adapt to new circumstances. This discovery of agency on the side of the police, embodied in the set-up of police associations, clashed with the state's quest for authority as exemplified in its security policy from 1919 onwards. We find a situation in which the state felt that the trinity of state, order and control needed to be strengthened and, if necessary, supported by other security organizations, while policemen wanted to explore the rights and opportunities the new democratic state had to offer. The guardians of a crumbling state's monopoly on internal violence were not just confronted with political violence and a difficult security situation; policemen also felt that their relations to the state and to the people needed to be rethought.[9] The term *Volkspolizei* (people's police) was born in the revolution when *Volk*

---

7 This feeling did not just characterise police forces as Rüdiger Graf illustrates: Rüdiger Graf, Die Zukunft der Weimarer Republik, Munich 2008, 143-152.

8 For example: Johannes Buder, Die Reorganisation der preußischen Polizei 1918-1923, Frankfurt 1986; Peter Leßmann-Faust, Die preußische Schutzpolizei in der Weimarer Republik, Düsseldorf 1989, first chapter; Manfred Reuter, In Treue fest. Eine Studie über ausgewählte Polizeigewerkschaften und Polizeigewerkschafter in der Weimarer Republik, Frankfurt 2012.

9 For an overview concentrating on the difficult links between the police, violence and the state see Alf Lüdtke/Herbert Reinke/Michael Sturm (eds.), Polizei, Gewalt und Staat im 20. Jahrhundert, Wiesbaden 2011.

became a key political concept as charged and open to interpretations as another word of the time; the *Volksstaat* (people's state).[10]

By the mid and late 1920s, the integration of the police in the Weimar State meant that the new reference point for the police had changed to the Weimar Constitution. The revolutionary concept of the "people's police", a slogan from the winter of 1918/19 which was critically directed at the state's police reforms, survived but was filled by policemen and politicians with a number of changing meanings throughout the 1920s and 1930s. It changed to a concept by which the police could be linked to the republican state: the people's police in the people's state.

2. SECURITY AND INSECURITY: QUESTIONING POLICE AUTHORITY

The state's monopoly on violence, carried out through its security organizations, is questioned in any revolution and so is its domestic order. It is the speed by which new authorities re-establish order afterwards that determines the outcome and the consequences of revolutions. Short-term emergency decrees can be evoked to prevent the dangers of long-term insecurity or looming civil war. But provisional measures also form the basis for the political normality that should begin as soon as possible and extensions beyond acute emergency situations prove equally dangerous for new political state forms.[11] The German revolution in November 1918 surprised policemen, like many other Germans, mainly because of its speed. While domestic security and public order issues had already been difficult to deal with for police forces during war time, the break down of any military back up for the police, resulting from the lost war and revolutionary uprisings, meant that police stations were quickly handed over to workers and soldiers' councils in November 1918.[12] As early as the end of the month, the police journal *Preußische Schutzmanns-Zeitung* reported that major bloodshed had been avoided in Berlin and elsewhere. It claimed that "a peaceful transfor-

---

10 See Heiko Bollmeyer, "Das Volk" in den Verfassungsberatungen der Weimarer Nationalversammlung 1919 – ein demokratietheoretischer Schlüsselbegriff zwischen Kaiserreich und Republik, in: Alexander Gallus (ed.), Die vergessene Revolution 1918/19, Göttingen 2010, 57-83.

11 See Christoph Gusy, Verfassungsumbruch bei Kriegsende, in: Christoph Gusy (ed.), Demokratie in der Krise. Europa in der Zwischenkriegszeit, Baden-Baden 2008, 15-51 (here 42-44).

12 Leßmann-Faust, 11-17; Weinhauer, 75-76.

mation from the monarchy to the republic" had taken place which was based on "harmonious" relations between the police and the workers and soldiers' councils. This, so the journal, was largely due to exemplary police behavior.[13] Self-congratulations were combined with the sincere hope that two weeks of revolutionary unrest were enough. While police forces across Germany quickly put their service at the disposal of the new authorities, the alleged "harmonious" relations did not work out smoothly everywhere.

Already one of the first actions, namely stripping the police of its weapons and accompanying policemen on patrol with armed members of revolutionary security organizations, was interpreted as humiliating and counterproductive by many in the police at the end of 1918.[14] Needless to say that the occupation of police stations as former symbols of Imperial power, the collecting of weapons and the public demonstration – with new armbands or otherwise – that these policemen were now serving a new political regime belonged to important signs that visualized this power shift and were also personally felt by policemen. In some cases weapons were handed out again shortly after the councils had established their control. Other police forces remained without them well into 1919. Adalbert Oehler, the mayor of Düsseldorf who had been in his post from 1911 to 1919, retrospectively described the winter months 1918/19 in his Rhenish city as a succession of disarming, rearming and disarming policemen.[15] Also Berlin's police carried out its tasks without weapons. In contrast, policemen in Breslau continued their work with weapons and so did police forces in a number of other cities.[16]

Naturally, police weapons did not only have a symbolic value but mainly a practical one. At a time when there were more weapons accessible than in the Imperial period as many returning soldiers had kept theirs and others felt they needed to protect their houses, businesses or farms from plundering and looting, police equipment mattered tremendously to the fulfillment of basic police duties.[17] This situation deteriorated in the summer of 1919 when defense organiza-

---

13 Preußische Schutzmanns-Zeitung, 4, 23.11.1918, Unter dem neuen Regiment, 413-414.
14 Adalbert Oehler, Düsseldorf im Weltkrieg. Schicksal und Arbeit einer deutschen Großstadt, Düsseldorf 1927, 647.
15 Ibid, 637-640.
16 Preußische Schutzmanns-Zeitung, 5, 1.2.1919, Aus den Vereinen: Breslau, 41; Preußische Schutzmanns-Zeitung, 50, 14.12.1918, Der Achtstundentag für die Schutzmannschaft, 444.
17 Weinhauer, 75-78; Dirk Schumann, Political Violence in the Weimar Republic 1918-1933, New York 2009 (revised and shortened translation of the German edition from

tions (*Volkswehren/Einwohnerwehren*) were heavily armed to undermine the Allies demands regarding the reduction of militaristic weapons. According to historian Rüdiger Bergien, the head of the *Reichswehr* believed that only weapons in actual possession of the military were to be reduced as part of the Versailles Treaty and, therefore, weapons in possession of other defense organizations were hoped to remain untouched.[18] The fact that by September 1919 the *Landrat* (county manager) of Waldbröl could point out that there were enough weapons and ammunition around in the different villages of his area that citizens could defend themselves and did not need any defense organization anymore was a rather worrying outcome of this policy.[19] It also exemplified the difficulties of policemen, who, even in case they had kept their weapons, were confronted with a population that was often better armed than they were.

Political turmoil, reduced police numbers and missing support of the military had created a power vacuum in most parts of Germany. Cologne's police president stated at the end of December 1918 that 200 policemen posts remained vacant and that he needed 400 to 500 auxiliary police to deal with the ever increasing tasks of combating violence and of securing order.[20] This vacuum of power was filled with a number of temporary organizations that took up some police tasks and were often presented, at least officially, as working along side policemen or as being partly controlled by them. This could mean the organization of an unarmed neighborhood night watch as in Cologne,[21] *Bürgerwehren* often set-up in November 1918 as reaction to the diminished police numbers by mayors, and *Landräte*[22] as well as defense organizations (*Einwohnerwehr*) in the

---

2001), 11-25; Benjamin Ziemann, War Experiences in Rural Germany 1914-1923, Oxford 2007 (German edition published in 1997), 228.

18 Rüdiger Bergien, Mit „Kreiskommissaren" zur „Volkswehr": Die preußischen Einwohnerwehren als Organ einer republikanischen Sicherheitspolitik 1918-1920, in: Rüder Bergien/Reinhard Pröve (eds), Spießer, Patrioten und Revolutionäre. Militärische Mobilisierung und gesellschaftliche Ordnung in der Neuzeit, Göttingen 2010, 117-138, here 130-133.

19 Landesarchiv NRW (Düsseldorf), Reg. Köln, BR101, Nr. 7626, Landrat Waldbröl to Regierungspräsident Köln, 2.9.1919.

20 Landesarchiv NRW (Düsseldorf). Reg. Köln, BR1001, Nr. 7627, Polizeipräsident Köln to Regierungspräsident, 21.12.1918, Betr. Einstellung von Hilfspolizeibeamten und Erhöhung des Lohnes.

21 Landesarchiv NRW (Düsseldorf), Reg. Köln, BR1001, Nr. 7626, Polizeipräsident Köln to Regierungspräsident, 9.9.1920

22 Landesarchiv NRW (Düsseldorf), Reg. Düsseldorf, BR7, Nr. 30272. The material on the set-up of *Bürgerwehren* in the area around Düsseldorf illustrates that there were

countryside to protect food supplies against marauding gangs.[23] Under the control of the Ministry of the Interior, the official guidelines for *Einwohnerwehren* stressed in May 1919 that their auxiliary role denied them police powers – for example the power of arrest – and stated that support of police patrols always had to happen with at least one policeman present.[24] It seems questionable if these guidelines were met given the difficult security situation. Furthermore, *Einwohnerwehren* could "temporarily" arrest someone when the respective person was about to flee otherwise.[25] The fact that repeated demands for more policemen made by municipal councils were satisfied by recruiting auxiliary policemen or members of *Einwohnerwehren* instead of regular policemen did not strengthened the police's position within this power struggle of numerous security organizations.[26]

By far the greatest threat to police authority and to the police's role as sole guardians of the state's domestic monopoly on violence was not temporary defense organizations but the introduction of the security police (a militarized force with heavy weapons) in the late summer of 1919. The new force was introduced with the suggestion that security and order could be separated and, therefore, dealt with by different types of police forces. Unlike the set-up of security organizations with a temporary character, the new security police was meant to bring about a permanent change. In March 1919, the Prussian Ministry of the Interior and the Reich Ministry of Defense started thinking about the introduction of a security police consisting of young and heavily armed military men who were to be accommodated in barracks for quick mobilization. More than just a short-term fix of the difficult domestic situation in the spring of 1919, the security police were to take over all police tasks linked to security matters. This was justified with the damning evaluation by state officials that the police had been incapable of securing order from November 9th 1918 onwards, had completely

---

often attempts to have these organisations, including the selection of its members, supervised by the police.
23 See Ziemann, 227-240. Einwohnerwehren used to be characterised as reactionary, anti-spartacist and anti-republican symbolising some of the difficulties the republic was faced with. This has been challenged by Benjamin Ziemann and Dirk Schumann. Recently, Rüdiger Bergien suggests that Einwohnerwehren could be interpreted as part of the republic's security policy see Bergien, 117-138.
24 BArch Berlin, R43I/2729, May 1919, 30-31, 32, 42.
25 Einwohnerwehr, 8, 15.10.1919, Bestimmungen für die Einwohnerwehren in Preußen.
26 Landesarchiv NRW (Düsseldorf), Reg. Köln, BR1001, Nr.7627, 10.5.1919 Konferenz der Polizei-Inspektionen der Städte der Regierungsbezirks.

lost influence on security issues and had proven to be *unverwendbar* (unusable) when the force had stated that it wanted to be politically neutral.[27]

In unusual unity, leading police officials, heads of police associations and experts in police administration tried to refute this evaluation by reminding of successes in combating crime even in the difficult winter of 1918/1919. They also addressed the issue of the police's political neutrality by clarifying that police forces did not want to be involved in political policing, but supported the new democratic state and had shown this support in the fights in January and March 1919.[28] Furthermore, they found that the division of police tasks into order, to be dealt with by the police, and security, to be maintained by the new militarized security police, made little sense. In late October 1919, the vice president of the *Vereinigung der staatlichen höheren Polizei-Exekutiv-Beamten Preußens* (Association of the higher police officers in Prussia) Eiben remarked that this distinction between order and security was like separating "the body from the soul." Furthermore, he believed that local police forces with their knowledge of local circumstances could best maintain security *and* order.[29] Police experts stressed the difficulties the security police had caused and criticized its allegedly tactless behavior towards the public and other police forces.[30] Suggestions for alternative options varied. Increasing the number of ordinary police forces was the most common demand supported by the affirmation that soldiers and policemen had very different tasks and, therefore, could not easily joins forces.[31] Others suggested continuing the *Verbürgerlichung* of the police which could be accompanied by the set-up of a military police to be mobilized only in cases of acute state emergencies.[32] Further proposals aimed at strengthening the civilian character of the police including changes to the police uniform,

---

27 Buder, 47-54.
28 Ernst Schrader, Ein Wort zur Aufklärung. Warum soll die alte Schutzmannschaft beseitigt werde? Berlin 1919, 3-7; Gustav Francke (Generalsekretär d. Polizeibeamten Deutschlands), Die Neugestaltung der Polizei, Berlin 1919, 4-10.
29 Die Polizei, 15, 23.10.1919, Neubau der Exekutivpolizei, 389. See also Kurt Wolzendorff (Professor für Verwaltungsrecht), Polizei im Volksstaate, in: G. Francke (ed.), Die Neugestaltung der Polizei, Berlin 1919, 35-38, here 38; Ernst Schrader, Die Reorganisation der Polizei, in: Gustav Francke (ed.), Die Neugestaltung der Polizei, Berlin 1919, 39-45, here 41
30 Sächsische Polizei-Beamten Zeitung, 15.9.1919, Protestkundgebung des Reichsverbandes gegen die Gründung einer Militärpolizei, 122.
31 Heinrich Lindenau (Oberverwaltungsgerichtsrat), Schutzmann oder Sicherheitssoldat, in: Francke (ed.), Neugestaltung der Polizei, Berlin 1919, 23-27, here 26-27.
32 Wolzendorff, 36-37.

the introduction of the baton as police weapon, the increase of local police stations as well as placing names or numbers of policemen on their collars to enable the public to easily identify them.[33]

Supporters of the new security police argued that the police's main concerns were linked to the loss of power and status in the proposed arrangement rather than the public's well being.[34] Indeed, police authority was not just questioned by political uprisings and turmoil, by rising crime rates and a lack of weapons, but, more fundamentally, by plans to take away one of the police's main tasks: maintaining security. This meant that ideas to reform and reorganize the police were debated with a sense of urgency and with the ultimate aim to prove that the police could still do its job properly. From March 1919 onwards, when plans regarding the introduction of a security police leaked, previous debates about internal police reforms and efforts to contribute to the shaping of the republic's future changed to more defensive claims trying to convince state ministries and the public alike of the usefulness of the police for its key tasks.

3. A NEW POLICE FOR NEW TIMES?
POLICE ASSOCIATIONS, DEMANDS AND EXPECTATIONS

When we look at the German revolution and its aftermath, moving away from direct threats to state order as well as political violence, we need to focus on police agency in these developments. Far from passively waiting until they were told what to do, policemen prepared to have their say in future police matters. In a number of cases, this newly discovered agency clashed with the state's radicalized quest for state authority. Police associations were one way for policemen to participate in decision making processes in their forces. These associations had already existed in Imperial Germany but they had not been allowed to represent demands linked to areas as negotiating wages, influencing police education or altering police structures.[35] This changed in November 1918 with the set-up of numerous police associations.[36] In mid-December 1918, the journal *Rundschau*

---

33 Rundschau für deutsche Polizei Beamte, 15.3.1919, Zur Neuorganisation der Schutzmannschaft, 430.
34 Friedrich Bertkau, Die Sicherheitspolizei, Berlin 1920, 22, 27.
35 Reuter, 28-29.
36 Statut des Verbandes Düsseldorfer Polizeibeamten genehmigt in der Generalversammlung am 23.11.1918; Die Industrie Zeitung für Rheinland und Westfalen: Offizielles Organ für die Polizei und Verwaltungsbeamten (1.4.1919-1.2.1920); Sächsische Polizei-Beamten Zeitung. Organ des Verbandes sächsischer Polizeibeamten.

für deutsche Polizeibeamte encouraged members of the police to make the most of their new rights: "... we have achieved that we can freely express our opinion and make our voices heard like any other citizen. Make use of this and found local police associations!"[37] Ernst Schrader demanded even earlier, in late November 1918, "to open the windows in all police stations so that the old air could disappear and the new spirit could blow inside." He encouraged policemen to actively participate and not to remain spectators of the most recent political events. Instead, he wanted policemen to inform themselves which political parties would best support their demands. Schrader also expressed his hopes of the demilitarization of the police relating to police equipment, uniforms as well as the tone within the police and the behavior of the police to the public.[38]

Equally, the *Rundschau für deutsche Polizeibeamten* asked policemen to help taking part in the great changes of the time, even when its outcomes could not be predicted.[39] There was a clear sense present in these journal articles that members of the police had to be strongly reminded of their political options and had to be encourage to make use of them even when future developments were uncertain. Historian Christoph Gusy suggests that for many civil servants and other old elites the sense of loss rather than gains temporarily characterized their views and feelings after the end of the First World War and that the new openness and uncertainty of the situation hit individuals much more dramatically than we often assume.[40] Given the circumstances, police associations with their efforts to shape future developments were attempts to recreate a sense of order and to promise future gains for individual policemen.

But it was not just the police's interest in new democratic rights and the appeal of organizing to get meaningful change on the way that was behind this wave of newly founded police association. There was a long list of demands addressing policing problems that rooted in the Imperial period. They included an 8-hour working day, the demilitarization of external appearance and internal structures, a better salary and a better insurance policy. In addition to these practical demands, there was the fear that police forces could be sidelined in case they failed to articulate their wishes at a time when others did so too. Several articles in police journals from November 1918 to the summer of 1919 reminded policemen that a strong and united voice was needed. Ernst Schrader, heading

---

37 Rundschau für deutsche Polizei Beamte, 12, 15.12.1918, Miteinander – Füreinander, 384.
38 Preußische Schutzmanns-Zeitung, 48, 30.11.1918, Neuorientierung, 421.
39 Rundschau für deutsche Polizeibeamten, 12, 15.12.1918, Kameraden, erwachet! 379-380.
40 Gusy, 34.

the police association uniting lower ranking policemen in Prussia, cautioned that too many newly founded police associations were not helpful for the goal of one powerful and united national police union.[41]

The learning curve in democratic self-organization was a steep one. While mobilizing members of Germany's police forces under the rally cry of protesting against the introduction of the security police successfully took place in Berlin and elsewhere in autumn 1919,[42] other issues on the agenda remained unresolved and undecided. Despite high hopes, a strong national police union (*Reichsverband deutscher Polizeibeamten*) did not function as well as envisaged and regional police associations kept their strong positions.[43] One issue causing problems was the question whether the police were allowed to go on strike. At the founding event of the *Reichsverband* in early May 1919, Schrader spoke out against strikes. In response, a number of local police associations disagreed and pointed to a number of successful strikes. The Düsseldorf representative Mr. Zinner claimed that the strike of Düsseldorf's police on 5 February 1919 had been important to support other civil servants protesting against measures of the workers and soldiers' council.[44] The representatives of Elberfeld and Leipzig agreed. In Elberfeld, the threat of going on strike of the municipal civil servants had been enough to prevent the police of being stripped off its weapons and from sacking individual police officers.[45] Policemen in Halle participated in a general strike but reassured that they would continue their task as soon as the strike was over.[46]

Despite these local examples, the policy of the *Reichsverband* was against using strikes especially when these actions were debated as tools for supporting

---

41 Preußische Schutzmanns-Zeitung, 1, 4.1.1919, Die Organisation der Polizeibeamten, 1-2.

42 Sächsische Polizei Beamten Zeitung, 15, 15.9.1919, Protestkundgebung des Reichsverbandes gegen die Gründung einer Militärpolizei, 121-122; Preußische Schutzmanns-Zeitung, 31, 19.9.1919, Die Militarisierung der Polizei vor dem Forum der deutschen Polizeibeamten, 365-366; Die Polizei, 17, 20.11.1919, Jedem das seine, 441. In early September (8.9.1919), numerous police associations met in Berlin to protest against the creation of the security police. While the security police were only planned for Prussia at the beginning, the fear that this system was to be adopted by other German states made mobilisation easier than for other issues.

43 Reuter, 65-70.

44 Rundschau für deutsche Polizeibeamte, 5, 15.5.1919, Reichsverband, 464.

45 Ibid, 465-66.

46 Die Polizei, 24.4.1919, Polizeibeamte in Halle und der Terror der Unabhänigen, 44.

financial demands.[47] Nevertheless, a small, perhaps desperate, threat remained. When the setting up of a new security police was condemned by the *Preußische Schutzmanns-Zeitung*, the journal referred to police strikes in England as a warning sign for the Prussian government. It pointed out that Prussia's police might need to resort to these actions if "forced to fight for its existence."[48] While the English police strike – mainly carried by the Metropolitan Police and the City of London Police in August 1918 – led to substantial improvements,[49] the German reference to it remained timid. Going on a national strike would presumably have further strengthened Prussian and national authorities in their convictions that the police were not fit for purpose.

Efforts of police forces across Germany to prevent the set-up of the security police failed,[50] but they triggered an intensive debate within the police about its allegedly inefficient role in securing order and even more about a *neuzeitliche* police within the new German state. When reforms and demands for the future were aimed at the position of the police in fast changing circumstances, these suggestions were, from the summer of 1919 onwards, clearly directed against the plans of the Prussian Ministry of the Interior and the Reich Ministry of Defense. The alleged new police with its new spirit became more than a future vision – it was presented as clear alternative to the introduction of a security police which was attacked as backwards and militaristic impeding the creation of a new police that fitted to the new times.[51] In these debates, the police discovered its democratic heart and focused on the relations between the police, the people and the republic. The new plans for the police did not fit to the new democratic republic neither to the people's wishes and was "a step backwards to reactionary times", so Gustav Francke, the head of the *Polizeibeamtenbund*, in September 1919.[52]

---

47 Rundschau für deutsche Polizeibeamte, 4, 15.4.1919, Der Polizeibeamte und die neue Zeit (E. Schrader), 443-444.
48 Preußische Schutzmanns-Zeitung, 25, 21.6.1919, Vor der Abschiedsstunde, 245-246.
49 Clive Emsley, The Great British Bobby, London 2009, 192-197.
50 When the Allies demanded dissolving the security police (due to its militaristic character) in 1920 and the security police had already proven its lack of reliability by siding with the organisers of the Kapp Putsch, police journals pointed out that they had made these points all along: Preußische Schutzmanns-Zeitung, 12/13, 27.3.1920, Der Putsch von rechts; Preußische Schutzmanns-Zeitung, 14, 3.4.1920, Die notwendige Neugestaltung der Polizei; Die Polizei, 4, 13.5.1920, Die Forderung des Tages.
51 Preußische Schutzmanns-Zeitung, 23, 7.6.1919, Gegen den alten Geist, 217; Preußische Schutzmanns-Zeitung, 24, 14.6.1919, Die Militarisierung der Polizei, 233.
52 Sächsische Polizei Beamten Zeitung, 15, 15.9.1919, Protestkundgebung des Reichsverbandes.

The personnel of the security police, with its recruiting of young military men, was also negatively contrasted to a somewhat rosy image of ordinary policemen. The picture of an experienced educator and trusted state representative with tactful behavior, common sense and appropriate police schooling was painted.[53] If not all these qualities had been obvious to the public before the revolution, this was allegedly due to superiors, regulations and militaristic hierarchies of the police in Imperial Germany. Now the police officer, so the suggestion, had changed from the police soldier to the free citizen among citizens. The journal *Die Polizei* summarized in July 1919: "A policeman should be helper, friend and guide. He should enjoy the trust of the public and be the person to turn to in any emergency." In theory, so the article, this could also be achieved by a man of the security police but the public had had enough of the war and of the military and would regard the security police as "natural enemy."[54] In addition, it was pointed out that the police needed to be part of the people ("im Volke stehen") to do its task properly. Already by definition, a member of the security police who lived in barracks could not fulfill this task.[55] Furthermore, this concept of the policeman being part of the people and, therefore, a citizen and guardian also encapsulated self-control and rational behavior rather than the readiness to resort to violence. This strong suggestion on the necessity of being part of the people was not just emphasized to strengthen the distance between the policemen and the soldier of the security police; it also embodied the criticism on police behavior in Imperial Germany when policemen were seen as behaving as if they were far removed from those they were policing.

While police experts, ranging from heads of police associations to senior police officials, were genuinely unhappy that their expertise had not been taken into account, or even consulted, by the Prussian ministry and found the police unfairly accused of having failed in its job, their demilitarization argument was the most prominent one put forward. It allowed the police to shift negative connotations regarding military style policing upon a different organization and, in so doing, the police sided with the public on this issue. Supporting the police's opinion, Berlin lawyer Dr Abraham wrote: "For us democrats, the positive result of the revolution so far has been the abolition of militarism. The London police were our role model and now the first achievement of our democracy should be

---

53 Sächsische Polizei Beamten Zeitung, 15, 15.9.1919, Mit dem Volk und für das Volk.
54 Die Polizei, 9, 31.7.1919, Zur Reform der Polizei, 236.
55 Die Polizei, 1, 10.4.1919, Die Polizei in der Demokratie; Die Polizei, 9, 31.7.1919, Zur Reform der Polizei.

the militarization of the police."[56] This sense of disappointment was even more pronounced in an article by Ernst Schrader who started with the high hopes in November 1918: "After the Prussian military regiment had collapsed on November 9 and the free republic was proclaimed [...], we believed that reforms and *neuzeitliche* changes would be made to the police. We believed that here in Berlin, in the capital of the new Germany, the beginning would be made... Should the police exist for the public or just for the government?"[57]

Some of these arguments inspired political debates. The reports of the Saxon People's Chamber illustrate heated discussions in late 1919 linked to the set-up of a militarized auxiliary police which was praised by the Social Democratic minister president Dr Georg Gradnauer in late October 1919 as a force "to safeguard the outcomes of the revolution." An interpretation the USPD (Independent Social Democratic Party) delegate and vice president Lipinski did not share when he classified the new auxiliary police as simply another formation of the army far removed from the traditional meaning of the police.[58] His USPD fellow party member Menke developed this point further by suggesting that the ordinary police forces should be increased rather than the creating a new "military formation."[59] It was an unusual alliance, and for very different motifs, in which the heads of police associations, who did not share the political convictions of the USPD, agreed in their rejection of the employment of more militarized support for the police.

Police protest against the introduction of the security police did not achieve a change in this policy. A year after the German revolution, Ernst Schrader published a summary of the previous twelve months with bleak future prospects. The initial excitement about helping to shape the republic's future and to participate in this making of new country had suffered severe blows. It was not the memories of the revolution that caused the article's depressed tone, but the proposed changes to police structures that, according to Schrader, "had systematically excluded police experience and expertise."[60] While vanity combined with the annoyance of not being listened to or even consulted certainly played a part in Schrader's evaluation, this was also about disappointed expectations in the

---

56 Abraham, Die Militarisierung der Berliner Schutzmannschaft, in: G. Francke (ed.), Neugestaltung der Polizei Berlin 1919, 47
57 Preußische Schutzmanns-Zeitung, 24, 14.6.1919, Die Militarisierung der Polizei, 233.
58 Verhandlungen der Sächsischen Volkskammer, Vol. 3, 1919/20, Session 65, 29.10. 1919, 2256, 2258.
59 Ibid., Session 74, 17.12.1919, 2521.
60 Preußische Schutzmanns-Zeitung, 45, 8.11.1919, Zum Jahrestag der Staatsumwälzung, 461.

new 'people's state' which did not value, so it seemed, the contribution of those wanting to help shaping its future.[61] In fact, these contributions were ignored and reversed due to the state's radicalized security policy; a security policy classified by many in the police as reactionary. The year of 1920 saw a number of revisions on this policy and ended the short life of the security police, but the newly created Prussian *Schutzpolizei* recruited men from both forces and was far removed from the civilian police force envisaged earlier.

4. "THE REVOLUTION HAS CONFUSED PEOPLE'S MINDS!" HOSTILE POLICE-PUBLIC RELATIONS AND LOCAL SPACE

While it was fairly easy for police forces to link their reform ideas to alleged demands from the public asking for a less militaristic appearance of the police, different and less harmful police weapons and friendlier relations between police and public,[62] it seemed to have been much more difficult to convince the public of this 'new' police. The fact that the strict and often biased policing in Imperial Germany was still fresh on the public's memory meant that debates on public-police relations almost always started with the assurance that the police had changed since the revolution.[63]

Ernst Schrader found that "the revolution had confused people's minds" and that many citizens in Germany's urban centers felt that the new freedom created by the revolution also meant that police orders did not need to be followed anymore. The difficult security situation had, according to Schrader, strengthened

---

61 Thomas Mergel suggests that one of the difficulties of the Weimar Republic and especially of its politics could be linked to the unrealistically high expectations placed upon the Weimar state. See Thomas Mergel, High expectations – deep disappointment. Structures of the public perception of politics in the Weimar Republic, in: Kathleen Canning et al. (eds.), Weimar Politics/Weimar Subjects, New York 2010, 192-210.

62 Preußische Schutzmanns-Zeitung, 4, 25.1.1919, Die notwendige Reorganisation der Schutzmannschaft, 29-30; Rundschau für deutsche Polizeibeamte, 4, 15.4.1919, Der Polizeibeamte und die neue Zeit, 442.

63 It is striking that these assurances continued well into the mid-1920s suggesting that the German public as well as the police needed to be reminded constantly that the police had moved on from its imperial past, see for example Paul Schmidt, Der praktische Dienst der Straßenpolizei, Berlin, 1922, 9-11.

these developments.[64] Furthermore, he suggested that the press and politicians had failed to educate and inform the public about the necessity of a police force in a republican state. The intensity with which the newspapers were informing their readers on a daily basis on the difficult security situation and the need for a security police should rather have been concentrated on reminding the German public to follow police orders.[65] Here the anger and bitterness about the newly created security police became obvious but also the deep rooted assumption in the police that the sometimes hostile citizens need to be educated to behave 'correctly'. The MSPD (Majority Social Democratic Party) deputy Becker made a similar call for better public support of the police. Speaking in Bremen's national assembly in July 1919, Becker demanded that everything should be done so that the press and the public supported police actions and that especially the integration of the working class was needed in this process. But he also reminded that policemen needed a much better understanding for the difficulties of the people and had to react accordingly and with empathy.[66]

Indeed, police-public relations were severely determined by police actions. Police responses to hostility and violence from sections of the German society often meant overreacting on the side of the police. Especially Imperial Germany had seen a number of cases in which police reactions directed at members of the working class had resulted in violent incidents that were interpreted as excessive by the liberal and the Social Democratic press.[67] The lethal danger of police weapons, often including sabers, contributed substantially to the situation. When police reformers stressed in 1918/1919 that Prussia's police should never again be used against the population to secure class interest, it was the heavily biased policing of the Imperial years that served as the backdrop for these demands.

We have already seen that the initial handover of police stations to soldiers and workers' councils in November 1918 happened quickly and with limited problems. This was mainly due to the fact that diminished police forces throughout the country had no capacity to defend police stations against soldiers and

---

64 Preußische Schutzmanns-Zeitung, 4, 25.1.1919, Die notwendig Reorganisation der Schutzmannschaft, 29-30.

65 Schrader, 45.

66 Verhandlungen der verfassungsgebenden Bremschen Nationalversammlung vom Jahre 1919/20, Session 25.7.1919, 665-667.

67 Thomas Lindenberger, Vom Säbelhieb zum sanften Weg? Lektüre physischer Gewalt zwischen Bürgern und Polizisten im 20. Jahrhundert, in: Alf Lüdtke et al. (eds.), Polizei, Gewalt und Staat im 20. Jahrhundert, Wiesbaden 2011, 205-224 (here 206-213). More generally see Thomas Lindenberger, Straßenpolitik. Zur Sozialgeschichte der öffentlichen Ordnung in Berlin 1900-1914, Bonn 1995.

revolutionaries and, therefore, opted for cooperation based on a lack of alternative. But this initial smooth shift of power did not last throughout the winter of 1918/19. The violent beginning of 1919 turned police stations into contested territory as they did not only come under attack in Spartacist uprisings but also from those in search of weapons which had been stored in police stations.[68]

In the Easter days of April 1919, Hamburg's working-class areas experienced violent protests, shootings at police stations and efforts to release prisoners. A state of emergency was declared and Hamburg's police relied on *Volkswehren* and, more importantly, on the *Wachabteilung* Bahrendfeld consisting of uniformed and heavily armed men to deal with the situation.[69] In early May 1919, Hamburg's police turned to the citizens of Germany's second city with a declaration expressing the force's irritation with the security situation and with the hostility towards the police without referring explicitly to the events just a few days earlier:

"[...] The police are not a *Kampftruppe* and will never serve as one. It is our task to fight criminals and protect property but we are facing big problems. Maybe some find it appropriate to steal the weapons of policemen but can a police officer fight against criminals without weapons? And who suffers from this? And from whom do criminals frequently steal? Especially from the working classes [...]. We want to serve everyone but everyone needs to understand that policemen need to be able to defend themselves when attacked. We are only doing our duty. Leave our police stations alone, they are there for the good of the masses. When police stations are attacked, this is done by criminals and we are fighting criminals."[70]

Berlin's police pointed out that they completely agreed with their Hamburg colleagues.[71] The sentiment expressed here that police stations could turn into rather weak strongholds in a sea of insecurity or, at least, unpredictable public reactions clearly irritated Hamburg's police. The fact that the city's 'Easter unrest' had resulted in 18 dead and had seen the use of 600 uniformed and militarised men helping the police to gain control[72] strengths the impression of a police force that felt under attack and believed it had to react forcefully. It also exem-

---

68 Weinhauer, 88-89.
69 Ibid, 84-85.
70 Cited in Preußischen Schutzmanns-Zeitung, 19, 10.5.1919, Ein Aufruf der Hamburger Schutzmannschaft an die Bevölkerung, 177.
71 Ibid.
72 Weinhauer, 85.

plifies a break down of communications and a lack of understanding between the police and the public.

The issue of police stations as important local pillars within the spatial network to secure order of a particular area was also debated with an eye to the set-up of the security police. Those critical of a new militarised police force suggested that order and security could be maintained through more police presence and regular beat patrol by the same police officer who should get to know the local population.[73] This suggestion echoed the core concepts of the English Metropolitan Police with its main aim of crime prevention rather than crime detection. To increase the numbers of local police stations and to ensure that they were not far away from each other was also considered as having an important impact on police public relations.[74] Unlike Hamburg's police, where the force's stations were presented as almost under siege by the public, the spread of police stations could be used very deliberately to maintain state authority. Also those in favour of the new security police thought about the location of police stations. The security concept for Berlin in mid-1919 envisaged not only the introduction of the security police but also the reorganisation of the spread of its police stations and the reduction of local police stations by one third. In the city's Eastern and Northern working-class neighbourhoods, ordinary police stations were meant to be replaced with stations of the security police illustrating clearly which areas were considered to be in need of policing by heavily armed security policemen.[75]

5. LEGACIES OF THE REVOLUTION?
THE PEOPLE'S POLICE AND THE PEOPLE'S STATE IN THE MID-1920S

In 1928, the leading police journal *Die Polizei* celebrated its twenty-fifth anniversary. Good wishes filled the pages combined with reflections on the turbulent last twenty-five years and an emphasis on the successful path the police had taken.[76] The difficult winter months of 1918/19 seemed a long time away. Furthermore, the restructuring of Germany's police forces in the early years of the

---

73 Rundschau für deutsche Polizeibeamte, 3, 15.3.1919, Zur Neuorganisation der Schutzmannschaft. Einige praktische Ratschläge, 430.
74 Ibid.
75 Schrader, 44.
76 See Die Polizei, 7 (Festnummer), 10.4.1928.

Weimar Republic meant that Prussia's police could date its "re-birth" to 1920 instead of 1918.[77] By the mid-1920s, neither the Prussian nor the national government was keen on commemorating the revolution.[78] This is not surprising given the fact that the republic's founding document was the Weimar Constitution drafted by the national assembly and signed by Reich president Friedrich Ebert in August 1919.[79] Policemen, as other civil servants, had to ensure that their actions were in line with Germany's democratic constitution. Furthermore, the revolution had left ambivalent memories which did not fit neatly into a grand narrative of heroically overthrowing the monarchy and establishing a democratic republic. Ten years after the revolution, references to it remained scarce.[80]

Annual festivities celebrated the signing of the Weimar Constitution (11.8.1919). These celebrations involved policemen in parades, concerts, sporting competitions, children's festivals and other events staged to honor the constitution *and* to promote a positive police image.[81] Official narratives of leading republican politicians as Carl Severing and Albrecht Grzesinki called the police the most important instrument of republican state authority.[82] Republican newspapers reported impressed from these celebrations, particularly from the capital, stressing the large number of policemen attending.[83]

---

77 Deutsches Polizei Archiv, 19, 10.10.1930, Werdegang der preußischen Exekutivepolizei, 294-297.

78 The great attention given to the tenth anniversary of the Weimar Constitution in August 1929 strikingly illustrates the lack of interest in the anniversary of the revolution in November 1928.

79 Contemporaries and historians alike have questioned the usefulness of having a constitution as founding document rather than a heroic narrative of struggle for liberty and freedom.

80 Gavriel D. Rosenfeld's article on commemorating the Bavarian revolution makes the same point with mainly focusing on commemorative activities after 1945. See Gavriel D. Rosenfeld, Monuments and the Politics of Memory. Commemorating Kurt Eisner and the Bavarian Revolution of 1918-1919 in Postwar Munich, in: Central European History 30 (1998), 221-252; Alexander Gallus, Die vergessene Revolution von 1918/1919 – Erinnerung und Deutung im Wandel, in: Alexander Gallus (ed.), Die vergessene Revolution von 1918/19, Göttingen 2010, 14-38.

81 For photographs see A. Grzesinski's papers in Landesarchiv Berlin. See also Die Polizei, 16, 20.8.1929 title page; Deutsche Polizei-Archiv, 16, 25.8.1930.

82 BArch Berlin, R601/203, fiche 10; Landesarchiv Berlin, E-200-60, 3983, speech by Grzesinski in 1931, Vossische Zeitung, 12.8.1929 Die Verfassungsfeier der Polizei.

83 Vossische Zeitung, 375, 11.8.1930 Der Aufmarsch der Berliner Schupo; Das Reichsbanner, 17, 1.9.1926, Verfassungsfeiern in den Gauen.

There was one important concept close to the hearts and minds of police officials and politicians who wanted to create a convincing narrative for the German police in the republican state: the idea of the people's police (*Volkspolizei*) in the people's state.[84] Introduced in the Weimar years, the term 'people's police' was used by successive political systems always stressing that the current state had the one and only people's police.[85] While it was easy for Weimar politicians and senior police officials to point out that the police of Imperial Germany had served class interests, cemented societal hierarchies and, therefore, needed to change, it was difficult to pinpoint when this change to this alleged *Volkspolizei* had happened. In 1928, overview articles on the police's development in the previous ten years refrained from giving a precise date, but linked the term people's police to the vague description *Staatsumwälzung* (change of state form).[86] Depending on political preferences and individual circumstances, the revolution, the abdication of the monarch, the first meeting of the national assembly or being accountable to the new workers and soldiers' council could mark the beginning of this *Staatsumwälzung* for policemen. In this way, an explicit link to the revolution did not need to be made, but, at the same time, the emphasis on the police's development to an organization that fitted the new times could be kept. After all, already the years before the outbreak of the First World War, had seen mounting criticism on the police's behavior towards the general public and its policing practices.[87]

In the Weimar years the reference to the 'people's police' meant different things to different people. It was especially the police reformers of Schrader's association who had very specific ideas linked to this concept going well beyond

---

84 Today the term people's police (*Volkspolizei*) is linked to its use in the German Democratic Republic. Unlike the GDR, neither the Weimar nor the Nazi state called their policemen *Volkspolizisten* on a daily basis. But the term *Volkspolizei* was used in the Weimar and Nazi years when politicians and police officials wanted to stress the police's role as serving the people.

85 For Nazi interpretations see Der deutsche Polizeibeamte, 5, 1.11.1933, Die Bedeutung des Kameradschaftsbundes im NS Staat; Der deutsche Polizeibeamte, 15, 1.8.1936, Polizei und Presse "...stolz u. freudigen Herzens können wir sagen: wir haben die so lange ersehnte und erkämpfte deutsche Volkspolizei."

86 Die Polizei, 7, 10.4.1928, Die Bedeutung der Polizei für den Staatsgedanken (A. Grzesinski); Die Polizei, 7, 10.4.1928, Die Organisation der preußischen Polizei (E. Klausener).

87 Herbert Reinke, Armed as if for War. The State, the Military and the Professionalisation of the Prussian Police in Imperial Germany, in: Clive Emsley/Barbara Weinberger (eds.), Policing Western Europe, Westport 1991, 55- 73 (here 65-73).

allusions in festive speeches or commemorative articles. The slogan 'with the people, for the people and from the people' was in 1918/19 directed against militarizing efforts and stressed the importance of the civilian character of the police.[88] In later years, these demands related to expanding the circle of those recruited to the police and to abolish obstacles in career paths for higher police posts. The *Preußische Polizeibeamten Zeitung* (previous Preußische Schutzmanns-Zeitung) wrote in 1926:

"[...] class barriers that cannot be overcome by those who are well qualified for the post should not exist in the *Volkspolizei*. The new state demands from its *Volkspolizei* first and foremost service to the people and should enable everyone to rise up the ranks."[89]

Here the police association reminded Weimar politicians that the true idea behind the catchphrase of the people's police in the republican people's state still awaited its fulfillment and actually still meant unfulfilled demands. In fact, the popular 1930- publication *Volk und Schupo*, aimed at creating a positive image of the police, claimed that statistical evidence on professions, religious affiliations and educational background of those entering the police in 1928 illustrated that the police already had "the character of a people's police."[90] A claim that was not true for high ranking positions within the police.

But even when politicians and police officials did not mean quite the same when they alluded to the term *Volkpolizei*, they generally shared the republican constitution as their reference and starting point by the mid-1920s. An important exception to the Prussian police's settling on lobbying on issues as recruitment policy, salary scales and career opportunities within the police, came from criminal police officer Erich Klingelhöller. He was a dedicated member of Ernst Schrader's police association and wrote the *Festschrift* for the association's tenth anniversary in 1926.[91] In his writings, Klingelhöller looked at the connections between the revolution, the police and the people in more detail regretting that

---

88 Preußische Schutzmanns-Zeitung, 36, 6.9.1919, Mit dem Volk und für das Volk!, 353-354; Die Polizei, 2, 24.4.1919, Die Polizei der Demokratie, 31-33.

89 Preußische Polizeibeamten Zeitung, 4, 23.1.1926, Polizei und Politik (Polizei-Oberst a. D. Dr. Schützinger).

90 Volk und Schupo, Cologne 1930, 40-41.

91 Erich Klingelhöller, Der Verband der Preußischen Polizeibeamten in seinem Werden und Wirken, Berlin 1926. For the situation of the Schrader association as well as of other police associations in the Nazi period see Elisabeth Volquardts, Beamtenverbände im Nationalsozialismus. Gleichschaltung zum Zwecke der Ausschaltung aufgrund politischer oder weltanschaulicher Gegnerschaft, Munich 2001, 111-129.

the civil servants (including the police) had not been clearer and courageous enough in their public commitment to the revolution. [92] He also felt that the discussion on the police since the revolution, and especially on the police's distance to the public, had focused too much on police shortcomings of the Imperial years that needed to be corrected in the new republic. According to Klingelhöller, it was the trinity of revolution, constitution and *Volksstaat* that needed to determine the organization and the development of the Prussian police.[93]

Fiver years later, in March 1931, Klingelhöller extended his criticism on the narrow focus on the Weimar Constitution as dominant reference point for the police in the 1920s and early 1930s. Partly to blame, he found, was the term *Volkspolizei* which had never really caught on due to the revolutionary connotations of the prefix "Volk." Born in the revolution to demonstrate the difference between the new police and the police of the Imperial years, the idealistic connotations of the concept were difficult to communicate to police and public alike. Furthermore, the term *Volkspolizei* was looked at suspiciously by many in the police who had experienced the bitter political fights and hostile public reactions in the early years of the republic. Erich Klingelhöller wanted to re-connect the term *Volkspolizei* to the revolution *and* the constitution and reminded that not concepts but historical developments shaped police organizations. He also acknowledged that many did not want to remember the revolution, but found:

"The revolution cannot be ignored because it gave the state a new form, a new face...the police is a product of this revolution. We need to develop the new *Polizeigedanken* (police idea) based on the revolution and combine it with the state's idea anchored in the republican constitution."[94]

This, he stressed, needed to take place at police schools and training facilities.[95]

Klingelhöller was not the only one reflecting on the link between the police and the people. The head of the German police institute Ernst van den Bergh suggested a very organic idea of the relationship between the police and the people that was to develop slowly over time.[96] Also van den Bergh felt that the police had a role in these developments and that a new sense of community should be created but he believed that trust and cooperation between the police

---

92 Klingelhöller, Der Verband der Preußischen Polizeibeamten, 26-27.
93 Ibid, 126.
94 Die Polizeipraxis, 4, 15.3.1931, Der neue Polizeigedanke (E. Klingelhöller).
95 Ibid.
96 Ernst van den Bergh, Polizei und Volk. Seelische Zusammenhänge, Berlin 1926.

and the public meant a slow and organic development.[97] Unlike van den Bergh, Klingelhöller found it was the rupture of the revolution that should be used to redefine the role of the police in the new German state that got its face through the revolution first and only thereafter through the constitution.

6. CONCLUSION

In hindsight, Prussia's former ministerial president, the Social Democrat Otto Braun, captured the general changes that occurred in November 1918 with an image linked to the police. He wrote in his memoir published in 1949: "The Prussian *Schutzmann*, whose omnipotence used to frighten the average citizen, fearfully ducked out and eventually disappeared completely off the streets."[98] While Braun was correct concerning the speed by which a powerful force like the Prussian police had to adapt to new circumstances, there are more stories to be told about Germany's policemen and their interpretation of the winter 1918/19. Chaos and insecurity were combined with demands for reforms and more rights for policemen. Numerous police associations tried to give a voice to members of the police, to represent their interests and to re-think police relations to the public. The introduction of the security police clearly illustrated the helplessness of police leaders in influencing – or even changing – this decision but, at the same time, the militarized force provided a powerful point of contrast for re-defining the institutional identity of the police. In the end, external factors determined the final shape of the German police and not all demands were met, not all reforms carried out and not everyone had the same ideas about the future role(s) of German police forces.

Convincing state ministries that the police should have a prominent role and substantial input in the shaping of Germany's security organizations failed due to the state's strong quest for authority. Convincing the public of the police's new ideas and new interpretations of its role(s) in relation to the German people and the new democratic state proved equally difficult and slow. And it was not just looking back to Germany's Imperial past that created problems; also police actions in the first years after the revolution often resembled an overwhelmed,

---

97 Ibid, 130.
98 Cited in Axel Schildt, Der lange November – zur Historisierung einer deutschen Revolution, in Alexander Gallus (ed.), Die vergessene Revolution von 1918/19, Göttingen 2010, 223-244 (here 228).

and sometimes overreacting, police.[99] Attacks on police stations as well as the assumption that the public felt that police orders did not need to be followed anymore irritated police forces and might have strengthened resentments.

The brief debate in 1918/19 about the role of a *neuzeitliche* police in the new state never reached the same intensity again in the Weimar years. After the founding of the Prussian *Schutzpolizei* in 1920, the revolution became a neglected reference point as it was replaced by the Weimar Constitution as the state's founding document. Even the police journal of Schrader's association, in 1919 at the forefront of stating that the revolution and its consequences needed a reformed police to fit to the new times, published little more than cursory statements on the years 1918 to 1920. Police officials and politicians tried to smoothly integrate the police by promoting and re-interpreting the concept of the *Volkspolizei*. Originally used by police associations to distance their reform demands for a more civilian police from the state's security policy in 1919, it turned into a catchword used by politicians and police officials alike to stress the connection between the police and the democratic "people's state."

However, police associations did maintain that the "people's police" was a future promise rather than reality. By focusing on the force's inclusiveness and recruitment policy, they reminded Weimar politicians that the true "people's police" which recruited from all sections of society was far removed from reality in 1928. Prejudices, hierarchies and class barriers within the police and within its recruitment meant that German police forces contributed to this situation and were heavily criticized by police associations. After the end of the Second World War, it was East Germany that tried the experiment of forming a police force deliberately recruited from people with no past experience in the police to avoid hiring those who had served in the Weimar or the Nazi state. Quickly, the consequences of this policy proved to be difficult but the rhetoric behind its set-up reminds us of similar ideas formulated by the Prussian police in 1918.[100]

---

99 See Weinhauer, 69-102. Richard Bessel reminds us that the difficulties of making police aspirations regarding a changed relationship to the public and policing activities compatible with each other characterised the Weimar years. See Richard Bessel, Policing, Professionalisation and Politics in Weimar Germany, in: Clive Emsley/ Barbara Weinberger (eds.), Policing Western Europe, New York 1991, 187-218.

100 Richard Bessel, Policing East Germany in the wake of the Second World War, in Crime, History & Societies 7:2 (2003), 5-21, here 7.

Labour Conflict and Everyday Violence as "Revolution"?
Barcelona, 1919-23

FLORIAN GRAFL

1. INTRODUCTION

In 1910, a former Civil Governor of Barcelona, Angel Ossorio, wrote: "Barcelona is a place where revolution is always ready to take place".[1] What he was obviously referring to were mainly the events of late July 1909, when a local protest against the unpopular war fought by the Spanish army in Morocco had led to a week of street fighting and incendiarism in Barcelona.[2] These struggles, in which about hundred people lost their lives and dozens of church buildings were set on fire, became known as Semana Trágica (Tragic Week), and may well constitute the most dramatic popular uprising in central Europe before the First World War.[3] Almost exactly ten years later, the city experienced another apocalyptical event: a strike at the Canadiese factory, the most important electricity company in the city, brought Barcelona to a total standstill for more than 40

---

1 Angel Ossorio, Barcelona, Madrid 1910, 13-14.
2 In the course of the 100th anniversary of the Tragic Week, many new works have been published, for example: Alexia Domínguez Àlvarez, La Setmana Tràgica de Barcelona 1909, Valls 2009, as well as: Dolors Marín, La Semana Trágica. Barcelona en llamas, la revuelta popular y la Escuela Moderna, Madrid 2009, and David Martínez Fiol, La Semana Tràgica, Barcelona 2009.
3 Angel Smith, La Semana Trágica, una perspectiva europea, in: Soledad Bengoechea (ed.), Barcelona i la Setmana Tràgica, 1909. Arrels i conseqüències, Barcelona 2012, 13-32, here: 13.

days. The strike spread to other factories as well, and in total about 100,000 workers participated.[4] Reports from eyewitness say that nearly all felt that this event, in which the anarchist trade union CNT (Confederación Nacional del Trabajo) for the first time demonstrated its growing power, was the start of a new age.[5] The years that followed would prove them right. Only a few months after the strike, which ended in success for the workers, the Federación Patronal, the association of employers, struck back by organizing a lock-out affecting about 200,000 workers, in order to smash the hated CNT.[6] After these events, a peaceful solution to the labor struggles became almost unthinkable. Therefore, the workers started to blackmail factory owners in order to improve their working conditions. Some of the victims refused, and as a result, were shot. In response, the Federación Patronal, which saw the work of the police as completely inefficient, began to gather a group of assassins themselves in order to take revenge. In this bloody labor war, which became known as the time of "Pistolerismo", more than 800 people fell victim to this practice in the streets of Barcelona by 1923.[7] Barcelona, as well as Spain as a whole, once again was on the verge of revolution, which the anarchists led by Buenaventura Duruti had carefully planned.[8] However, the army struck first. They responded to the demands of the Catalan employers for an "Iron Surgeon", and by a coup d'etat, General Primo de Rivera in September 1923 established a firm dictatorship which violently suppressed everything which he saw as a potential danger to the Spanish

---

4 Obviously, this event has already been thoroughly investigated. starting with Albert Balcells, El Sindicalismo en Barcelona (1916-1923), Barcelona 1965 to recent monographs by Angel Smith, Anarchism, Revolution and Reaction. Catalan Labour and the Crisis of the Central State, 1898-1923, New York 2007.

5 See for example: Coromines, Pere, Cartes d'un visionari, Barcelona 192, 218-219 and Alfaro Baratech, Los sindicatos libres de España. Su origen – su actuación – su ideario, Barcelona 1927, 51.

6 The lock-out apart from the two books mentioned above, is extensively covered in Soledad Bengoechea, El locaut de Barcelona (1919-1920). Els precedents de la Dictadura de Primo de Rivera, Barcelona 1998.

7 For a general overview of the events of the Pistolerismo, see the monograph by Albert Balcells, El pistolerisme, Barcelona 2009, or the article by Francisco Romero Salvadó, "'Si vis pacem para bellum". The Catalan Employers' Dirty War 1919-23', in: Francisco Romero Salvadó /Angel Smith (eds.), The agony of Spanish liberalism. From revolution to dictatorship 1913-1923, London 2010, 175-201.

8 See the extensive monograph by Abel Paz, Durruti. Leben und Tod des spanischen Anarchisten, Hamburg 1994.

state: anarchism, labor unions and Catalan nationalism.[9] However, when Primo de Rivera gave way after he losing the support of his benefactors in 1930, it only took a while until the conflicts once again turned into the violent struggles that finally led to the Civil War, the biggest catastrophe in the history of modern Spain.[10]

Given the large impact of the events in Barcelona between 1919 and 1923, it is rather strange that while the violence of the interwar-period in Europe gained a lot of recognition recently, the Spanish case so far has been almost neglected. One recent example is the book edited by Robert Gerwarth on paramilitary violence in Europe in the interwar-period. Although the book is doubtlessly an impressive work with a remarkably wide scale in geographical terms, covering not only well-known examples as Germany and Italy, but also Ireland and the Baltic countries in Northern Europe, as well as Russia and Ukraine in the East and the Ottoman Empire in the South, it nevertheless excludes Spain without further explanation.[11] Without going into much detail on the historiography of Spain in the first half of the 20th century, the exclusion of the Spanish case in monographs on the violence of the revolutionary years following the First World War, seems to stem from two reasons. Firstly, a rather trivial explanation is that due to the language barrier, many of the extant works on mostly political violence in Spain during the first half of the 20th century, as for example the groundbreaking work by Eduardo González Calleja, remain almost unknown.[12] The second reason is that Spain did not take part in the First World War, and therefore seemingly, the thesis of brutalization does not necessarily apply. This thesis claims that civil societies in the European states were brutalized during their

---

9 Once again, it should be enough to cite a classic work such as Ben-Ami, Shlomo. Faciscm from Above: The Dictatorship of Primo de Rivera 1923-1930, Oxford 1983 as well as a recent monograph: Eduardo González Calleja, La España de Primo de Rivera (1923-1930). La modernización autoritaria, Madrid 2005.

10 For the dimensions of this massive bloodshed, it is enough to have a look at the recent book by Paul Preston, The Spanish Holocaust, Inquisition and Extermination in Twentieth-Century Spain, London 2012.

11 Gerwarth, Robert/Horne, John (eds.), War in Peace. Paramilitary Violence in Europe after the First World War, Oxford 2012.

12 See Eduardo González Calleja, El máuser y el sufragio. Orden público, subversión y violencia política en la crisis de la Restauración 1917-1931, Madrid 1999 as well as the recent Contrarrevolucionarios. Radicalización violenta de las derechas durante la Segunda República, 1931-1936, Madrid 2011.

service in the First World War.[13] In terms of the Spanish case, however, the assumption that Spain, due to its neutrality during the First World War did not undergo a process of brutalization is based on a very superficial knowledge of its contemporary history. In fact, even without having participated actively in the bloody battles of the First World War, the Spaniards nevertheless suffered from various instances of collective violence, beginning with the 19th century when the country was shaken by the bloody guerrilla war fought against the occupation army of Napoleon, and later by the violence in the remaining Spanish colonies, i.e. Cuba, the Philippines and Morocco[14].

These considerations make it worthwhile to examine the Spanish case more closely in the context of the revolution of 1918/19 to make comparisons to other European countries. So far, most collective violence in Spain in the first decades of the 20th century was examined to explain the excesses of violence during the Civil War.[15] This article instead aims to show that the collective violence which put Spain on the verge of revolution in 1923 has to be seen not only in the context of the history of collective violence in contemporary Spain, but also in the context of the European revolutions which are dealt with in this book. One might argue that, for example, in comparison to the revolutionary events in Germany, it is questionable whether one could speak of a "revolution" in the Spanish case. It is true that the violent events in Spain were motivated largely socially, rather than politically and might not have had the same dimension as in Germany. However, not only did contemporaries have a sense of the impending Civil War as early as the late 1910s, but also recent Spanish historians speak of an ongoing

---

13 See for example the first issue of the Journal of Modern European History (2003), which focused on Violence and Society after the First World War.

14 For an overview of the history of Spain in the 19th century, see for example: Mary Vincent, Spain 1833-2002. People and State, Oxford 2007, the Spanish army and its struggle in the colonies was first examined by Stanley Payne, Politics and the Military in Modern Spain, Stanford 1967. A recent article would be: Sebastian Balfour, The Making of an Interventionalist Army 1898-1923, in: Francisco Romero Salvadó/Angel Smith (eds.), The agony of Spanish liberalism. From Revolution to Dictatorship 1913-1923, London 2010, 255-274.

15 The classical example is Gerald Brenan's The Spanish Labyrinth. The social and political background of the Spanish Civil War, Cambridge 2009. Modern examples are the books by Julián Casanova and Stanley Payne, for example Julián Casanova, The Spanish Republic and Civil War, Cambridge 2010 and Stanley Payne, The Collapse of the Spanish Republic 1933-1936. Origins of the Civil War, Yale 2006.

revolution during that period.[16] Thus, revolution in those years was and is present as a powerful concept. Given the limits of this essay, it seems necessary to focus on Barcelona, a city which – as will be shown – serves as a microcosm of all the conflicts Spain has faced in modern times. Before doing so, however, it seems sensible to give a more general overview on these struggles, as well as arguing to what extent the Spanish state was able to regulate these conflicts.

2. SPAIN AND ITS MAIN CONFLICTS AT THE BEGINNING OF THE 20TH CENTURY

Florentino Monroy, who was a close friend of Buenaventura Durruti when they were young, recalled an event from their childhood: "We often went to the orchards. Durruti always wanted to share everything we found there with the others. One day, one of the landowners caught us in the act and shouted: 'You over there, get out of here' and Durruti responded: 'We are not in a hurry actually'. Then the land owner said: 'This is my orchard' and Durruti asked him: 'And my orchard, where is it? Why don't I have any orchard?'."[17] Later Durruti wrote a letter to his sister Rosa about those years: "In my childhood, the most significant thing I realized was the suffering of the people, not just of our family, but also of our neighbors. Intuitively, I was already a rebel. I guess it was already back then when my destiny was decided".[18] This enormous gap between rich and poor, which Durruti came to understand in his youth, might be seen as the source of all the conflicts existing in contemporary Spain. At the beginning of the 20th century, life expectancy for the 18.6 million inhabitants of Spain was no more than about 35 years, much less than that of other European states. Even if was largely due to poor conditions in the health system, resulting in a high childhood mortality, it seems that the living conditions in general in Spain during that period were very tough.[19] This situation worsened during the First World War, when high inflation caused food prices to rise by 90% from May 1915 to May 1921.[20]

---

16 See for example, Eduardo González Calleja/ Fernando del Rey Reguillo, La defensa armada contra la revolución. Una historia de las guardias cívicas en la España del siglo XX, Madrid, 1995 or: Àngel Herrerín López, Anarquía, Dinamita y Revolución social. Violencia y represión en la España de entre siglos (1868-1909), Madrid 2011.
17 Hans Magnus Enzensberger, Der kurze Sommer der Anarchie, Frankfurt am Main 1972.
18 Paz, Durruti, 15.
19 Julián Casanova/Carlos Gil Andrés, Historia de España en el siglo XX, Barcelona 2009.

The poor in Spain did not have much hope that politics could improve their situation. A welfare system similar to that of other European states did not exist really in Spain, and it seemed that this was not to change soon. It may appear as if people had the opportunity to influence politics with their votes for the Cortes, the Spanish parliament. But in reality, this did not count for much, and they had almost no influence on policy. This was due to the fact that the leading parties, the Conservatives and the Liberals, had agreed to a system of *turno pacífico* (peaceful change). This meant that by manipulating the elections, they alternated in leading the government.[21] At the local level, this system was supported by the *caciques*, local elites who influenced the elections, and in return received wide administrative privileges. This led to client politics, and a disregard for the people's real needs.[22]

However, in Spain, as in many other European countries at the turn of the century, the desire of the lower classes to participate in the political process grew.[23] Given that this seemed impossible, many turned to the new political philosophy which had entered Spain in the 1870s: Anarchism. Two decades later, it was deeply routed in the political culture of Spain.[24] Although it started as a peaceful political movement, it led to a profound split in Spanish society. While the upper and middle classes saw anarchism as a severe threat to public order, it contributed to a feeling of community among the workers, pitted against

---

20 Balcells, Pistolerisme, 11, for a detailed overview of the influence of the First World War on Spain, see the works of Franciso Romero Salvadó, Spain 1914-1918. Between war and revolution, London1999, as well as: The foundations of Civil War. Revolution, social conflict and reaction in liberal Spain 1916-1923, London 2008.

21 Walther Bernecker, Geschichte Spaniens im 20. Jahrhundert, München 2010, 33.

22 For a recent overview of the Spanish political system in the decade of World War I, see: Javier Moreno Luzón, The Government, the Parties and the King, 1913-23, in: Francisco Romero Salvadó/Angel Smith (eds.), The agony of Spanish liberalism. From revolution to dictatorship 1913-1923, London 2010, 32-61.

23 Francisco Romero Salvadó and Angel Smith, in their introductory article The agony of Spanish Liberalism and the Origins of Dictatorship: A European Framwork, in: Francisco Romero Salvadó/Angel Smith (eds.), The agony of Spanish liberalism. From revolution to dictatorship 1913-1923, London 2010, 1-31, give a very instructive comparison of the Spanish case with political developments in other European countries.

24 For a recent overview of Anarchism in Spain, see the article by Teresa Abelló, Anarchism in the Catalan-speaking countries. Between syndicalism and propaganda (1868-1931), in: Catalan Historical Review 3 (2010), 87-102.

to the "criminal" entrepreneurs who were depicted as their enemies.²⁵ These controversial sentiments intensified when Spain was struck by a wave of anarchist terrorism in the 1890s. There were three major terror attacks which all took place in Barcelona. On 24 September 1893, Paulino Pallás attempted to assassinate the military general Arsenio Martínez Campos. Little more than a month later, on 7 November, Salvador Santiago dropped two bombs in the Liceo opera and killed 20 people. Three years later, a bomb exploded during the Corpus Christ procession, caused 12 deaths, and leaving many more injured. These three attacks were directed at whom the Anarchists saw as their main enemies: the military as the main security force of the state, the upper class, which regularly met in the Liceo and used this events to show their wealth – a strong provocation to the workers who faced the daily struggle to survive - and the church, seen as a representative of the state and despised for the inquisition, which lived on in the collective memory of Spaniards.

When it became obvious at the end of the 19th century that "propaganda by deed" was as Romero Maura put it "a thing of the past", the anarchists looked for other ways to seize power.²⁶ They now turned to collective actions in form of general strikes, and in doing so forming close ties with the working class movement. The question of the improvement of working conditions had been a major dispute since industrialization began in Spain in the second half of the 19th century. Now the worker's demands for higher wages, and a shortage of working hours were mixed with the anarchist's dreams of insurrection. The general strikes – as did that of 1902 – became violent affairs with shoot-outs with the police, and attacks on employers.²⁷ During the first two decades of the 20th century, trade-unionism grew in popularity to such a degree that the most powerful union, the CNT, had reached about 700,000 members by the end of the 1910s. It was not only the rise of the trade-unions but also developments in Russia that filled Spanish business owners with fear.²⁸

Apart from the anarchist threat to the government, and the polarization of the conflict between workers and employers, another challenge for the Spanish

---

25 Chris Ealham, Class, Culture and Conflict in Barcelona, 1898-1937, London 2005, 39.
26 Joaquín Romero Maura, 'Terrorism in Barcelona and its Impact on Spanish Politics. 1904-1909', in: Past and Present 41 (1968), 130-183, here: 130.
27 For the latest monograph on the anarchist terror attacks in the 1890s, see: Angel Herrerin López, Anarquía.
28 For a recent article on the CNT, see: Katharina Biberauer, Anarchismus mit oder versus Syndikalismus. Die ideologische Entwicklung der CNT (1910-1936), in: Friedrich Edelmayer (ed.), Anarchismus in Spanien. Anarquismo en España, Wien 2008, 109-161.

central state was the growing regionalism in the country's most powerful industrial regions, the Basque country and Catalonia. In both regions, regional sentiments began to grow in the second half of the 19th century as cultural movements. However, after the painful defeat Spain suffered in the war against the United States, and the resulting loss of its last important colonies, namely Cuba, the Philippines and Puerto Rico, the dissatisfaction with the Spanish Central State resulted in the foundation of political parties demanding a state of autonomy. Especially in Catalonia, this separatist movement became a serious challenge for the Spanish Central State by the end of the First World War. This was due to hopes raised by Woodrow Wilson's concept of self-determination for smaller nations, as well as by the participation of about 40,000 Catalans in the Allied forces, for which the Catalans now hoped to receive support in their struggle for independence.[29] The overview of the conflicts in Spain during that period of time, raises the question of how the Spanish central state was able to control the violent struggles by imposing law and order. As such, in the next part of this chapter, the connection between violence, state and order, the central question in this chapter, will be investigated using Spain and Barcelona as a case study.

3. LAW AND ORDER IN SPAIN IN THE FIRST THIRD OF THE 20TH CENTURY

"[…] My son, our trial was an absurdity. So absurd, that they did not dare to judge us in public as they usually do when they think that justice is on their side. They did not announce the trial in advance, they did not let anyone in. They are going to assassinate us. You should know that your father died a happy man, convinced that in his life he followed a great and just idea. His death and the death of his companions will serve to shed light on the crimes that the authorities are committing beyond the law [....]."

This is an excerpt from the letter Manuel Archs wrote on 17 May 1894, one day before he was executed because of his presumed participation in the anarchist terror attacks described above. It is addressed to his son Ramon who suffered a similar fate in 1921. He was arrested because he was suspected of having taken

---

29 Aside from the countless Catalan studies on Catalan nationalism, which obviously exist, two works from international historians should be mentioned here: Klaus-Jürgen Nagel, Arbeiterschaft und Nationale Frage, Saarbrücken 1991, as well as Angel Smith, The Origins of Catalan Nationalism, 1770-1898, Basingstoke 2014.

part in planning the assassination of the prime Minister Eduardo Dato. He was beaten to death during police questioning.[30]

The Archs' family were not the only people affected by the state's reprisal measures, although probably few suffer as severely. But mass detentions, mistreatment and torture were quite frequent and affected many working class people. In Barcelona, many had at least had one family member in jail. These practices were first applied during the mass hysteria after the first anarchist terror attacks in the 1890s. In order to expose an anarchist complot, hundreds of anarchists were put into prison – many without any clear evidence about their interference in the terror attacks. As was later made public by former anarchist convicts, torture was frequent, and among the anarchists found guilty and executed, not all – as in the case of Manuel Archs - were ever proven guilty.

The practice of arrest without trial was common between 1918 and 1923 as well. For example, on 20 November 1920, 64 labor leaders were arrested, among them, famous figures of the labor movement including Salvador Seguí.[31] Following court reports in contemporary newspapers, if convict report are to be believed, mistreatment by the police was again used regularly to force suspects to confess to their crimes. While these accusations are difficult to verify given that there are no objective sources available. Further, although it is possible that these reports were used by suspects to escape condemnation, it is generally accepted that in 1921, another violence-condoning law was passed called the "Ley de Fugas" (Law of the fugitives). This law permitted policemen to shoot suspects when they intended to escape, a practice that was first proposed in 1870 by the Governor of Cordoba in order to fight the local bandits.[32] In Barcelona, cases where suspects were shot stretched from 5 December 1920 to 24 October 1922, and it reached its climax between 19-21 January 1921 when as revenge for the murder of a policeman, more than twenty suspects were killed.[33]

Because of these practices, it is quite common in Spanish historiography to speak of state-sponsored terrorism.[34] While these policies were, on the one hand, arguably justified, on the other hand, it is undeniable that the seeming failure of

---

30 The letter and the story behind it can be found (in Catalan) in: Antoni Dalmau, El Procés de Montjuic. Barcelona al final del segle XIX, Barcelona 2010, 214-215.
31 Nagel, 460-461.
32 González Calleja, Mauser, 186.
33 Maria Pradas Baena, L'Anarquisme i les lluites socials a Barcelona 1918-1923. La repressió obrera i la violència, Barcelona: Publicacions de l'Abadia de Montserrat, 2003, 172-174. The conservative press still in 1922 defended the enforcement of this law, see for example in El Correo Catalan, 1 November 1922.
34 Vincent, Spain, 1.

the authorities to guarantee law and order was lamented by many contemporaries. In fact, a possible motivator for the "Ley de Fugas" was the courts' considerable inefficiency as evidenced by the fact that most suspects were released due to lack of evidence.[35]

This raises the question of what forces were in charge of guaranteeing law and order during the Spanish Restoration Monarchy. After the War of Independence against the French, the Spanish army had become the protector of the Spanish state, not only against foreign enemies, but also from domestic unrest. Although the Guardia Civil began to take over the task of preserving law and order from the second half of the 19th century. Soldiers nevertheless remained a common sight in the streets of Barcelona since they often served to reinforce the police. In order to legalize this measure, martial law was frequently called during the first decades of the 20th century. Nevertheless, it seems that soldiers, apart from fights during strikes, were not often involved in violent acts. However, there was one incident which caused a large scandal and made obvious the tensions between the military and public opinion. In 1905, the satirical magazine "Cu-Cut!" (Cuckoo!) published a cartoon showing two civilians in conversation: "What is celebrated here?" "It's a victory celebration" – "So then it cannot have anything to do with the army". The publication of this cartoon poured salt in the wounds suffered by the Spanish military, who was facing a severe crisis after the defeat of 1898. The following night, in an act of fury, several officers stormed the publishing house of *Cu-Cut!* and of *La Veu de Catalunya*, (The Voice of Catalonia), a Catalanist newspaper, and destroyed its facilities. This however, remained the only incident implicating the military in Barcelona in the decades before the Civil War.[36]

More significant was the impact of the civil governors, the leaders of the military garrison who had significant influence on law and order in Barcelona. As such, it is not coincidental that the *Ley de Fugas* was attributed to Severiano Martinez Anido, a general who had served in several colonial wars. He served as civil governor of Barcelona from November 1920 to October 1922. As early as the date of his appointed on 8 November 1920, he left no doubts about his inten-

---

35 This becomes obvious in a letter from the civil Governor of Barcelona to the Minister of the Government in Madrid from the 1st July 1923, Archivo Nacional Histórico, 58A(13), telegramm 32.

36 For these incidents, as well as the role of the military in general in Barcelona until the coup d'etat by Primo de Rivera see: Eduardo González Calleja, El ejército y orden publico durante la Restauración. La lucha por el control gubernativo en Barcelona (1897-1923), in: Jordi Cassasas (ed.), Els fets del Cu-cut! Cent anys després, Barcelona 2006, 59-118.

tions: "I have worked in Cuba and the Philippines, I should have been in Africa. The Government decided to send me to Barcelona and I will act as though I were in active service".[37] Given the brutality with which the Spanish army had dealt with the rebels in the colonies, it was clear from Martinez Anido's statement that clemency would not be forthcoming to anyone.[38]

The Spanish Police, the *Guardia Civil* (The Civil Guard) was founded in 1844 in order to prevent banditry in the countryside.[39] The policemen were sent directly from Madrid, and were not familiar with local practices. As such, they remained outsiders in their new environments, which was probably in the sense of the authorities.[40] The police in Barcelona at the turn of the 20th century was in terrible condition. In 1893, the year of the first anarchist terror attacks, a French commissioner wrote in his report that the police in Barcelona were poorly organized and paid.[41] The inspectors were corrupt, as for example, one among them, Antonio Tressols made significant amounts of money by blackmailing criminals.[42] Although in the first decade of the 20th century serious attempts were made to improve the quality of the policeforce, the police never was seen as being very efficient.[43] This was mainly due to the small number of policemen in relation to the fast-growing population, which was 1:5,000 in 1919. This was far less than in other European cities during the time. London, for example, counted with a ratio of 1:360 in favor of the civilian population.[44] Hence, the police force in Barcelona was very small by European standards, and despite reforms at the beginning of the century, remained underpaid. Yet, while some policemen had other part-time jobs, others supplemented their income through corruption.[45]

Given that the police in Barcelona was rather inefficient, it makes a certain logic that attempts were made to reinforce the power of the authorities. The first was to hire informants, and the second was to establish an independent security force in Barcelona. Both efforts, however, had already failed rather tragicomically by the beginning of the 20th century. In 1907, the case of Joan Rull caused a scandal, and shook confidence in the authorities even further. Rull was an anar-

---

37 Smith, Anarchism, 331.
38 Balfour, 270.
39 Vincent, 31.
40 Temma Kaplan, Red City. Blue Period. Social movements in Picasso's Barcelona, Berkeley 1992, 7.
41 Dalmau, Procés, 29.
42 Maura, Terrorism, 174.
43 Herrerín López, Anarquía, 256.
44 Balcells, Pistolerismo, S. 21f.
45 Ealham, Class, 17.

chist convicted of a bomb attack. In order to regain his freedom, he promised the police to provide them with valuable information that would help them to thwart further anarchist bomb attacks. As it turned out later, he took the money they gave him without providing the required information, and when they refused to continue paying him, he himself bombed the city centre to underline the importance of his "work".

At the same time, the authorities, possibly influenced by the highly popular Sherlock Holmes stories by Arthur Conan Doyle, hired Scotland Yard officer Charles Arrows, for a considerable amount of money, to establish a new police force in Barcelona. The fact that the Englishmen spoke neither Spanish nor had any idea about his work conditions exposed him to the mockery of the local press from the first day of his arrival in the summer of 1907. The well-intentioned Arrow fell victim to the jealousy of the local police inspectors. Not much longer than a year later, the Englishmen resigned in frustration.[46]

A more serious alternative to the Guardia Civil were the "Somaten". This was a vigilante group that originated in medieval times. Through the centuries, it served largely in rural Catalonia where it imposes law and order. In the first decades of the 20th century, the Somaten also made an appearance to help control labour conflicts in Barcelona, and went on to play an important role during the Canadiese strike.[47] Later, this paramilitary organization, comprised mostly of the conservative upper- and middle-class, organized patrols to feign armed robberies.[48]

4. REVOLUTION IN ITS EVERYDAY SETTING IN BARCELONA

In the previous section, it became obvious that maintaining law and order in the Spanish state mainly involved dealing with challenges to the authorities. The city on the Mediterranean Sea, beyond the first decade of the 19th century, as observed by Angel Ossorio, but also in the following quarter of a century remained a place where revolution was always in the air. This was mainly due to the fact that Barcelona not only was the capital of Catalonia, and therefore the stage for growing Catalan nationalism, but also the most important industrial city in Spain where the social tensions between workers and entrepreneurs affected more people than in any other Spanish city. Consequently, the third main challenge to

---

46 Both cases ar extensively covered in Antoni Dalmau, El cas Rull. Viure del terror a la Ciutat de les Bombes (1901-1908), Barcelona 2008
47 The most extensive case study on the Somaten is: González Calleja/del Rey, Defensa.
48 El Diluvio, 10 August 1923.

the Spanish central state, anarchism, also had its stronghold in Barcelona. In order to show how in Barcelona revolution took place in its everyday setting, the development of these three main lines of conflict should be described by explaining how each practiced of violence.

4.1 "Visca Catalunya!" – "Long live Catalonia!"

The first violent clash involving Catalan nationalists had taken place on 29 of September 1918, the first anniversary of the death of Prat de la Riba, the first president of the Mancomunitat, the local Catalan government. A group of young Catalanists had entered the Paseo de Gracia, a popular boulevard in the city center, with American and Catalan flags and was violently dissolved by the police.[49] Incidents like this also occurred on various occasions in the week of the armistice.[50] It became a common ritual for the Catalanists to come together in the evenings and walk along the Ramblas, waving Catalan flags and screaming "Visca Catalunya!".[51]

The walk through the streets as a collective act can be traced in Barcelona to the tradition of celebrations and processions. This ritual constituted a feeling of community among the poorer population, independent of the aristocracy, who did not take part in the events.[52] During the second half of the 19th century, street protest had become the main expression of Barcelona's largely illiterate population.[53]

The clashes became more violent in December 1918 after political negotiations in favor of a separate Catalan state failed definitely. The evening of 22 December, after a mass meeting in a theatre, about 100 people with Catalan flags entered the Ramblas. When a group of about ten policemen tried to dissolve the demonstrations, one was shot and injured.[54] The clashes reached their peak in the

---

49 González Calleja, Mauser, 346.
50 For example, see: El Día Gráfico, 17 November 1918.
51 Nagel, Arbeiterschaft, 429.
52 James Amelang, Public Ceremonies and Private Fetes. Social Segregation and Aristocratic Culture in Barcelona, ca. 1500-1800, in: Gary McDonogh (ed.), Conflict in Catalonia. Images of an urban society, Florida 1986, 17-32, here: 21-23.
53 Kaplan, Red City, 14.
54 A report on these events from the civil Governor of Barcelona to the Minister of the Government in Madrid from the 15 January 1919, Archivo Nacional Histórico, 54A (21), blames the Catalanists for having started the attacks, while El Diluvio on the 24 December 1918 said that the policemen shot first.

second half of January, 1919. The continuous fighting between Catalanists and Spanish patriots on the streets, led to with many injured people, and the murder of one Catalanist. The escalation produced protests all over Spain. The government reacted by forbidding Catalan symbols on 28 January.[55] The events of the Canadiese strike the following month pushed the conflicts between Catalans and Spaniards completely to the background. By the end of the Restoration monarchy in 1923, only one more incident was reported, when on 2 May 1920, during the celebration of the Jocs Florals, the traditional Catalan poetry competition, a group sang the popular Catalan folk song „Els Segadors" (The mowers), that referred to a Catalan popular uprising in Early Modern times, and shouted "Mori Espanya" (Death to Spain) and "Visca Catalunya lliure" (Long live the free Catalonia).[56] On 11 September 1923, date of the most important Catalan holiday, once again there was fighting in the streets between Catalan nationalists, Spanish patriots and the police, resulting in 30 injured. These events made Primo de Rivera move up his coup d'etat, originally planned for 15 September, to the night 12 September.[57]

4.2 "Quan mataven pels carrers" – "When they Murdered on the Streets"

In the morning of 5 January of 1920, rumors spread in Barcelona that there had been an assassination attempt on Felix Graupera.[58] The construction tycoon aged only 29 in 1902, had become part of the directory board of the *Centro de Contratistas Generales de Obras y Maestros Albañiles* which later turned into the *Federación Patronal*, a powerful union of Barcelona's leading entrepreneurs. Graupera became its president on 15 March 1919, and was responsible for the lock-out which from November 1919 to January 1920 affected about 200,000 workers in Barcelona, bringing them close to starvation.[59]

---

55 González Calleja, Mauser, 346-347.
56 El Noticiero Universal, 3 May 1920 published a short note on this event, while a court report is found in El Correo Catalan, 19 April 1922.
57 Alejandro Quiroga, Nation and Raction, in: Francisco Romero Salvadó/Angel Smith (eds.), The agony of Spanish liberalism. From revolution to dictatorship 1913-1923, London 2010, 202-229, here: 202.
58 Bengochea, Lock-Out, 144.
59 Bengoechea, Organització patronal i conflictivitat social a Cataluya, Barcelona 1994, 342.

Graupera had been blackmailed to cancel the lock-out within 24 hours, but he, protected by two policemen who served as his bodyguards, seemed to feel safe. However, 30 minutes before the end of the ultimatum, when he – traveling by car – was about to return home, he was fired upon by ten gunmen. Graupera himself, as well as his companion Modest Batlle, another member of the directory board of the *Federación Patronal*, were wounded, whereas one of the policemen succumbed to the injuries he had received during the shoot-out.[60]

The assassination attempt on Graupera, constitutes, by its brutality without a doubt the climax of the so-called *atentados sociales*. This expression, used by the local press, referred to armed aggressions between business owners and workers. The attacks had begun before the First World War – Cucurull gives the figure at 376 between 1910 and 1914 – spontaneous attacks during strikes or demonstrations.[61]

Most sources agree that things changed in 1916 when the spontaneous attacks turned into carefully planned assassination attempts that one Graupera later fell victim to. Apart from the change in quality, there was also a significant change in the quantity of the attacks. Balcells states that of the 1116 *atentados sociales* in Barcelona and its surroundings, 85% took place between 1918 and 1923.[62] In that period, which became known as "Pistolerismo", shoot-outs in the streets became part of daily life in Barcelona, and consequently, Joan Oller i Rabasa, refers to this time by the title of his novel "Quan mataven pels carrers" (When they murdered in the streets).[63]

Taking a closer look at the conditions of the *atentados sociales*, it seems that three different types of aggressions can be documented. Firstly, aggressions between employers and workers were the result of private motives.[64] One example was the murder of Jaime Raurell, the owner of a bakery, on 24 March 1920. Pedro Ruiz Martí was tried for this crime later. Apparently, had been working for the victim for seven years before he was suddenly fired.[65] The high number of these cases was due to the concept of the *patrono*, i.e. employers who had

---

60 Bengochea, Lock-Out, 144.
61 Fèlix Cucurull, Panoràmica del nacionalisme català, IV, Del 1914 al 1931, Paris 1975, 75.
62 Balcells, Violéncia social i poder polític. Sis estudis històrics sobre la Catalunya contemporània, Barcelona 2001, 16.
63 Joan Oller i Rabasa, Quan mataven pels carrers, Barcelona 1930.
64 Miguel Ángel Serrano, La ciudad de las bombas. Barcelona y los años trágicos del movimiento obrero, Madrid 1997, 65.
65 El Correo Catalan, 6 April 1921.

close relations with his workers, a common occurrence in Barcelona until the Civil War.[66]

Nevertheless, as the assassination attempt on Felix Graupera shows, many of the attacks were directed against representatives of the two sides of the conflicts. As such, in the first place, leading industrials fell victim to assassinations, as did Antonio Barret on 8 January 1918. Barret together with his brother had owned the company *Industrias Mecanicas Consolidadas*, where about 1,000 people worked. Rumors had it that in this factory weapons were produced for the Allied forces.[67] Not surprisingly, the anti-German newspaper *El Radical*, claimed that the German Secret Service in Barcelona was responsible for the assassinations of factory owners during the war.[68] While it seems true that the German consulate in Barcelona tried to create ties with the CNT in order to provoke strikes to stop the production of goods for the Allied forces, the sources in the German Foreign Office denied any connection with Pistolerismo.[69] One also has to take into account that the workers' newspaper *Solidaridad Obrera* applauded the death of Barret by writing „For all pigs, the day of Saint Martin arrives sometimes" (Saint Martin is the day when in Spain pigs are traditionally slaughtered).[70]

In order to defend themselves, the employers's hired a group of gunmen themselves. This gang, which the local press referred to as *Banda negra* (Black gang), was lead by Fritz Stallmann, a German who came to Barcelona in the course of the First World War. He took the name Baron von König, pretending to be of aristocratic origin. Under his command, the *Banda Negra* murdered important figures of the labor movement, and was involved in shoot-outs with the Pistoleros of the CNT. But in May 1920, the *Federación Patronal*, which had sponsored the *Banda Negra*, decided that they did not want to rely on the services of Stallmann any longer and he was forced to leave the country.[71]

After von König's expulsion, the policy of fighting violence with counter-violence continued in the form of the *Sindicato Libres*. This new trade union, which was under the influence of the factory owners, was founded in 1919 in

---

66 Marin, Semana Trágica, 37.
67 Bengoechea, Organització, 327.
68 El Radical, 8 June 1918.
69 See the files by von Rolland, the chief of the German consulate in Barcelona during the First World War in the Politisches Archiv des Auswärtigen Amtes, file: Madrid 365 // 7317, special file: von Rolland P1c.
70 Smith, Anarchism, 250-252.
71 The gang is documented in great detail in the memoires of the former police officer Manuel Casal Gómez: La Banda Negra. Origen y actuación del pistolerismo en Barcelona 1918-1921, Barcelona 1977.

order to divide the workers.[72] The Pistolerismo now turned into a syndicate war in which members of both syndicates fell victim to tit-for-tat assassinations. After a short period of peace in 1922, the killings continued in 1923 when a new wave of strikes, comparably to the Canadiese strike in 1919, affected Barcelona and made the Catalan industrialists call for an "iron surgeon", who they found in the person of Primo de Rivera.[73]

4.3 "La Ciudad de las Bombas" – "The City of Bombs"

When in November 1919, in only 12 hours, three explosive devices detonated in the Calle de Simón Oller, and one bomb was found at the monument of Doctor Robert near the Plaza de la Universidad, the Republican newspaper *El Diluvio* saw the first signs of the re-establishment of terrorism.[74] The reference was to the 1890s, when according to the anarchist dogma of propaganda by deed, a series of determined bomb attacks had shaken the Catalan city, and became known as "La Ciudad de las Bombas" (The City of Bombs).[75]

However, spectacular bomb attacks such as the ones on the Liceo opera in 1893 or on the Corpus Christ procession in 1896, producing dozens of injured and many deaths, were rarely seen in the period of the Pistolerismo. In total, only four large bomb explosions took place, all between August 1919 and July 1921. On 6 August 1919, a bomb exploded in the Paseo de Gracia near the Palace of the Duke of Mariano, caused eight injuries.[76] Much more spectacular was the bomb attack on 12 September 1920 in the *Pompeya*, one of the music halls in the Parallelo, highly popular with the working class. The explosion caused three deaths and 20 injuries. Since most of the victims were workers, it is likely that the bomb attack was the result of the conflict between the two syndicates, as described in the previous paragraph.[77] Another fatal bomb explosion took place on 2 May 1921 in the Calle de Toledo 10 in the worker's district Sants. This explosion, however, was not a bomb attack but was instead caused accidently by a group of young anarchists who fabricated bombs in their home. It seems that

---

72 The Sindicatos Libres are still best examined in: Colin Winston, Workers and the Right in Spain, 1900-1936, Princeton 1984.
73 Romero Salvadó, Dirty War, 188-192.
74 El Diluvio, 27 November 1919.
75 Angel Smith, Barcelona through the European mirror. From red and black to claret and blue, in: Angel Smith (ed.), Red Barcelona. Social protest and labour mobilization in the twentieth century, London 2002, 1-16, here: 7.
76 El Diluvio, 7 August 1919.
77 González Calleja, Mauser, 169.

this group, one week before, had attempted to launch a bomb attack during a parade with 40,000 members of the Somaten in the centre of Barcelona. They tried to transport the bomb by car, but were not able to come close to their goal. In the end, the bomb exploded far from the parade without causing any major damage.[78] The last bomb attack took place on 30 June 1921, when five smaller bombs were set off on the Placa de Cataluña, also without causing casualties.[79]

From the second half of 1921 to the end of the Pistolerimo in 1923, the anarchists changed from bomb attacks to armed robberies. The most spectacular happened in September 1922 when a train was robbed in Pueblo Nuevo.[80] In 1923 *Los Solidarios*, headed by Buenaventura Durruti, carried out various robberies, mainly on banks. According to one of its members, Ricardo Sanz, the group, at the end of 1923, had purchased weapons for 200,000 Pesetas. The weapons were to be used for a revolution, but after the coup d'etat by Primo de Rivera, Durruti and his companions were force to escape Spain and seek refuge abroad.[81]

5. CONCLUSION

From the foregoing, one should better understand why the former Civil Governor of Barcelona, Angel Ossorio, felt that Barcelona was a place where revolution always was ready to take place. On the one hand, the city on the Mediterranean was center stage for the three major conflicts that affected Spain during the first decades of the 20th century: regionalisms as Basque and Catalan nationalism as a challenge to the unity of the Spanish Central state, anarchism as a threat to the conservative political system, and the social tensions between business owners and the workers. On the other hand, it became obvious that due to the weakness and backwardness of security forces such as the *Guardia Civil*, it became impossible to maintain law and order. That revolution that came closer in the intermediate years after the First World War, was due to the fact that, as in other parts of Europe, conflicts intensified and took more violent form, with a broad repertoire of violent practices – street fighting, assassinations, bomb attacks and armed robberies. As a consequence, in 1923, after almost half a century, the Spanish restoration monarchy came to an end. Not by a social revolution as the

---

78 González Calleja, Mauser, 195.
79 El Correo Catalan, 2 July 1921.
80 For a detailed description of this event, see for example the reports on the trial in El Diluvio, 1 September 1926.
81 Enzensberger, Sommer, 38-49.

anarchists and workers had hoped for, but by military coup, lead by General Primo de Rivera.

Gender and the Imaginary of Revolution in Germany

KATHLEEN CANNING

> „Wie macht man eine Revolution, wie macht man keine, war es eine?" (Brecht on his *Trommeln in der Nacht*)[1]

1. INTRODUCTION

The German revolution of November 1918 is scarcely present in the annals of the "great revolutions" of modern history that inspired emulation, celebration or commemoration. Although frequently cast as a "failed revolution," the events of November 1918-January 1919 fulfill some of the criteria Eric Hobsbawm outlined in his classic essay of 1986 on modern revolutions. While these events did "break through or overturn" institutions of state and law and did arise as a sudden shock to contemporaries, the violence they unleashed was more episodic than prolonged. The revolution did involve movements of groups and masses and actions of open resistance but it hardly took the intellectual form of a programmatic idea or ideology.[2] The 1918-19 revolution also shares some of the attributes that Jack Goldstone's typology of revolution proposes, most notably the paralysis of the state and/or its subsequent loss of legitimacy in the face of the invigorated desire of citizens/subjects to participate in politics.[3] Although the November revolution originated in the specific national/dynastic/military context

---

1 As cited in Astrid Oesmann, The Theatrical Destruction of Subjectivity and History. Brecht's Trommeln in der Nacht, in: The German Quarterly 70 (1997), 136-150.
2 Eric J. Hobsbawm, Revolution, in: Roy Porter/ Mikulas Teich (eds.), Revolution in History, Cambridge 1986, 5-6.
3 Jack Goldstone (ed.), Revolutions. Theoretical, Comparative, and Historical Studies, 3rd Edition, Belmont 2003, 2, 5-6.

of Germany at war, it also constituted one site in a wider transnational uprising against the European imperial order.[4] The extensive wave of strikes, revolts, and revolutions that erupted across Central Europe during the last months of the First World War had national, sub-national and transnational dimensions as the long-term social costs of war and the mass conscription and militarization of citizens (and of subjects without citizenship) rekindled pre-war claims of national and civic belonging, lending them a new urgency.[5]

Inspired by the last decade of new cultural histories of the First World War and the Weimar Republic, this essay explores the experience, imaginary, and emotions of the prolonged revolutionary moment of 1918-19 in which Germany's war, defeat and revolution became inextricably entwined. The conventional scholarly division between the history of war, with its emphasis on diplomacy, military and foreign policy, and that of *Innenpolitik*, which approached the revolution in terms of domestic political conflicts, has obscured what Michael Geyer has termed the in-between character of 1918/19, marked by the coincidence of Germany's defeat and the popular uprising against monarchy and military. That the revolution involved both "Kriegsbeendigung und Kriegsbewältigung" and was thus entangled with the inception of the peace process has, as Geyer notes, "been absent in the historiography."[6] Adam Seipp's recent study of demobilization in Germany and Britain similarly bridges "the chasm between wartime and postwar" in its extension of "the lived experience of societies at war beyond the conclusion of hostilities and the diplomatic agreements that periodize warfare in the historical consciousness."[7]

Not only did the conditions of war mobilize and politicize hundreds of thousands of disparate and largely unorganized civilians, but the sailors and soldiers who seized ships, barracks and city halls in November 1918 revolted against the

---

4   On the November Revolution as a fragment of transnational protest, see Michael Geyer, Zwischen Krieg und Nachkrieg – die deutsche Revolution 1918/19 im Zeichen blockierter Transnationalität, in: Alexander Gallus (ed.), Die vergessene Revolution, Göttingen 2010, 187-222.

5   On the transnational dimensions of demobilization between 1917-21, see Adam R. Seipp, The Ordeal of Peace: Demobilization and the Urban Experience in Britain and Germany, 1917-21, Farnham 2009, Introduction. On cultural demobilization, see John Horne, Demobilizing the Mind. France and the Legacy of the Great War, 1919-1939, in: French History and Civilization 2 (2009), 101-119.

6   Geyer, Zwischen Krieg und Nachkrieg, 193-94. Also see Conan Fischer, A Very German Revolution? The Post 1918 Settlement Re-Evaluated, in: German Historical Institute Bulletin 28:2 (2006), 6-32.

7   Seipp, The Ordeal of Peace, 6.

war itself, that is, against German military's relentless pursuit of hostilities in the face of the troops' utter depletion and looming defeat.[8] Thus in Geyer's view the revolution, as a *"Kriegsbeendigungsrevolution,"* was remarkably successful: it ended the war, overthrowing both the Hohenzollern monarchy and the militarized state of Hindenburg and Ludendorff.[9] The triumphant celebrations of the war's end, the Kaiser's abdication, and the promise of equal citizenship soon dissipated as the shock of Germany's defeat set in. In the face of hunger, cold, epidemic, and grief, the step by step process of postwar reordering began: the crafting of new forms of governance, the demobilization of soldiers, and the realignments of gender, labor, and family. While recent scholarship on the First World War has taken a pronounced cultural turn towards the study of experience, language, emotion, gender and memory, studies of the war's *aftermath* have remained preoccupied with the political, social, and economic consequences of war, defeat, peace and the founding of the Weimar republic.[10] An important exception here is the study of psychic and bodily injuries that veterans carried back from the front and the attempts of the medical and social welfare estab-

8   Benjamin Ziemann, The German Revolution in 1918/1919. Romance, Tragedy or Satire? Unpublished paper presented to conference, "Approaching Revolutions," University of Virginia, March 25-27, 2010, 2-3.
9   Geyer, Zwischen Krieg und Nachkrieg. Also see Geyer's Insurrectionary Warfare. The German Debate about a Levee en Masse in October 1918, in: Journal of Modern History 73 (2001), 462-463 and Endkampf 1918 and 1945. German Nationalism, Annihilation and Self-Destruction, in: Alf Lüdtke/Bernd Weisbrod (eds.), No Man's Land of Violence. Extreme Wars in the 20th Century. Göttingen 2006, 35-68.
10 Some of the classic studies of war experience include: Gerhard Hirschfeld, Gerd Krumeich/Irina Renz, (eds.), Keiner fühlt sich hier mehr als Mensch. Erlebnis und Wirkung des Ersten Weltkriegs, Frankfurt 1996; Gerhard Hirschfeld etc. (eds.), Kriegserfahrungen. Studien zur Sozial- und Mentalitätsgeschichte des Ersten Weltkriegs, (Schriften der Bibliothek für Zeitgeschichte, N.F. Bd. 5), Essen 1997; Benjamin Ziemann, Front und Heimat. Ländliche Kriegserfahrungen im südlichen Bayern 1914-1923, Essen 1997; Ute Daniel, The War from Within. German Working-Class Women in the First World War. Oxford etc. 1997; Jay Winter/Jean-Louis Robert (eds.), Capital Cities at War. Paris, London, Berlin 1914-19, Cambridge 1997; Karen Hagemann/Stefanie Schüler-Springorum (eds.), Heimat-Front. Militär und Geschlechterverhältnisse im Zeitalter der Weltkriege, Frankfurt 2002. Also see the urban histories of wartime experience by Belinda Davis, Home Fires Burning. Food, Politics, and Everyday Life in World War I Berlin, Chapel Hill 2000; Maureen Healy, Vienna and the Fall of the Habsburg Empire. Total War and Everyday Life in World War I, Cambridge 2004; and Roger Chickering, The Great War and Urban Life in Germany. Freiburg 1914-18, Cambridge 2007.

lishment to categorize and treat them, which became emblematic for the state's contention with the living memory of war.[11] Historian Karin Hausen's signature essays on war widows and on the effacement of women's mourning and grief in public memory were among the first to investigate the longer-term war injuries, bodily and psychic, suffered by female civilians.[12]

2. PERCEPTIONS OF REVOLUTION: RUPTURES IN TIME AND SPACE

This essay examines the intertwined and often dissonant experiences of living through the war's aftermath while envisioning and enacting a new future. Wolfgang Schivelbusch's analysis of *The Culture of Defeat* highlights the "dreamland" state that characterizes the aftermath of wars "that mobilize the nation to a high degree," such as the First World War.[13] In Schivelbusch's schema a dreamland or euphoria follows military collapse and internal revolution as citizens begin to imagine a different, even utopian future. Most notable in witness accounts of living through the revolution is the prevalent sense that the revolution represented an utterly unexpected, sudden *Sturmwind* (a heavy gale) that swept through Germany without warning. This experience of shock, of an unanticipated collapse, is puzzling in view of the increasingly militant civilian protests on the home front during 1917 and 1918, the failure of the German Army's summer offensive of 1918, and the mutinous sentiments among soldiers at the front during the spring and summer of 1918. Other diaries and memoirs of November

---

11 See, for example, Paul Lerner, Hysterical Men. War, Psychiatry, and the Politics of Trauma in Germany, 1890-1930, Ithaca, NY 2003; Sabine Kienitz, Beschädigte Helden. Kriegsinvalidität und Körperbilder 1914-1923, Paderborn 2008; Deborah Cohen, The War Come Home. Disabled Veterans in Britain and Germany, 1914-1939, Berkeley 2001; and Jason Crouthamel, The Great War and German Memory. Society, Politics and Psychological Trauma, 1914-45, Exeter 2009.

12 Karin Hausen, The German Nation's Obligations to Heroes' Widows of World War I, in: Anne Higonnet etc. (eds.), Behind the Lines. Gender and the Two World Wars, New Haven 1987, 185-199 and The 'Day of National Mourning' in Germany, in: Gerald Sider/Gavin Smith (eds .), Between History and Histories. The Making of Silences and Commemorations, Toronto 1997, 127-145. Both appear in German in: Karin Hausen, Geschlechtergeschichte als Gesellschaftschaftsgeschichte, Göttingen 2012.

13 Schivelbusch, The Culture of Defeat, 10. His notion of "dreamland" stems from theologian Ernst Troeltsch's observations of 1918-19 as explicated in Troeltsch's Spektatorbriefe.

1918 chronicle unprecedented occurrences but seem uncertain about whether they constituted a revolution, or when it began or came to an end. Even the most politically attuned intellectuals and activists were unsure of the origins or outcomes of town hall seizures or the declaration of the new German republic. Germans living at a distance from the scenes of revolutionary action wondered about the geography of revolution: where its centers were and how it might spill over to the peripheries, small towns and countryside. They pondered whether it was a German revolution or one carried into Germany from Bolshevik Russia and through which communicative channels was it sweeping through Germany - by train, by print, by word of mouth? Victor Klemperer, best known for his prolific diary entries while in hiding during the Third Reich, found that daily life seemed to go on rather peacefully during the November days of 1918, despite the reports he had read in the press of intensifying chaos in the cities. The revolution, he noted, "seems to be taking place on a subterranean surface below our daily perceptions," adding laconically that "those who are in the midst of these events would appear to notice or comprehend them the least."[14]

Count Harry Kessler, diplomat, cosmopolitan aristocrat and art collector, observed the revolutionary atmosphere in Berlin on November 12, 1918 from inside the Reichstag building where the provisional government of independent and majority Socialists convened:

"Cigarette butts everywhere, wastepaper, dust and dirt from the streets litter the carpets. The corridors and lobby teem with armed civilians, soldiers and sailors. In the lobby rifles are piled on the carpet and sailors lounge in the easy chairs. The disorder is vast, but quiet reigns."[15]

Despite the disorderly interior spaces of improvised governance, Kessler noted that outside the city's factories were working; electricity, water and telephone service continued; the trams ran on their regular schedules "irrespective of street fighting;" and there were "remarkably few dead or wounded." On November 12th it still seemed to Kessler that "the colossal, world-shaking, upheaval scurried across Berlin's day to day life much like an incident in a crime film."[16]

---

14 Victor Klemperer, Leben sammeln, nicht fragen wozu und warum. Tagebücher 1918-24, Walter Nowojski/Christian Löser (eds.), Berlin 1996, 11 as cited in Schildt, Der lange November, 235.
15 Berlin in Lights. The Diaries of Count Harry Kessler (1918-1937), translated and edited by Charles Kessler, New York 1999, 10-11.
16 Kessler, Berlin in Lights, 11.

The conjuncture of war's end and popular uprising meant that grief and mourning inflected the experience of revolution and the attempts to make sense of the symbolic and sensory transformations of the moment.[17] Socialist sculptor and artist Käthe Kollwitz, made the following diary entry on November 9, 1918:

"Today it is actually happening here in Berlin. This afternoon...I walked from the zoo to the Brandenburg Gate where leaflets were distributed announcing the Kaiser's abdication. A demonstration moved through the gate and I joined...In front of the Reichstag an assembly. Scheidemann announced the republic, then nearby a soldier addressed the crowd; he was aggravated and confused....We moved to unter den Linden. Trucks passed full of soldiers and sailors. Red flags. I saw soldiers who ripped off their cockades and laughing, tossed them on the ground.
So this *is* really happening. We experience it but can scarcely grasp it. I am continuously thinking of Peter. If he had lived, he would have joined them. He would have ripped off those insignias as well. But he did not live and when I last laid eyes upon him he had the same hat with the cockade and his face was shining."[18]

Kollwitz recounts these events with sympathy for the revolutionaries but it was also a moment of renewed grief for her son Peter, who was killed in October 1914 at age 18 after a mere two weeks at the front. Revolution brought an end to the murderous war, yet it also prompted Kollwitz to relive Peter's death, to reimagine him as a revolutionary soldier. Amidst her subsequent entries, there are fragmented mentions of shots heard in the night, street battles, of her attendance at countless political assemblies, her fears of civil war, of an Allied invasion and a punitive peace. Her diary captures the aftermath of war and revolution, when uncertainty hovered over the future terms of governance, citizenship, and the definition of national boundaries.

3. THE IMAGINARY OF REVOLUTION

The November Revolution was the catalytic event that both brought the war to an end and set in motion the work of imagining Germany's future in a Europe

---

17 On this point see Geyer, Zwischen Krieg und Nachkrieg, 195-196.
18 Käthe Kollwitz, Die Tagebücher 1908-1943, Entry for Nov. 9, 1918, 378-379. Also see Claudia Siebrecht, Imagining the Absent Dead. Rituals of Bereavement and the Place of Women's Bereavement in German Women's Art during the First World War, in: German History 29 (2011), 202-223; and Regina Schulte, Käthe Kollwitz's Sacrifice, in: History Workshop 41 (1996), 193-221, translated by Pamela Selwyn.

shattered by four years of war. The November days of upheaval and uncertainty called up disparate standpoints, from the longing for revolutionary socialism to the demands for a revived nationalism or even for a future that would resuscitate the pre-war past. This essay posits a view of revolution as a new social, political and cultural imaginary that authorized new actors, subjects, and publics, new rhetorics, visions and symbols that took shape within the popular mobilizations for a new state and society. These new formations left ineffaceable marks on the Weimar Republic that defy the simple question of revolutionary success or failure. Conceiving of the revolution in terms of a social imaginary highlights the changing perceptions of social and political existence that ordinary Germans experienced in the course of the revolution. In Charles Taylor's definition, social imaginary is seldom expressed in theoretical terms, but is carried instead "in images, stories and legends" and can still constitute a "common understanding that makes possible common practices and a widely shared sense of legitimacy."[19] Political scientist Anne Phillips defines "political imaginary" in similar terms as "a context of thought that sets people in motion," and that generates new forms of political agency.[20]

Social imaginary seems a particularly apt term for the revolutionary moment of 1918-19 when the coinciding forces of war, defeat and revolution ruptured more than political frameworks of *Herrschaft*, but also seemed to shatter the cultural registers of belief, opinion, and feeling about nation and state, religion and society, gender, sex, and family. While the sailors', soldiers' and workers' councils formed the governing center of the revolution and sought to enact new forms of political representation, "the revolution" marked a cultural break as well, enlisting journalists, playwrights, painters, and photomontage artists whose poems, short stories, novels and early postwar films contended with the revolution's rupturing effects. This essay is concerned with the convergences and disjunctures between political and cultural representations that forged new citizenships, subjectivities and notions of governance in the course of the political settlements of 1918/19, but it is also attentive to the meanings, emotions, and consciousness that formed beyond or beneath these formal political restructurings.

That gender was a critical dimension of the transformations of 1918/19 is another central argument of this essay. The German revolution of 1918-19 has scarcely earned attention from historians of gender; nor have social and political historians of Germany considered gender a significant aspect of the defeat, revo-

---

19 Charles Taylor, Modern Social Imaginaries, Durham 2003, 23-26.
20 Anne Phillips, Citizenship and Feminist Theory, in: Geoff Andrews (ed.), Citizenship, London 1991, 77.

lution, or the founding of the republic. The almost complete absence of gender in political history of the revolution contrasts sharply with the presence of volatile, uncertain, changing and contested masculinities and femininities in the visual art, film, theater, and fiction of the immediate postwar period and in the diaries and memoirs of many of its leading intellectuals and artists. The gender of the political revolution – the overwhelmingly masculine membership in the revolutionary *Räte* – has been so obvious as to remain unnamed in most historical accounts. The female actors who appear in the annals of the revolution usually figure as peripheral to the high-stakes contests over governance and political representation in the councils and newly formed political parties. The occasions in which gender is impossible to overlook in 1918-19, such as the nearly immediate declaration of equal suffrage for women and men over the age of 20; the subsequent outpouring of attention to schooling and recruiting female voters; the demobilization of soldiers and the expulsion of women from their wartime jobs, and the negotiation of female citizenship in the writing of the Weimar constitution, have scarcely counted as salient in either the founding or longer-term fate of the Republic.

This essay questions the stark – and counterintuitive – separation between historical study of the revolution and the gendered experience of war on the home front, including the self-authorization of female citizens who staked claims to a role in shaping the new state. The revolutionary declaration of equal suffrage for men and women on November 12 represented the first and most fundamental gender policy of the revolutionary government and laid the foundation for that of the Republic. That the home front had become a laboratory of citizenship during the war is a crucial backdrop for the abrupt realization of equal suffrage at the war's end. While middle-class women were mobilized and nationalized into various sectors of war support, working-class women and "women of lesser means" experienced a new politicization on the bread lines and in the munitions factories.[21] Female participation in the expanding protests over bread, coal, and peace on the home front fueled their increasingly vociferous self-authorizations as citizens and claimants for new participatory rights. Demobilization might be viewed as the enactment of a second highly significant gender policy, one that aimed to fulfill a massive project of gender realignment. A high-stakes undertaking for the provisional government, demobilization became a fundamental test of its legitimacy, of its capacity to rectify the material, social and political crises of the war's end through an essential realignment of the sexual division of labor. As hallmarks of revolutionary gender policy, suffrage

---

21 See Davis, Home Fires Burning; Daniel, The War from Within; and Healty, Vienna and the Fall of the Habsburg Empire.

and demobilization set in motion new political and social practices in 1918-19: new initiatives aimed to recruit and educate the new female voters on the one hand and on the other hand, the enactment of demobilization decrees the mass dismissals of women from their wartime jobs.[22]

The gendered outcomes of war spilled over into the revolutionary period in fields beyond the realms of citizenship law and labor policy. The simmering sense of an impending crisis of gender or sexuality, detectable in the records of military and medical authorities from 1916 on, intensified in the wake of the Germany's unanticipated defeat.[23] Conservatives and military authorities had interpreted soaring rates of sexual promiscuity, prostitution, and venereal disease as evidence of the sexual ungovernability of German women, particularly soldiers' wives, in wartime.[24] At the same time, the steady decline of the birth rate along with rising rates of infant mortality and child neglect seemed to signal the fracturing of marriage and motherhood under the hardships of war. Not only state and military authorities, but also the Social Democrats, worried about containing women's spontaneous and localized protests over food, coal, peace and suffrage. Bound by the "peace of the fortress," the SPD was increasingly unable to predict or control the actions of women and young workers who eluded the organizational and disciplining efforts of both unions and socialist parties in 1917 and 1918.[25] Further anxieties about the wartime "feminization" of produc-

---

22 On the mobilization of new female voters in 1919, see Julia Sneeringer, Winning Women's Votes. Propaganda and Politics in Weimar Germany, Chapel Hill 2002. On the gender politics of demobilization, see: Susanne Rouette, Sozialpolitik als Geschlechterpolitik. Die Regulierung der Frauenarbeit nach dem Ersten Weltkrieg, Frankfurt etc. 1993; and Richard Bessel, Was bleibt vom Krieg? Deutsche Nachkriegsgeschichte(n) aus geschlechtergeschichtlicher Perspektive, in: Militärgeschichtliche Mitteilungen 2:2 (2001), 297-305.

23 Kathleen Canning, Sexual Crisis and the Writing of Citizenship: Reflections on States of Exception in Germany, 1914-1920, in: Alf Lüdtke/Michael Wildt (eds.), Ausnahmezustand und Polizeigewalt, Göttingen 2008, 168-211.

24 Lisa Todd, 'The Soldier's Wife Who Ran Away with the Russian.' Sexual Infidelities in World War I Germany, in: Central European History 44 (2011), 257-278; and Cornelie Usborne, Pregnancy is the Woman's Active Service. Pronatalism in Germany during the First World War, in: Richard Wall/Jay Winter (eds.), The Upheaval of War. Family, Work and Welfare in Europe, 1914-1918, Cambridge 1988, 389-416.

25 Ullrich, Kriegsalltag, 610-611. Also see Willy Albrecht etc., Frauenfrage und deutsche Sozialdemokratie vom Ende des 19. Jahrhunderts bis zum Beginn der zwanziger Jahre, in: Archiv für Sozialgeschichte 19 (1979), 459-510; and Rolf Helbig/Wilhelm Langbein/Lothar Zymara, Beiträge zur Lage des weiblichen Proletariats und dessen

tion and social reproduction also intensified in the face of the inexorable growth of the female population "surplus" that resulted from the death of two million German men by the fall of 1918. The conjuncture of Germany's defeat and the revolutionary declaration of female suffrage changed the political meanings of this surplus, which was soon figured as the demographic foundation for an irrevocable "emancipation" of German women. In authorizing women as new political subjects, the revolution appeared to affirm and even to render permanent the wartime shattering of the gender order.

4. THE GENDER OF REVOLUTION AS IMAGINARY

Intellectuals and reformers who sought to analyze the origins of the crisis surrounding women, gender, or sexuality from the vantage point of the later Weimar Republic most often looked back to the war or to the upheaval of the revolution as a definitive turning point that "shattered all foundations into pieces," most notably that of gender norms and hierarchies.[26] Manes Sperber, Communist, novelist and psychologist, explained in his memoir, *Die vergebliche Warnung*, the "sexual problem" he had observed in his patients during the 1920s as stemming from the "social earthquake of the war and the postwar period." Women, "widowed before they could even marry," became the "avant garde of a radical emancipation, a sexual revolution" through their questioning of the purpose of any long-term relationship.[27] While the political revolutions in Berlin and Munich in 1918 and 1919 scarcely initiated or fulfilled anything like a sexual revolution, a more capacious understanding of revolution as an imaginary rather than a sequence of strictly political events allows for the inclusion of the perceived rupturing of gender and sexual regimes in 1918-19 under the rubric of "revolution." That gender and sexuality remained a node of recurrent crisis throughout the Republic can thus be viewed as one of the legacies of the 1918-19 revolution.

---

aktive Einbeziehung in den Kampf der deutschen Arbeiterklasse gegen Imperialismus, Militarismus und Krieg in der dritten Hauptperiode der Geschichte der deutschen Arbeiterbewegung, Leipzig, 1973, 131-132, 140-141, 400-401.

26 Manes Sperber, Die Vergebliche Warnung, Vienna 1975.
27 Sperber, Die vergebliche Warnung, 212-213. Also cited in Grossmann, Continuities and Ruptures. Sexuality in Twentieth-Century Germany, Historiography and its Discontents, in: Karen Hagemann/Jean Quataert (eds.), Gendering Modern German History, New York 2008, 212.

The war's end and revolutionary upheaval set the stage for the scenes of betrayal or estrangement between husbands returning from the front and their wives or lovers as portrayed in dramas such as Brecht's *Trommeln in der Nacht* and Ernst Toller's *Hinkemann*. Both male and female figures share the attributes of disorientation and self-estrangement, their subjectivities shattered by four grinding years of war and by the unexpected cataclysm of defeat and revolution. In Brecht's *Trommeln in der Nacht*, which he wrote in Augsburg in early 1919, Andreas Kragler returns from his wartime post in Africa in search of his fiancé Anna, who thinks Kragler is long dead. Pregnant by another man, Anna is pressured by her wealthy parents to forget Kragler – "a corpse rotting in the earth" – and to marry Murk. When Kragler appears at the betrothal party to reclaim Anna, she turns her back on Murk and leaves to join Kragler and the revolutionary forces engaged in a battle over the press headquarters. While the revolution reunites the estranged lovers, Kragler ultimately decides to forsake the revolutionary uprising in favor of a new life and individual happiness with Anna.[28]

As in Brecht's *Trommeln in der Nacht*, the main character in Ernst Toller's *Hinkemann* is a soldier returning from the front to his wife, Grete. A military commander in the Munich Räterepublik, Toller penned the play, originally titled *Der deutsche Hinkemann*, in 1922 after serving a prison term for his revolutionary activities. It was first staged in 1923, generating vitriolic protests by nationalists and conservatives against Toller's representation of war veterans as emasculated and impotent.[29] Returning injured from war in 1918, Eugen Hinkemann reveals to his wife that he has been castrated by a gunshot. Describing his return, Hinkemann recalls seeing "no people in the streets, just bits and pieces of humans…and endless need."[30] Impoverished and despairing at their respective plights, he and Grete each sink into bitterness and contemplate suicide. Grete takes up an affair with her husband's friend Paul and becomes pregnant, while Eugen, hoping to provide for his wife at least financially, joins a freak show where he is hailed as a German hero and strongman for biting the heads off of rats. Hinkemann bleakly dismisses all hope of personal or revolutionary redemp-

---

28 Bertolt Brecht, Trommeln in der Nacht, Gesammelte Werke I, Stücke I, Frankfurt 1967, 69-124. See also Hans Kaufmann, Drama der Revolution und des Individualismus, in: Wolfgang M. Schwiedrzik (ed.), Brechts Trommeln in der Nacht, Frankfurt 1990, 367-85 and Astrid Oesmann, The Theatrical Destruction of Subjectivity and History. Brecht's Trommeln in der Nacht, in: The German Quarterly 70:2 (Spring 1997), 136-150.
29 Carol Poore, Disability in Twentieth-Century German Culture, Ann Arbor 2007, 42-44.
30 Ernst Toller, Hinkemann. Eine Tragödie, Stuttgart 1971.

tion, decrying the rancor, mistrust and hatred that divided comrades and friends along party and class lines, proclaiming "Keine Tat, die nicht erstickt in Hader und Verrat!" In the play's last act Hinkemann terms himself "a laughable figure, as sadly laughable as these times in which we live." Noting that "these times have no soul and I have no gender," he concedes that he and Grete should each go their own way.[31] Consumed by shame and despair, Grete springs to her death from the window, leaving Hinkemann alone with her corpse, itself now broken into pieces. While Brecht's *Trommeln in der Nacht* concludes with the reconciliation of Kragler and Anna, in Toller's *Hinkemann* such a reunion is thwarted by the bodily and psychic damage of war and the impossibility of redemption through revolution, ultimately shattering Grete as well as Eugen.

Robert Reinert's recently rediscovered film, *Nerven*, shot in Munich in the summer of 1919, "encapsulates like no other film the anguish of the turbulent months that saw the end of military action and a subsequent civil war," according to film scholar Anton Kaes.[32] The film is also unusual in its exploration of "secondary trauma," which like shell-shock, spread like a "contagious disease" on the home front, shattering the nerves of the film's male and female characters. In the first scene of *Nerven*, two contrasting male figures contend with what one film reviewer termed the "nervous epidemic that has gripped mankind and has driven it to actions and guilt."[33] In the first scene the manufacturing magnate, Roloff, hosts a triumphant celebration of his company's jubilee. In the middle of his speech rallying hundreds of employees and guests for the company's renewed quest to "conquer the world" with its advanced products, the factory smokestacks explode, spewing fire and smoke through the crowd and dispersing them into the streets. Roloff retreats to his home seeking comfort from his wife when he is seized by flashbacks from the battlefield and must confess to her that the war had destroyed his "nerves of steel." The other male figure, Johann, assumes the role of a socialist preacher and, is first shown making his way through a battlefield comforting dying soldiers and lamenting the corpses that litter the landscape. The scene then flashes to the unnamed city in the aftermath of the factory's explosion, where Johann rallies the workers with patient explications of the social and political conditions they now face. Armed workers then pour into the streets in a scene that evokes the November revolution. Back at the Roloff family villa, his sister, Marja, who is to be married the next day, tries on her

---

31 Toller, Hinkemann, 30, 33, 51.
32 Anton Kaes, Shell Shock Cinema. Weimar Culture and the Wounds of War, Princeton 2009, 39. The film was pieced together from fragments found in various film museums by Stefan Drössler and reissued in 2008 by Edition Filmmuseum (41).
33 As cited in Kaes, Shell Shock Cinema, 43.

wedding gown, only to abruptly cast it aside, revealing to her nursemaid that she can only love a man like Johann who enjoys the trust of the people. Marja asks whether she, too, feels how the "mysterious currents quiver through the air, how the earth shakes under something unprecedented and monstrous?"[34] Frantic and unnerved, Marja runs to the balcony as the workers march by in formation; she then sets out in search of Johann in the crowd, eluding her fiancé, who arrives on horseback on the eve of their wedding. Subsequent scenes reveal Johann as the clandestine lover of Roloff's wife, who finds solace from her husband's war-damaged nerves in Johann's arms. While Marja's love for Johann remains unfulfilled, she seeks his company and comfort by kindling a friendship with his blind sister, who appears oblivious to the traumatized people around her. Reinert's film thus refuses the post-war gender settlement that Georg Jacoby's propaganda film of 1917, *Dem Licht Entgegen*, idealized, which depicted women nurturing shell shocked men back into civilian life by reintegrating them into the intimate spaces of family and domesticity.[35]

At the center of the dramas by Brecht and Toller and Reinert's 1919 film was the emergence of a new female subject, one whose actions and inclinations were crucial to the reintegration or estrangement of the returning soldier. The perception of a new female sexual agency that originated in the experiences of war, defeat and revolution was still pronounced in cultural critic Hans Ostwald's *Sittengeschichte der Inflation* of 1931. Positing the inflation of 1922-23 as a particularly volatile turning point with respect to gender relations, Ostwald traced this crisis back to the war, noting that:

"…If during the war women were forced to take over many male jobs, they did not allow themselves afterward to be pushed quite all the way back into home and family. That had its effect on relations between the sexes as well. And the last stage of this development, there arose the female bachelor – the woman in charge of her own life, whether unmarried, divorced, or widowed."[36]

---

34 Kaes, Shell Shock Cinema, 42.
35 Kaes, Shell-Shock Cinema, 6-10.
36 See Hans Ostwald, Sittengeschichte der Inflation. Ein Kulturdokument aus den Jahren des Marktsturzes, Berlin 1931, 7-9. This text from Ostwald is also featured in the German Historical Institute's online Deutsche Geschichte in Dokumenten und Bilder, Bd. 6, Die Weimarer Republik 1918/19-1933 (http://germanhistorydocs.ghidc.org). Bernd Widdig's examination of "Gender and Inflation" in his Culture and Inflation in Weimar Germany, Berkeley 2001, 200-201, drew my attention to Ostwald's text.

Ostwald observed that in the wake of the inflation "women in many respects [had] completely transformed themselves. They asserted their demands, particularly their sexual demands, much more clearly. In every conceivable way they intensified their claim to experience life more fully and intensely."[37] The social scientific study of "Authority and the Family," conducted by the Institute for Social Research in 1927, included an unprecedented survey of 360 medical doctors about women's sexual behavior in which the respondents identified a "loosening of sexual morals" in the postwar period on the part of both sexes. Promiscuity was more pronounced among women, the authors concluded, because their prospects of marrying had decreased so markedly after the war.[38]

Perceptions of gender or sexual crisis during the Weimar Republic were frequently attached to the figure of the "new woman." Ubiquitous in the realms of consumption, fashion, advertising, visual culture, popular fiction and film during the 1920s, the new woman figure also troubled political, philosophical and literary explorations of gender, family and sexuality. The brisance of the new woman is usually understood in terms of her embrace of individuality and sexual freedom, as well as her pleasure in fashioning and displaying the self in the spheres of popular culture during the 1920s. While the political backdrop of the revolution seldom seems relevant to the sense of crisis surrounding the new woman, it is possible to posit at least two highly volatile political links to the conjoined processes of defeat and revolution. First, the "girl phenomenon" can be situated in the context of Germany's defeat, as Wolfgang Schivelbusch argues in his *Culture of Defeat*. The fact that men did not return from war as victors meant they had little choice, he suggests, but to accommodate themselves to the will of women. "German girlism of the 1920s," he notes, "was the result of such accommodation, reflecting a shift in power relations in favor of women."[39] Secondly, consideration of female suffrage as one platform for the new woman reveals an important link to one of the first acts of the revolution. Although it would be mistaken to understand suffrage as marking a moment of "emancipation," it unquestionably authorized German women to engage in a new "politics

---

37 Ostwald, Sittengeschichte der Inflation, 7-9, as cited in and translated by Bernd Widdig, Culture and Inflation, 201.

38 Max Horkheimer, Erhebung über Sexualmoral, Studien über Autorität und Familie, Paris 1936, 245, 277-280. See Grossmann, Continuities and Ruptures, which drew my attention to this intriguing study.

39 Schivelbusch, The Culture of Defeat, 274-275.

of presence" in the expanding and increasingly political and cultural publics of the Weimar Republic.[40]

A highly porous figure, the new woman became an emblem of female economic independence in the form of wage-earning and consumption that was both self-directed and fashion-driven; this figure also represented the sexually self-aware single woman who disavowed marriage and motherhood.[41] Enmeshed in the consumption of sex and material goods, the new woman usually appears as deeply apolitical. Yet contemporaries who puzzled over the meanings of the new woman for Weimar political and moral culture situated her origins in the experiences of war and the deeply political ruptures of defeat and revolution. Atina Grossmann has argued persuasively that the new woman was not merely "a media myth or a demographer's paranoid fantasy, but a social reality that can be researched and documented" and who "existed in office and factory, bedroom and kitchen, just as surely in café, cabaret, and film."[42] The serialization of Irmgard Keun's popular new woman novel, *Gilgi: eine von uns*, in the Social Democratic daily, *Vorwärts* in 1932 attests not only to the SPD's attempt to reach out to young women but its recognition of the Gilgi figure as emblematic of some of the party's own female readers and voters.[43] The dramas, films, and memoirs of the post-war and interwar period analyzed briefly here appear to confirm the recent claim of Ingrid Sharp and Matthew Stibbe that the years 1918-23 "constitute a distinctive period full of radical potential during which the renegotiation of gender relations took place under unstable and highly volatile conditions of unprecedented social, economic, and political strain."[44] Yet the fact that the revolutionary events of 1918-19 usually remain enmeshed in the processes of

---

40 On the politics of presence, see political theorist Anne Phillips, The Politics of Presence, Oxford 1995.

41 See Julia Sneeringer, The Shopper as Voter. Women, Advertising, and Politics in Post-Inflation Germany, in: German Studies Review 27 (2004), 477-501.

42 Atina Grossmann, Girlkultur or Thoroughly Rationalized Female. A New Woman in Weimar Germany? in: Friedlander etc. (eds.), Women in Culture and Politics. A Century of Change, Bloomington 1986, 62-80; and Ann Snitow/Christine Stansell/Sharon Thompson (eds.), The New Woman and the Rationalization of Sexuality in Weimar Germany, in: Powers of Desire. The Politics of Sexuality, New York 1983. Also see Katharina von Ankum, (ed.), Women in the Metropolis. Gender and Modernity in Weimar Culture Berkeley 1997.

43 Kerstin Barndt, Sentiment und Sachlichkeit. Der Roman der Neuen Frau in der Weimarer Republik Cologne 2003, 150-153.

44 Ingrid Sharp/Matthew Stibbe (eds.), Aftermaths of War. Women's Movements and Female Activists, 1918-23, Leiden 2011, 4-5.

Germany's defeat and in the inception of the Weimar Republic makes it difficult to distinguish the particular place of the revolution in this gender transformation.

5. THE GENDER OF REVOLUTION AS EXPERIENCE

While we may readily recognize the period of revolution as coinciding temporally with a phase of particularly volatile gender relations, few historians have posited a causal connection between the political events of revolution and the renegotiation of gender relations. In the space remaining in this essay, I propose a modest agenda for assessing the gender of revolution. *First,* both the presence and absence of female actors in the popular revolutionary events that took place on local and national stages in November 1918 requires explanation and analysis. The overwhelming masculinity of the revolutionary actors in the first days of the revolution should not inhibit consideration of the ways in which female civilians, who led the bread protests on the home front since 1916 and were active participants in the munitions strikes of 1917 and 1918, are present in memoirs and photographs of revolutionary events such as mass demonstrations, town hall gatherings, and spontaneous local assemblies.[45] As a spontaneous mass anti-war movement, the first phase of the German revolution involved "multiple constituent forces,"[46] including disparate male and female actors, sentiments, and sites of action, as well as a considerable degree of improvisation.[47] Ernst Toller's memoir, *I Was a German,* recounts the first days of the revolution in Berlin:

"First Kiel, then Munich, then Hanover, Hamburg, the Rhineland, Berlin. On Nov. 9, 1918, the Berlin workers left the factories and marched in thousands from north, south and east to the center of the city – old grey men and women who had stood for years at the munitions benches, men invalided out of the army, boys who had taken over their fathers' work. The processions were joined by men on leave, war-widows, wounded soldiers, students and solid citizens. No leader had arranged this uprising. The revolutionary leaders at the factories had reckoned on a later day. The Social Democratic deputies were sur-

---

45 See Claudie Weill, Women in the German Revolution. Rosa Luxemburg and the Workers' Councils, in: Christine Fauré (ed.), Political and Historical Encyclopedia of Women, London etc. 2003, 267-268.
46 Geyer, Zwischen Krieg und Nachkrieg, 193-195.
47 Peter Caldwell, The Weimar Constitution. Counterrevolutionary Tool or Document of Revolution? Unpublished paper presented to the German Studies Association conference Oct. 2010.

prised and dismayed. They were even then discussing ways and means of saving the monarchy with the Chancellor, Prince Max of Baden."[48]

Anecdotal and disparate pieces of evidence from memoirs, newspaper reportage, and police reports, confirm the presence of women in the spontaneously-formed revolutionary crowds.[49] Martha Arendsee, who belonged to the USPD during the revolution and became the editor of the KPD paper *Die Kommunistin* during the 1920s, further recounted that women surrounded the factories on November 9th, cheering on the workers as they streamed out and then moved on to the barracks to summon the soldiers.[50] In Hamburg in the days following the Kaiser's abdication, Lida Gustava Heymann described "the convening of a large public assembly at which only women were supposed to speak." She noted the sense of celebration in the crowded hall about "the end of the war, the revolution without bloodshed, the young republic," and the reclaiming of women's right to speak in public without the strictures of censorship.[51]

While female activists comprised an indisputable minority in both the Majority and Independent Social Democratic Parties, and in the circles of left liberal social reformers, the revolutionary events of November prompted most of those with a public reputation and political experience, such as Klara Zetkin (USPD, after December 1918: KPD) and Luise Zietz (USPD) to take public positions – in speeches, pamphlets, in the pages of newspapers, on the meaning of defeat, revolution and council rule for women's future in a new Germany. A *second* significant inquiry might seek to move beyond this presumption of women's absence to probe how female actors experienced the revolutionary moment, positioned themselves within it, or sought to challenge its terms to accommodate their needs, claims, and visions. It may be helpful to differentiate here between

---

48 Ernst Toller, I Was a German. The Autobiography of a Revolutionary. The Political Turmoil in Germany during and after World War I, New York 1991, 139.
49 See, for example, Lida Gustava Heymann's account of the concerns she and Anita Augspurg brought directly to Kurt Eisner in late November 1918. Heymann, Erlebtes-Erschautes, 163-164. Also see Christiane Sternsdorf-Hauck, Brotmarken und rote Fahnen. Frauen in der bayrischen Revolution und Räterepublik 1918/19, Frankfurt, 1989.
50 I argued this point as well in my essay, Das Geschlecht der Revolution. Stimmrecht und Staatsbürgertum 1918/19, in: Alexander Gallus (ed.), Die vergessene Revolution von 1918/19, Göttingen 2010, 84-116. See Arendsee, Die Novemberrevolution und die Frauen, 915-16; and Helbig/Langbein/Zymara, Beiträge zur Lage des weiblichen Proletariats.
51 Heymann, Erlebtes-Erschautes, 162.

those spontaneous and unauthorized female participants in the popular uprising and those female activists who, schooled by pre-war political experience and by the four years of war, seized the opportunity to realize a new form of political subjectivity. Lesser known than Zetkin or Zietz, Toni Sender's autobiography recounts her role as chair of a shop stewards' meeting in Frankfurt and her decision to authorize the arrest of the city's police chief and place him in the custody of the Frankfurt Soldiers' and Workers' Councils during the first heady days of the revolution. Although a young woman in her twenties amidst many "greybeards" in the Independent Socialist movement, Sender was elected to the Executive of the Frankfurt Council and oversaw the dissemination of information to the public regarding the Council's deliberations.[52] Although women could be elected to the newly-formed councils ("Frauen waren wählbar"), it appears that only a few women became *Rätevertreterinnen* at the city or provincial level, for example in Frankfurt am Main, Ulm, and Braunschweig.[53] With elections to the workers' councils taking place at the level of the shopfloor or the labor council (*Betriebsrrat*), the elected representatives included almost no housewives, agricultural and domestic workers, or part-time, temporary, or marginally employed workers.[54] Among the members of the 800 workers' councils in greater Berlin were 37 women, most of whom represented the largely female work force in the Berlin department stores or other female professions, such as nurses.[55] Only nineteen women were among the 370 representatives elected to the Workers' Council of Greater Stuttgart.[56] Among the 496 delegates elected to the General Congress of Workers- and Soldiers' Councils that convened in mid-December in Berlin were two women, one each from the USPD and the SPD. Despite the paucity of female representatives at the Congress, its members nonetheless approved the measure proposed by delegate Käthe Leu from Danzig, "to seize

---

52 Toni Sender, The Autobiography of a German Rebel, New York 1939, 103, 105-108, 114.

53 Arendsee, Die Novemberrevolution und die Frauen, 915-916. Arendsee recalled the election of only two female Rätevertreterinnen, but Weberling notes that women were present here and there as members of the local councils. See Weberling, Zwischen Räten und Parteien, 14-15.

54 Weill, Women in the German Revolution, 268-269.

55 Weberling, Zwischen Räten und Parteien, 14-15; Sternsdorf-Hauck, Brotmarken und rote Fahnen, 41-47.

56 Weill, Women in the German Revolution. 268.

every opportunity to advance the interests of women, which have been marginalized in all realms of life."[57]

The *third proposal* is to widen the scope of revolution beyond the council movement to encompass the proclamation of equal suffrage for women and men.[58] Not only did the suffrage declaration of November 12, 1918 mark one of the first revolutionary acts, but it also set in motion new waves of mass mobilizations of voters that would ultimately constitute another front of revolution. Sudden and unanticipated by all parties, the decree catapulted experienced activists into politics, while also appealing to "unpolitical" German women to take an active role in the "Neuformung Deutschlands."[59] The acute awareness of the *Frauenüberschuss* – the "surplus" of over two million women – lent female voters unprecedented visibility both as political actors and as objects of vigorous campaigns by all parties across the political and religious spectrum. The energetic attention devoted to mobilizing German women as first-time voters produced an extraordinary influx of women into unions and parties through late 1919, which contrasts starkly with the scant and often unnamed presence of women in the council movement.

The unanticipated announcement of equal suffrage prompted searching debates in party and voters' assemblies as to *why and how* women had suddenly gained citizenship rights when just weeks before the revolution both the Reichstag and the Prussian Landtag had rejected suffrage petitions without extensive consideration. Certainly the pre-war struggle of socialists and workers against the Prussian three-class suffrage system, and the campaigns of middle-class and socialist feminists in favor of female suffrage had laid the groundwork for this "citizenship moment" of 1918. Yet the particular conditions of war – the sharpened tenor of relations between militarized state and civil society that arose in the face of military law, censorship and the state's failed provisioning of the civilian populace – fostered the new participatory claims of citizenship, demarcating them from the fields of meaning surrounding the formal terms of

---

57 Der Zentralrat der deutschen sozialistischen Republik 19.12.2918 - 8.4.1919, bearb. Von Eberhard Kolb unter Mitwirkung von Reinhard Rürup; Quellen zur Geschichte der Rätebewegung in Deutschland 1918/19. Bd. 1. Leiden 1968, 7; also see Weberling, Zwischen Räten und Parteien, 15. The precise formulation of Leu's motion was in favor of: "die bisher auf allen Lebensgebieten zurückgesetzten Interessen der Frauen überall tatkräftig zu fördern."

58 See Canning, Das Geschlecht der Revolution.

59 Magnus Hirschfeld/Franziska Mann, Was jede Frau vom Wahlrecht wissen muss! Berlin 1918, 7.

Staatsangehörigkeit (national belonging).[60] While some contemporaries explained the ascription of citizenship rights as a just reward, granted to women and workers in recognition of their profound sacrifices on behalf of Germany's war efforts, others noted that equal suffrage constituted a vital step towards quelling the revolutionary upheaval through the promise of elections. If by the end of the war the right to vote was no longer controversial within the various wings of the German feminist movement, the fact that suffrage arrived through revolution was particularly distressing to conservative and nationalist women. In their view the revolution, following upon the German defeat, represented a national catastrophe, one that they called upon women to defeat through their political participation.[61] In a retrospective of 1921, Emma Föllmer remembered: "Many of us had not hoped for or even desired the right to vote that the revolution bestowed upon us."[62] Föllmer and others reluctantly accepted the right to vote as an unwelcome burden, but one that represented their only means to prevent further upheavals and instabilities in the realm of politics.[63] By contrast, female activists in the radical, pacifist, and Social Democratic movements urged German women to express their gratitude to the revolution for its swift enactment of suffrage, which gave them an unparalleled opportunity to influence "the internal remaking of Germany." In a series of speeches and pamphlets in December and January 1918/19 Social Democratic activist Adele Schreiber illuminated the historical precedents for this turning point in women's rights, which she embedded in analysis of European revolutions since 1789.[64]

Confusion and uncertainty prevailed as contemporaries envisioned and debated how precisely German women's new rights would be enacted, ascribed or restricted. Bourgeois and socialist feminists issued urgent calls to educate female citizens, authoring handbooks and convening courses and assemblies that aimed to offer training in citizenship (*staatsbürgerliche Erziehung*) to female voters who would soon exercise influence on the political and social transformation of Germany. The work of schooling female voters for political participation relied upon the political knowledge of those long-time activists who did not find a place for their expertise within the councils. After all of their own years of training for participatory citizenship, including the last four years on the home front,

---

60 This argument is elaborated in greater detail in Canning, Sexual Crisis.
61 Weberling, Zwischen Räten und Parteien, 21-23.
62 Emma Föllmer, Zwei Jahre politisches Frauenwahlrecht, Vom Vaterländischer Volksbund (ed.), Berlin 1921, 3. See also Gerhard, Unerhört, 329.
63 Weberling, Zwischen Räten und Parteien, 33.
64 Adele Schreiber, Revolution und Frauenwahlrecht. Frauen! Lernt wählen! Berlin 1919, 3-10. Bundesarchiv Koblenz Nachlass Schreiber 1173/58, 159; 1173/59, 18-24.

feminist activists sought to prove their own capacity to instruct the masses of politically inexperienced female voters in citizenship. As Social Democrat Adele Schreiber asserted in 1918:

"Millions of women, who had no knowledge of politics, are now in need of enlightenment. The training of young women for citizenship has been thus far utterly neglected. And now the training period that remains for German women is terribly brief. 'Learn to vote' is the slogan of the day. But it is very difficult to learn to be a voter in such a short time, for that means becoming a conscious citizen with the capacity for independent judgments. And now begins the massive competition of all of the parties for the woman voter!"[65]

In underlining the "extraordinary responsibility and the somber duty" of educating and mobilizing female voters, activists recognized that there was no turning back, no return to "the old system" and that the making of a "future-oriented state" (*Zukunftsstaat*) was now in the hands of the female majority.[66] That the stakes were very high for those feminists who sought to reimagine politics was clear in Franziska Mann's observation that "the eyes of the world are now directed at German women" in 1918-19.[67] Their most urgent tasks involved crafting a future state that departed markedly from that of the authoritarian Kaiserreich as well as training female citizens who would not conform to "the existent conditions and to that which had already occurred" and who instead welcomed the prospect of pushing these political "openings towards something new, towards that which was still becoming."[68]

A *fourth* proposal for gendering the German revolutions of 1918-19 is the exploration of the political interpretations, critiques and challenges that female activists posed on the course, organizational forms, outcomes, and missed chances as they became "active, newly autonomous, and self-defining subjects."[69] In some respects this quest coincides with Moritz Föllmer's investigation of the "acts of subjective liberation and novel self-expression" that took place among intellectual activists, gay rights advocates and feminists under the

---

65 Schreiber, Revolution und Frauenrecht, 10, 12.
66 Schreiber, Revolution und Frauenwahlrecht, 14-15.
67 Hirschfeld/Mann, Was jede Frau vom Wahlrecht wissen muss! 7.
68 Cauer, Einige Betrachtungen über die Wirkungen des Krieges, 50.
69 Rita Felski, The Gender of Modernity, Cambridge 1995, 2, 14. See also Rüdiger Graf, Anticipating the Future in the Present. 'New Women' and Other Beings of the Future in Weimar Germany, in: Central European History 42 (2009), 647-673.

broad rubric of revolution.[70] While feminist activists may have taken pride in their unprecedented opportunity to influence the form of governance and the negotiation of peace in 1919, their hopes and visions of the future were cast against the shadow of mass death and mourning. The somber acknowledgement by liberal feminist Agnes von Harnack that "an entire sea of blood and tears" overshadowed Germany's first democratic election opened an unusual space for the recognition of emotion as a component of political decision-making.[71] Yet this recognition of mass grief as a political force also offered an entirely rational assessment of the war's devastation of military and civilian life and of female voters' desire to create a new sort of polity. Some feminists sought to cast politics in new discursive terms, drawing sharp lines between their political visions and inclinations and those of the men who had led Germany into war and the disastrous defeat, pointing to the capacities of female citizens who were not encumbered by their past failures, to imagine a new future for state and citizens by "saturating the state with the influence of women."[72]

Additional matters of contention that were most acute in the months between November 1918 and January 1919 were the radically different political visions regarding the form of governance and the capacity for political representation.[73] Self-governance through the *Räte* on the one hand, and the mass enlistment and schooling of voters for the first democratic elections to the National Assembly on the other, constituted two fronts in the revolutions of 1918/19. Liberal feminists and intellectuals argued, for example, that democratic suffrage and the council movement constituted fundamentally different, even opposing forms of political representation, which also had divergent implications for gendered citizenship. In the view of Gertrud Bäumer, who led the Federation of German Women's Associations from 1910 through 1919 and joined the DDP in 1919, the

---

70 Moritz Föllmer, In Search of the Revolutionary Subject. Unpublished paper, presented to the conference, In Search of Revolution.

71 Agnes von Harnack, Die Frauen und das Wahlrecht (Ausschuss der Frauenverbände Deutschlands, (no publication date), 2-3. This brochure most likely appeared in late November or December of 1918.

72 See von Harnack, Die Frauen und das Wahlrecht, 5 and Schreiber, Revolution und Frauenrecht, 9. Schreiber's formulation was: "Wir treten unbelastet in die Politik." Schreiber noted that women "werden gerufen beinahe am Sterbebette des Vaterlandes, um mitzuhelfen, zu retten und gesund zu pflegen." In her study of Left-Liberal women, Angelika Schaser notes: "Nach dem Ende des Krieges, nach der Niederlage, die den männlichen Politikern angelastet wurde, konnten Frauen unbeschwerter Propaganda für Parteien machen." Schaser, "Bürgerliche Frauen," 670-671.

73 These arguments were first outlined in Canning, Das Geschlecht der Revolution.

councils represented a "new danger for women's right to vote:" the "Russian council system, she noted, would replace the *Rechtsstaat* with a *Machtstaat* that was "fundamentally founded on the basis of violence."[74] The councils, "as a system of representation based solely on profession (Beruf) with essentially economic goals," could not embody or represent the political interests of most female workers, housewives, or domestic workers. That this debate about the form of governance coincided with demobilization and the massive displacement of women from their wartime jobs deepened feminist skepticism about council rule, fostering alternative visions such as women's councils and a vigorous investment in the recruitment and training of female voters. This dispute widens the scope of revolution to reveal the gendered dimensions of the struggles over political representation, governance and the terms of political participation for women and men.

6. Conclusion

Approaching the German revolution 1918-19 as an imaginary constituted by the conjuncture of war, defeat, and political upheaval opens a place for the gender of revolution, while firmly resisting adjudications of the revolution's success or failure, or of the fulfillment or miscarriage of women's emancipation. Instead, I have emphasized the emergence of new forms of male and female subjectivity that took shape at the conjuncture of defeat, revolution, and the founding of the Weimar Republic. If the perception of a profound rupture in gender and sexual hierarchies was part of the imaginary and legacy of the revolution, the analysis of the experience of revolution makes clear the significance of gender to its politics of participation and claims of political representation, that is, to the visions of citizenship it fostered. The writing of citizenship into the constitution of the Weimar Republic established not only new terms of governance and political representation, but also sought to define the "ordering principles" of national boundaries, of social and sexual order. The uncertain topography of the nation, followed by the punitive terms of peace in June 1919, would infuse the terms of citizenship with nationalist sentiment, entangling the ordering principles of the national body with those of social and sexual order. Deliberated over a period of six months in 1919, the Weimar constitution sought to reconcile men and women, citizens and state, and to expunge the sense of gender rupture from the poli-

---

74 Gertrud Bäumer, Die neue Gefahr für das Frauenstimmrecht, Die Frauenfrage 21 Jg. (Mai 1919): 36-37. See also Anja Weberling, Zwischen Räten und Parteien. Frauenbewegung in Deutschland 1918/19, Pfaffenweiler 1994, 37-38.

tics of the republic by ascribing rights to men and women on the basis of sexually differentiated capacities. As much as the new republic sought to overcome its revolutionary beginnings, its authorization of new political subjects and notions of self recast the political and cultural landscape of the republic and the terms by which gender, sexuality, citizenship and national belonging would be governed.

Fear of Revolution
Germany 1918/19 and the US-Palmer Raids

NORMA LISA FLORES

1. INTRODUCTION

On Friday, 7 November 1919, the second anniversary of the Russian Revolution, local police along with federal agents stormed the headquarters of the Union of Russian Workers (URW), located in the Russian People's House at 133 East 15th Street in New York. Armed with only 27 warrants, the police proceeded to openly attack and arrest 200 people inside.[1] While the New York headquarters of the URW was being turned over, simultaneous attacks were occurring in 19 other cities, including Detroit, Michigan; Philadelphia, Pennsylvania; Newark, New Jersey; and Ansonia, Connecticut.[2] Two days later, *The New York Times* ran an article claiming that the arrests of the 7 November raids "ended the first phase of a campaign which the Department of Justice is waging to rid the United States of alien radical agitators who are urging the overthrow by violence of the Government."[3] Among those arrested were anarchists Emma Goldman and Alexander Berkman who, along with 247 others, were placed aboard the *USS Buford* and deported, without trial, to Russia on 21 December 1919.

Two months later, the Department of Justice launched a second synchronized attack against suspected communists. Beginning at 9 PM on Friday, 2 January 1920, federal, state, and local authorities targeted members of the Communist

---

1 Edwin P. Hoyt, The Palmer Raids, 1919-1920. An Attempt to Suppress Dissent, New York 1969, 52.
2 The Ogden Standard, 8.11.1919, 1.
3 The New York Times, 9.11.1919.

and Communist Labor Parties in thirty-five cities across the United States.[4] The following day, the *New York Tribune* reported that "the round-up[s] had been carefully planned for three months," and "agents of the Department of Justice . . . charge[d] that these organizations advocate and teach the overthrow of the United States government by force and violence."[5] As a result of the 2 January raids, nearly 3,000 individuals – alien and citizens alike – were taken into custody. A. Mitchell Palmer, Attorney General for the United States since March 1919, later defended the Department's actions writing:

"I am constrained to believe that these activities on the part of the government have halted the advance of 'red radicalism' in the United States and that what once seemed like a serious menace or organized revolution has been successfully met. Peace and order have, in the main, been maintained and the public has learned to recognize the horrible face of Bolshevism under the disguise of political parties; labor unions have largely purged themselves of these crafty 'borers from within'; it has come to be plainly seen that this is no fight between capital and labor, as the ultra-radical agitator insist, but that it is a fight between organized government and anarchy."[6]

With civil liberties suspended as a result of wartime legislation, the Department of Justice took full advantage of post-war fears regarding bolshevism to further expand their own powers. Even though civil liberties had been denied and laws clearly bent, postwar hysteria induced so much panic within the United States that the American public easily gave in to government sponsored propaganda and virtually allowed Palmer to produce the First Red Scare without the threat of any type of legal or even executive reprimand. By focusing his time and attention on the problems of Europe in the war's aftermath and opening of the peace negotiations, President Woodrow Wilson failed to address domestic issues regarding race, gender, and class. Consequently, the President's absence from the nation from 4 December 1918 until July 1919 not only meant that there was a deficiency of executive power, but that domestic problems were left to be addressed by inept individuals, like Palmer, who were attempting to advance their own political careers rather than restore public order.

---

4   New York Tribune, 3.1.1920, 1.
5   New York Tribune, 3.1.1920, 1.
6   "Statement of the Attorney General before the Committee on Rules, House of Representatives." 2 June 1920 in Department of Justice Memorandum from J. E. Hoover, 19 October 1920, 33. Federal Bureau of Investigation. The Palmer Raids, 1919-1920, 84002.

Although the United States did not experience the drastic upheaval within its national hierarchy as Germany did, there were still valid concerns among political leaders and citizens alike that the current state of domestic affairs would lead to a Bolshevik revolution if national concerns were not amply addressed. As a result, nations that had survived the war quickly attempted to maintain the status quo – or at least keep power firmly held by an organized executive – with the administrative heads encouraging the creation of national security states, where power was retained firmly by the central government. In 1919, Robert Laird Borden, Canadian Prime Minister noted that:

"In Canada, as elsewhere, the conditions of business and employment were abnormal [...]. There was a distinctive lack of the usual balance; the agitator, sometimes sincere, sometimes merely malevolent, self-seeking and designing, found quick response to insidious propaganda. In some cities there was [a] deliberate attempt to overthrow the Government and to supersede it by crude, fantastic methods founded upon absurd conceptions of what had been accomplished in Russia. It became necessary in some communities to repress revolutionary methods with a stern hand and from this I did not shrink."[7]

And neither did the officials in Germany or the United States. On 11 May 1919, *The New York Times*, further propelled public fears regarding the spread of bolshevist ideals by reporting that since the signing of the armistice, there were "Sixteen Wars Now Raging" in Europe, of which "the Bolsheviki are fighting nine wars" against the Allies in Russia, Russian Loyalists, Ukrainians, Germans, Poles, Rumanians, Letts, Finns, and Lithuanians.[8] While another Bolshevik revolution had yet to occur outside of the Soviet Union, uprisings in Munich, Budapest and Vienna, though short-lived, continued to remind both the state and public that bolshevism could take hold in a weakened industrialized world facing post-war labor strikes, bids for self-determination, or a rise in immigration. That prospect alone was enough motivation to grant the national government all rights and responsibilities necessary to begin policing domestic affairs.

Though at the time public surveillance was deemed to be a political necessity in the global war against bolshevism, the long-term consequences of the national security state inadvertently led to the gradual acceptance of government sponsored terrorist organizations during moments of domestic peril. By the end of 1917, the All-Russian Extraordinary Commission for Combating Counterrevolution and Sabotage or the Cheka had been implemented under the direction of Vladimir Lenin and by 1919 paramilitary groups like Germany's *Freikorps* units

---

7   Robert Laird Borden, His Memoirs, Henry Borden (ed.), Toronto 1938, 972.
8   The New York Times, 11.5.1919, 1.

were being used as counterrevolutionary measures in Berlin. On 11 August 1919, Germany began to implement a national security state with the passage of the Weimar Constitution and containing Article 48, which "empowered the president to restore public law and order in the Reich as a whole, if necessary by armed force. To this end he could temporarily suspend some of the basic rights guaranteed by the constitution."[9] Since the United States did not suffer a change in central authority immediately following the war, the Federal Government did in fact extend wartime laws which granted the authorities the right to suspend civil liberties, including the *Espionage Act* of 1917, which has been revised throughout the twentieth century. Once the threat of the First Red Scare expired after 1921, however, the United States instead relied on the use of government offices as a means of public surveillance beginning with the formation of the Federal Bureau of Investigation (FBI) in 1924, which was headed by J. Edgar Hoover until his death in 1972. Additional agencies were also established beginning in 1938 with the creation of the House of Un-American Activities Committee (HUAC) and the Office of Strategic Services (OSS) in 1942, which was the frontrunner for the Central Intelligence Agency (CIA), signed under the National Security Act of 1947, and on 4 November 1952, the National Security Agency (NSA) was established. In light of this brief, and by no means complete history, the question then becomes, how did the post-World War I period impact two nations in regards to domestic policing? And more specifically, how did the challenge against the state's centralized power during World War I grant public officials the power to reassert the federal government's authority based on using the fear of a potential Bolshevik revolution as a means of manipulating public opinion?

2. HISTORIOGRAPHY

To date, the uprisings of 1919 and indeed revolutions of the post-war period have been restricted to geographical regions and timeframes that are limited to the events surrounding the Great War. In most instances, the Russian Revolution of 1917 is often viewed as the bases of radical activity during this time period, which leaves little room for other interpretations of uprisings to be accounted for on their own. Also, particularly questionable is the use of the term revolution as well as the theory of rebellion and how it is projected onto historical moments during periods of political and social upheaval. Among academic scholars, the

---

9 Edgar J. Feuchtwanger, From Weimar to Hitler. Germany 1918-1933, New York 1993, 41.

word revolution has now taken on a broader understanding that in order to be a deemed a success violent action must always be at the center of the struggle.[10] While the post-war period in Europe absolutely lent itself to the notion that the surviving nations were indeed altered, for nations in the west, the basic idea of revolution manifested fears that times of turmoil, public execution, and mass chaos was going to descend upon the nation's shores if something was not done to specifically combat the growing terrorist threat. Examining two nations, which were each dealing in similar matters, but operating in diverse situations, offers an exemplary comment on a moment of global significance, when the state, driven by the fear of the unknown substituted all manner of sound reasoning. Though the post-war era has been published in both Europe and the United States, there was renewed interest in the German Revolution and the First Red Scare following World War II and the start of the Cold War. Whereas the main body of research in the United States from the 1940s and 1950s has remained untouched, in Germany, the last few years have stimulated a revival in works on the subject of both the November Revolution and Weimar Republic.[11] Even so,

---

10   Among others, refer to Theda Skocpol, States and Social Revolutions. A Comparative Analysis of France, Russia and China, Cambridge 1979; Crane Brinton, The Anatomy of Revolution, New York 1938; Hannah Arendt, On Revolution, New York 1963; James DeFronzo, Revolutions and Revolutionary Movements, New York 2011; Jack A. Goldstone, Revolutions. Theoretical, Comparative, and Historical Studies, New York 2002; Jeff Goodwin, No Other Way Out. States and Revolutionary Movements, 1945-1991, Cambridge 2001.

11   See, among others, Walter Tormin, Zwischen Rätediktatur und sozialer Demokratie. Die Geschichte der Rätebewegung in der deutschen Revolution 1918/19, Düsseldorf 1954; Eberhard Kolb, Die Arbeiterräte in der deutschen Innenpolitik, 1918-1919, Düsseldorf 1962; Robert W. Dunn, The Palmer Raids, New York 1948; and Robert K. Murray, Red Scare. Study in National Hysteria, 1919-1920, New York 1955; Eric Waldman, The Spartacist Uprising of 1919 and the Crisis of the German Socialist Movement, Milwaukee1958. Renewed interests in German studies stem from Anthony McElligott, Rethinking the Weimar Republic, London 2014; Dirk Schumann, Political Violence in the Weimar Republic, 1918-1933. Fight for the Streets and Fear of Civil War, New York 2012, edited volumes like Anthony McElligott (ed.), Weimar Germany, Oxford 2009; Helga Grebing (ed.), Die Deutsche Revolution 1918/19, Berlin 2008; and Karl Christian Führer et al. (eds.), Revolution und Arbeiterbewegung in Deutschland 1918-1920, Essen 2013; Alexander Gallus, Die vergessene Revolution von 1918/19, Göttingen 2010; Volker Ullrich, Die Revolution von 1918/19, Munich 2009; and Stefan Danz, Rechtswissenschaft und Revolution, Hamburg 2008. For the United States see Regin Schmidt, Red Scare. FBI and the Origins of Anticommunism

none of these studies, either from Germany or the United States, offer, at book length, a broader transnational understanding or even world perspective of 1919. Despite the interest in the subject, literature concerning both countries is based on specific instances that do not venture beyond their geographical locations. As a result, current understanding of the time period remains segmented. And while both Germany and the United States possessed diverse problems in the post-World War I period, their responses to the threat of bolshevism remains fundamentally similar.

While the current field of literature is vital to move the discussion of the post-war period forward, in this case, it is necessary to go back to the basic use of primary literature in regards to the Palmer Raids in order to specifically readdress how the impact of revolutions and uprisings in Europe influenced matters in the United States. The Spartacist Uprising, which occurred before the opening of the Paris Peace Conference and the Seattle Strikes, impacted the United States and propagated fears that a similar situation would also arise in North America. Even though the term "Spartacist Uprising" is debatable, the fact remains that the situation has come to represent a period of fear rather than a specific movement. Nevertheless, for many Americans, Germany was seen as a modern advanced society and should the nation succumb to bolshevism, then the radical red ideals of the Soviet Union would eventually overrun France and England and ultimately threaten the United States. By demonstrating the impact of Germany's November Revolution and the drastic shift in central authority, one begins to understand how individuals in positions of authority in the United States used the German situation to propel fears that unrest from labor organizations and immigration were a threat to the overall stability of the country.

Whereas Germany's Kaiser Wilhelm II abdicated the throne and inadvertently created a near political catastrophe, President Wilson's volunteered absence meant that the position of executive power was more or less vacant from 4 December 1918 through 4 March 1921, when his term ended. While Vice President Thomas R. Marshall did preside over the Executive Cabinet meetings while President Wilson was in Paris, the sudden collapse of the President on 2 October 1919 from a stroke did not propel the Vice President to again assume control as a

---

in the United States, 1919-1943, New York 2000; Christopher M. Finan, From the Palmer Raids to the Patriot Act, New York 2007; Christopher Capozzola, Uncle Sam Wants You. World War I and the Making of the Modern American Citizen, New York 2008.

state leader.[12] In fact, the Vice President did not have any direct communication with the President until their tenure in office ended and President Wilson left the White House.[13] In the meantime, the Vice President claimed that he did not inquire after the President's health "for fear that people would accuse him of "longing for his place"[14] and as such, members of President Wilson's Executive Cabinet were also never directly informed about the severity of his condition. Even so, the Executive Cabinet convened "twenty-one times" between October 1919 and April 1920, without the express confidence of either the President or Vice President.[15] Consequently, as Palmer made ready for the first of two raids, neither the President, Vice President, Secretary of State, Secretary of Treasury, or the Secretary of War were in a position to effectively call the Attorney General's motives into question, particularly during the debate over ratification of the Treaty of Versailles. And so, as the only individual in full possession of a domestic affairs office at the time, Palmer saw himself as the one person who was able to restore social order in the United States. This is of particular interest seeing that the central government was in fact in a state of crisis, due to circumstances far beyond any influence from Europe.

While both Germany and the United States struggled to maintain some semblance of central authority from 1918 through 1920, they did so in the shadow of collapsing regimes, rising republics, and global uncertainties. Instead of entering into a period of peace, the postwar era was marred with uprisings and assassinations, labor strikes and domestic terrorism that engulfed nations on both sides of the Atlantic. According to "A Report" issued by the Legislative Committee of the People's Freedom Union in March 1920,

"Soon after the armistice, labor began to exhibit signs of unrest. During the war, workingmen had listened to speeches promising, in the event of Allied victory, a new society more equitably adjusted to the demands of the rank and file of the producers of wealth. But there was no evidence on the part of program of reconstruction. President Wilson left the rehabilitation of industry to the business men and went to Paris. Meanwhile, prices were steadily mounting. One hundred thousand men and women were out of work in

---

12 The Executive Office of the United States consists not only of the President and Vice President, but also of the Presidential Cabinet, which constitutes 15 executive departments.
13 Farrell, 17.
14 Mark O. Hatfield. Vice Presidents of the United States, 1789-1993, Washington D.C. 1997, 340-341.
15 Farrell, 17.

March 1919, on the East Side of New York city alone. [...] At such a time American labor naturally showed interest in labor movements abroad.

A casual reading of newspapers in the six months following the armistice indicates the alarm felt over this awakening interest, and the attempts made to picture the unrest in America, due to economic causes, as the product of Bolshevist atrocities. [...] The whole propaganda apparatus of war diverted its hate-stream from Germany to Russia."[16]

As a result, the radical nature of 1919/1920 ignited fears – irrational or not – throughout the Western World that the growing social, political, and economic instability could quickly produce a succession of Bolshevik inspired revolutions. And for the United States, the one European nation that appeared to be the division between Bolshevik radicalism and western democracy was Germany, which in the immediate aftermath of the war appeared to be one of the many countries on the continent that was vulnerable to extremism.

3. THE SPARTACIST UPRISING

In the weeks leading up to the armistice, Germany was already struggling to maintain order and stability both on the frontlines and at home. By 3 October 1918, the power and authority of Kaiser Wilhelm II was usurped when Prince Max von Baden was "named Chancellor of the German empire and under the threat of a military dictatorship" sent "the note requesting an armistice [...] through the Swiss government to President Wilson."[17] As both sides entered into labored agreements for terms of peace, Germany's military rebelled. Sailors first mutinied in Wilhelmshaven on 29-30 October and were eventually supported by protestors in Kiel on 2 November, resulting in a full military takeover on the 4th.[18] Klaus Schwabe remarks that "when the first reports of the Kiel mutinies reached Washington on November 7, 1918, Breckinridge Long, an Assistant Secretary of State, noted in his diary: 'This is the worst news of many months. If

---

16 The Truth About the Lusk Committee. A Report Prepared by The Legislative Committee of the People's Freedom Union, New York/New York, March 1920, 6-7.

17 Ralph Haswell Lutz, The German Revolution, 1918-1919, Stanford/California 1922, 24.

18 Gabriel Kuhn (ed.), All Power to the Councils. A Documentary History of the German Revolution of 1918-1919 Oakland 2012, xxv.

true, it means the advent of Bolshevism in force in Germany'."[19] Shortly thereafter, "mass demonstrations and armed uprisings spread to several German cities, including Hanover, Brunswick, Frankfurt, Stuttgart, and Munich."[20] The abdication of the Kaiser, Crown Prince, and Imperial Chancellor on 9 November, created a political power vacuum that threatened to overrun the state. Although Friedrich Ebert, one leader of the German Social Democratic Party (SPD), had been appointed to take command, there were still suspicions that because of Germany's weakened state, the radical left – supported by individuals like Karl Liebknecht – might use the opportunity to generate public support and incite an open rebellion that would bring Russian Bolshevism to Berlin.

Driven by the thought that Germany was about to erupt in revolution, Philip Scheidemann, who was then acting as Secretary of State, hastily announced the establishment of the Weimar Republic on 9 November, in what he later described as an attempt "to forestall the proclamation of a Soviet Republic by Karl Liebknecht."[21] Though Scheidemann's open declaration of the Republic solidified the right's attempt to out-maneuver the radical minority and retain political power, his actions did little to placate disgruntled members on the left. As President Wilson and other members of the Allied forces prepared to travel to Europe and open the Paris Peace Talks, Germany's newly appointed leaders struggled to maintain unity within their own Social Democratic Party. Disagreements that had threatened the stability of the SPD throughout the war quickly unraveled after 11 November and by the end of December 1918, the relationship between the SPD and the Independent Social Democratic Party of Germany (USPD) reached a breaking point. Political fallout within the USPD continued and on 30 December 1918 "Liebknecht and the other Spartacist leaders" severed all ties with the SPD and created the first Communist Party of Germany (KPD) "with the suffix Spartakusbund."[22] Even though it has been noted that Rosa Luxemburg "remained bitterly opposed to the élitist revolutionary strategy developed and applied by the Russian Bolsheviks," it nevertheless appeared to Germany

---

19 Klaus Schwabe, Woodrow Wilson, Revolutionary Germany, and Peacemaking, 1918-1919. Missionary Diplomacy and the Realities of Power, Chapel Hill/North Carolina 1985, 118.
20 All Power to the Councils, xxv.
21 Philip Scheidemann, Memoirs of a Social Democrat. In Two Volumes. Volume Two, Freeport/New York 1970, 581-582.
22 Helmut Trotnow, Karl Liebknecht (1871-1919). A Political Biography, Hamden/Connecticut 1984, 192.

and the world that the Spartacist were at the forefront of a bolshevist movement in Central Europe.[23]

Schwabe points out that "as late as October 1918, the American press was still hailing Karl Liebknecht as the true champion of German freedom. From this point of view, the Spartacus League was a genuine ally of the Associated Powers, and there was no Bolshevist problem at all."[24] By the time the Spartacist split from the majority, public opinion in the United States was already turning following the circulation of the Sisson Documents. Published as part of the War Information Series and entitled "The German-Bolshevik Conspiracy" by the Committee of Public Information in October 1918, the documents were reported to prove that Lenin and Leon Trotsky were German agents and prove "that the Bolshevik Revolution was arranged for by the German Great General Staff, and financed by the German Imperial Bank and other German financial institutions."[25] Although the authenticity of the communications was called into question, Schwabe argues that "the impact of these documents [...] had by no means faded among American diplomats by the time that the German revolution broke out."[26] Allegations of a Bolshevik backed uprising went beyond the United States and were also reported in Great Britain in a memorandum submitted to the War Cabinet on 7 November 1918 by Diplomat Robert H. B. Lockhart, maintaining that "it should be recognized at once that Lenin and Liebknecht represent one and the same thing, and that the latter is as great a danger to Europe as the former."[27] As public opinion throughout the Western World was assaulted with intrigues linking radicals in Germany with the Bolshevik Revolution in Russia, the Spartacist Uprising in January 1919 solidified in the minds of many living in the United States that a worldwide communist assault against stable governments was nearing.

Reacting to the increasing division between the right and the left, Germany sought to eradicate all radicals from within their administrative ranks in an attempt to retain control of the government. These efforts, however, soon back-

---

23 Conan Fischer, The German Communists and the Rise of Nazism, New York 1991, 4-5.
24 Schwabe, 118.
25 "Bolshevik Propaganda." Hearings before a Subcommittee on the Judiciary United States Senate. Sixty-Fifth Congress. 11 February 1919 to 10 March 1919, Washington D.C. 1919, 1125.
26 Schwabe, 119.
27 "Mr. Lockhart to Mr. Balfour." Enclosure. "Memorandum on the Internal Situation in Russia." 7 November 1918 (Received 8 November 1918). National Archives, Kew Garden, England. CAB/24/73.

fired after Berlin Police President Robert Emil Eichhorn, who was a member of the Independent left, refused to leave his post for right-wing supporter Eugen Ernst on 3 January 1919.[28] Eichhorn's struggle against the state was quickly backed by members of the radical left and served as a rallying point for a general revolution. Despite reservations that Germany was not yet ready for an uprising, when the Revolutionary Shop Stewards called for a public protest on Sunday, 5 January 1919, the left-wing organizations united. While differences in opinion among strike leaders hindered the progress of the uprising as early as 6 January, the state was still intent on destroying the opposition through the use of open force.[29] Though the Spartacist did not make any open attacks on permanent political institutions, on 8 January, Gustav Noske issued a call that "gradually drew into the city the skeleton regiments of the old Imperial Army."[30] Claiming that should the revolt succeed the people's voices would be silenced, Noske reasoned that "the Government is [...] taking the necessary measures to end the reign of terror and prevent its recurrence once and for all."[31] For a city that had not witnessed firsthand any of the battles during the Great War, Berlin suddenly found itself under siege on account of its government. On 11 January, state sponsored volunteer forces entered Berlin and quickly overran the revolutionaries. Two days later, members of the local citizen guard murdered Liebknecht and Luxemburg, although it was later reported that both had been "shot while trying to escape."[32] Despite the fact that the Spartacist Uprising failed to permanently disrupt the practices of the state or economy, Palmer referred to Germany as an example that "the Bolshevik notion [was] spread[ing], literally, like wildfire."[33] Such logic allowed Palmer to brand labor unrest within the United States as a Bolshevist threat and use existing legislation as a means of restraining all forms of radicalism.

---

28 Lutz, The German Revolution, 1918-1919, 94.
29 Trotnow, 197.
30 Ralph H. Lutz. The Spartacan Uprising in Germany, in: Current History: A Monthly Magazine of The New York Times 14 (April-September 1921), 83.
31 Ibid.
32 Eric Waldman, The Spartacist Uprising of 1919 and the Crisis of the German Socialist Movement: A Study of the Relation of Political Theory and Party Practice, Milwaukee/Wisconsin 1958, 194-195.
33 "Statement of the Attorney General before the Committee on Rules, House of Representatives," 19.

4. THE PALMER RAIDS

Since the Alien and Sedition Acts of 1798, the United States has relied on federal statues to renounce civil liberties and exclude certain persons under the guise of protecting the national borders during times of crisis. By the late 19th century, growing intolerance of new immigrants led to the *Chinese Exclusion Act of 1882*, which used race to deny individual settlement in the United States for the first time in the country's history. Further exclusions came on 3 March 1903 with passage of the *Immigration Law* which "marked a new era for the control of immigration" by excluding, among others, "anarchists, or persons who believed in or advocated the overthrow by force or violence of the Government of the United States or of all government or of all forms of law."[34] Incidentally, the 1903 law was revised on 5 February 1917 to include the "provision for the *expulsion* of anarchists as well as for their exclusion."[35] Coincidently, before the United States declared war on 6 April 1917, the federal government already possessed the right to expel social dissidents without the fear of public scrutiny. With the passage of the *Espionage Act* of 15 June 1917 and the *Sedition Act* of 16 May 1918, "the federal government prosecuted 2,000 people for merely speaking out against the war."[36] Even though these laws were enacted late in the war, they nevertheless set the foundation for the persecution of "untrustworthy" citizens including any and all strikers.

At the time, journalist Paul Sann noted that when the soldiers started to arrive in the United States, they "did [not] march back into the short day and high pay he was enjoying when Uncle Sam tapped him to go make the world safe for democracy. Oh no [...] The Hun quit too soon; our factories were over expanded, our shelves glutted, our foreign markets devastated by the years of havoc and destruction, our price structure shot. The wartime honeymoon between labor and capital blew up in fearful strife."[37] For the United States, the first major labor demonstration denounced as bolshevism occurred when 35,000 shipyard workers in Seattle, Washington walked off their jobs on 21 January 1919, demanding better wages. Speculation that the strike was somehow influenced by the Bol-

---

34 Sidney Kansas, U.S. Immigration. Exclusion and Deportation and Citizenship of the United States of America, Albany/New York 1948, 7.
35 Constantine M. Panunzio. The Deportation Cases of 1919 – 1920, New York 1921, 13.
36 David Cole, Enemy Aliens. Double Standards and Constitutional Freedoms in the War on Terrorism, New York 2003, 106.
37 Paul Sann, The Lawless Decade. Bullets, Broads & Bathtub Gin, Mineola/New York 2010, 15-16.

sheviks was fanned further by members of the media, like *The Seattle Star*, which on 4 February printed a full page editorial warning against the dangers of radicalism and declared that "the use of force by Bolsheviks would be, and should be, quickly dealt with by the army of the United States."[38] Nevertheless, two days later nearly 60,000 sympathetic union employees throughout the Seattle area also went on strike in a show of solidarity.[39] Despite the fact that Seattle "business men took out riot insurance on their warehouses and purchased guns," the general strike began without incident and peacefully ended on the 11th.[40] And while a federal agent, from the Bureau of Investigation commented that "the strike as far as union labor is concerned is lost and amounted to nothing, simply inconveniencing people for two or three days," the damage to the public psyche was already done.[41]

On 4 February members of the U.S. Senate voted unanimously for the formation of the Overman Judiciary Subcommittee, headed by Senator Lee S. Overman of North Carolina, which was charged with examining "Bolshevism and all other forms of anti-American radicalism in the United States."[42] Without substantial evidence to warrant the necessity of such a committee, government agencies out of Washington D.C. and in other cities across the United States, used the situation in Seattle to further promote old wartime agendas aimed at riding the country of any type of "foreign ideals." According to Evans Clark, "the New York 'Lusk Committee', officially known as the Joint Legislative Committee Investigating Seditious Activities, was appointed in March 1919, at the suggestion and stimulation of the Union League Club of New York, a body of the most prominent, wealthy and influential Republicans in the United States."[43] Even though the Overman and Lusk Committees did not produce a substantial amount of evidence to support their claims of a Bolshevik menace, their incessant fear mongering continued to perpetuate wartime propaganda directed against radicals, labor unions, and immigrants in a time of peace. In fact, Clark notes that "from February 11 until March 10, 1919, the American

---

38 The Seattle Star, 4.2.1919, 1.
39 Robert K. Murray, Red Scare. A Study in National Hysteria, 1919 – 1920, Minneapolis/Minnesota 1955, 59-61.
40 The Seattle General Strike. An Account of What Happened in Seattle and especially in the Seattle Labor Movement, during the General Strikes, February 6 to 11, 1919, Seattle/Washington 1919, 3.
41 Regin Schmidt, Red Scare. FBI and the Origins of Anticommunism in the United States, 1919-1943, Copenhagen 2000, 134.
42 The New York Times, 02.1919.
43 Evans Clark. Facts and Fabrications about Soviet Russia, New York 1920, 17.

papers were screaming in scare heads, and in columns upon columns of news stories, the most scandalous misrepresentation about Soviet Russia, brought to light by the careful manipulation of the United States Senate Committee Investigating Bolshevism."[44] While the nation did endure the occasional raid or public speech in the early months of 1919 the danger of a Bolshevik revolution seemed minimal until 28 April, when a mail bomb was delivered to the office of Seattle Mayor, and ardent anti-Bolshevik spokesman, Ole Hanson.

Although the bomb failed to explode, news of the incident quickly circulated throughout the country, generating even more interest when a second homemade bomb was detonated by the unsuspecting maid of former Senator and Chairman of the Immigration Committee Thomas W. Hardwick at his home in Atlanta.[45] Any notion that the bombs sent to Mayor Hanson and Senator Hardwick was simply a matter of coincidence shattered the following day, when an additional sixteen suspicious packages were recovered from a Post Office in New York and others were discovered in Salisbury, North Carolina and Salt Lake City, Utah.[46] In testimony presented to the House of Representatives Committee on Rules on 1 June 1920, Palmer alleged that it "became apparent from the mailing dates of these bombs that the conspirators had attempted to arrange that delivery thereof would all be made on May 1 the date set for celebration of the Communist Internationale," citing that "it was the premature delivery of the bombs directed to Senator Hardwick and Mayor Hansen and the quick action and vigilance of the postal authorities that none of the other bombs resulted in injury to the persons for whom they were intended."[47] For local and federal authorities investigating the bombings, there was little evidence to explain the meaning of the bombers actions.

Since the bombs were similarly wrapped, intended for prominent government officials, and bore the label of Gimbel Bros. of New York, the press immediately reported that "a nation-wide bomb conspiracy," was underway to which "police authorities say has every earmark of the I.W.W.-Bolshevik origin."[48] While the May Day celebrations occurred without further incident, Joel Kovel argues that "the logic of hysteria is that it exaggerates something real," and therefore, "the reality which hysteria elaborated was the *evil* of the Communists,

---

44 Ibid., 15-16.
45 Frederick Lewis Allen. Only Yesterday. An Informal History of the 1920s, New York 1959, 43.
46 Robert Dunn (ed.), The Palmer Raids, New York 1948, 14.
47 Attorney General A. Mitchell Palmer on Charges Made Against Department of Justice by Louis F. Post and Others, 157.
48 The New York Times, 1.5.1919.

but the *threat* they, and a number of other radical workers' movements, posed to the established powers in the wake of the Great War and the breakup of empire."[49] For many, the fact that the bomb investigation failed to produce any guilty individuals further perpetuated speculation that an attack against the United States by radicals was imminent. A month later, public fears were bona fide when a bomb detonated on the front porch of Palmer's home in Washington D.C., killing the attacker and damaging the front of the house on the night of 2 June. At the same time that Palmer's house was hit, bombs were also detonated at the residences of Justice Robert F. Hayden, municipal judge of Boston; Mayor Harry L. Davis, Cleveland, Ohio; Justice Charles C. Notts, Jr. of general sessions of New York City; Judge W. P. Thompson of Pittsburgh, Pennsylvania; Representative Leland W. Powers of Newtonville, Massachusetts; Max Gold, a silk manufacturer of Paterson, New Jersey; and "two bombs at the Church of Our Lady of Victory in Philadelphia, Pennsylvania."[50] Despite the fact that damage was inflicted, and two men were killed, the bomber at Palmer's home and "the watchman at Judge Nott's [...] none of the intended victims received physical injury" from the attempted bombings.[51]

Unlike the lack of physical evidence associated with the failed May Day bombings, at each of the targets of the 2 June attacks, authorities discovered a leaflet printed on pink paper, entitled "Plain Words" and signed "The Anarchist Fighters," which declared "there will have to be bloodshed; we will not dodge; there will have to be murder; we will kill because it is necessary; there will have to be destruction; we will destroy to rid the world of your tyrannical institutions."[52] Though, further investigations into the origins of the bombs proved unsuccessful and the authorities again failed to specifically locate the source of a larger terrorist plot, some Americans still bought into the theory that Bolshevism was on the rise in the United States. Two days after the bombings, Washington Attorney Jesse W. Tull sent a letter to Palmer stating "every true American citizen will join you in annihilating all such people from the Nation."[53] While evi-

---

49 Joel Kovel, Red Hunting in the Promised Land. Anticommunism and the Making of America, New York 1994, 14-15.
50 Attorney General A. Mitchell Palmer on Charges Made Against Department of Justice by Louis F. Post and Others, 158-159.
51 Ibid., 159.
52 Ibid.
53 "Letter from Jesse W. Tull, Attorney-At-Law to A. Mitchell Palmer." Washington, D.C., 4.6.1919. Misspellings in the origins. National Archives. R. G. 60. Department of Justice Central Files. Straight Numerical Files. 202600. Sections 1-3. Box 3134. Entry 112.

dence did not permit the federal government to launch a full scale investigation of suspected Bolshevism throughout the country, smaller state sponsored agencies, like the Lusk Committee, seized the opportunity to specifically denounce local organizations, beginning with a raid on the office of the "the representative of the Russian Government in the United States, Mr. L. Martens and his staff" on 12 June.[54] The following day, "at 3 P.M., Lusk's agents simultaneously invaded the Rand School of Social Science at 7 East 15th Street, the headquarters of the Socialist Party 'left wing' at 43 West 20th Street, and the I.W.W. at 27 East 4th Street. Participating in the raids were 'volunteers' from an outfit calling itself the American Protective League."[55] Although the summer raids of 1919 yielded little evidence that a Bolshevik uprising was afoot in New York City, the idea that radicalism could potentially be brought into the United States via foreign institutions only furthered the resolve of government offices to react before anything happened.

While the circumstances of the post-war period eventually gave away to the Spartacist Uprising, the United States also faced a series of uncertainties in the immediate aftermath of the Great War that led both the people and government agencies to fear the worst. Already by the end of July 1919, there had been an estimated 1,279 labor strikes in the United States.[56] Along with the bombing attempts, race riots were also becoming a frequent occurrence including a two day riot in Chicago that started on 27 July and ended with the deaths of "at least thirty-eight people."[57] Considering the events of the summer of 1919, including the attempt on his own life, Palmer concluded "that there must be established a systematic and thorough handling of the unlawful elements in the United States, whose sole purpose it was to commit acts of terrorism and circulate literature advocating the overthrow of the Government of the United States."[58] As a result, on 1 August 1919, Palmer was able to secure "an appropriation of $500,000 from Congress" and established the General Intelligence (GID) or Radical Division, naming his special assistant, J. Edgar Hoover as its director.[59] Created with the intent of "collecting evidence and data upon the revolutionary and ultraradical movements," the GID quickly gained recognition for perfecting surveillance

---

54 Clark, 17 – Ludwig C. A. K. Martens.
55 Dunn, 21.
56 Hanson, 287.
57 Capozzola, 136.
58 Attorney General A. Mitchell Palmer on Charges Made Against Department of Justice by Louis F. Post et al., 166.
59 Murray, 193.

against suspect radical activity in the United States.[60] Under Hoover, the GID created an elaborate index system that came to include "over 200,000 cards, giving detailed data not only upon individual agitators connected with the ultra-radical movement, but also upon organizations, associations, societies, [and]publications."[61] Shortly after its formation, GID was called upon to investigate the Spanish anarchist society, *El Ariete*, the Union of Russian Workers of the United States and Canada, as well as the steel and coal strikes of 1919.[62] With the attention of the federal government already involved in cataloging suspected radicals, the United States once again appeared on the brink of a radical revolution when the Socialist Party of America split into to two new factions, the Communist Party of America and the Communist Labor Party in September 1919.

Shortly after the collapse of President Wilson on 2 October 1919, Senate Resolution No. 213 informed Palmer that he was "requested to advise and inform the Senate whether or not the Department of Justice has taken legal proceedings, and if not, why not, and if so, to what extent, for the arrest and punishment of the various persons within the United States who during recent days and weeks and for a considerable time continuously previous thereto, it is alleged, have attempted to bring about the forcible overthrow of the Government of the United States; who it is alleged, have preached anarchy, and sedition."[63] Given that there had already been raids against suspected radicals by the Overman and Lusk Committees, Palmer's used the Senate's inquest to further justify the Department of Justice's actions of 7 November. Utilizing the authority provided under "An Act to Exclude and Expel from the United States Aliens who are Members of the Anarchistic and Similar Cases," Palmer was granted the power to denounce radical notables like Goldman and Berkman, who for years

---

60 The Abridgment 1920 Containing the Annual Message of the President of the United States to the Two Houses of Congress. 66th Congress, 3rd Session. With Reports of Departments and Selections from Accompanying Papers, Washington, D.C. 1921, 490.
61 Ibid.
62 Ibid., 492.
63 Investigation Activities of the Department of Justice. Letter from the Attorney General Transmitting in Response to a Senate Resolution of October 17, 1919, A Report on the Activities of the Bureau of Investigation of the Department of Justice Against Persons Advising Anarchy, Sedition, and the Forcible Overthrow of the Government. 66th Congress, 1st Session. Senate. Document No. 153. 17 November 1919, Washington, D.C. 1919, 5.

had been targeted by federal authorities for their involvement in extremism.[64] Consequently, by linking their names to the 7 November raids, the arrest and deportation of 249 suspected radicals was capped as a success and thereby alleviated public backlash against government agencies. Though Palmer later admitted that "the government's first efforts were directed against individual agitators, amongst whom Emma Goldman and Alexander Berkman were perhaps the most conspicuous," he also claimed that "many other active and dangerous persons were apprehended and held for deportation,"[65] including Adolf Schnabel and Peter Bianki.[66] Despite Palmer's attempt to used the deportation of 249 radicals aboard the *USS Buford* as a positive step in the government's attempt to rid the country of Bolshevism, Louis F. Post, Assistant Secretary of Labor, contradicted the Attorney General commenting that "of that number [...] 199 were deported because they were members of the Union of Russian Workers," and "43 who were said to be Anarchists."[67] Post also concluded "that there was not a particle of evidence which indicated that" any of the deportees "were violent or a menace to the American government."[68] While these accusations came after the fact, at the time there was little backlash against either Palmer or the Department of Justice for the raids of 7 November. Consequently, just six days after the *USS Buford* set sail for Russia, a confidential letter to George E. Kelleher of Boston, Massachusetts from Frank Burke, Assistant Director and Chief of the Bureau of

---

64 Approved on 16 October 1919, Section Two of and "Act To Exclude and Expel from the United States Aliens who are Members of the Anarchistic and Similar Classes," declared "that any alien who, at any time after entering the United States, is found to have been at the time of entry, or to have become thereafter, a member of any one of this Act, shall, upon the warrant of the Secretary of Labor, be taken into custody and deported in the manner provided in the Immigration Act of February fifth, nineteen hundred and seventeen (Approved, 16 October 1918 – [Public – No. 221 – 65th Congress.] [H.R. 12402.] – An Act to Exclude and Expel from the United States Aliens who are Members of the Anarchistic and Similar Classes." Record Group 60. Department of Justice. Central Files. Straight Numerical Files 202600. Sections 4-7. Box 3135. Entry 112. National Archives II, College Park, Maryland.
65 "Statement of the Attorney General before the Committee on Rules, House of Representatives," 33.
66 The Abridgment 1920, 493.
67 "Louis F. Post: Former Assistant Secretary of Labor, Washington, D.C. Speech at Harvard Student's Liberal Club, Harvard University, Cambridge," 1-2, 23.3.1921. Report Made by William E. Hill. Federal Bureau of Investigation. The Palmer Raids, 1919-1920. [8]392[3].
68 Ibid.

Investigation in Washington D.C. already revealed the plans for a second raid, affirming "that the tentative date fixed for the arrests of the Communists is Friday evening, January 2, 1920."[69] This time, targeting members of the Communist Labor Party and the Communist Party of America, the raids were expanded and 5,000 warrants were requested.[70]

Although the Department of Justice vowed on 5 January 1920 "that its agents would continue their activities [upon suspected radicals] until a complete round-up had been made," the January raids have instead come to signify the last major assault against radicalism.[71] Part of the issue was that the Bureau failed to uncover a large radical organization operating within the United States. In spite of the accusations of the Bureau of Investigation against radicalism, estimates of membership to the Socialist Party, Communist Labor Party, and the Communist Party in December 1919 stood somewhere between 79,000 and 129,000 people.[72] And since supporters of these organizations made up "a rather slender nucleus" of the population, Frederick Lewis Allen observed that their numbers would have been hardly capable of sustaining "a revolutionary movement" that would have rivaled those in Europe and specifically challenged the authority of the federal government.[73] While the January raid included simultaneous assaults in 33 towns, of the near 3,000 arrests, "2,202 were subsequently canceled by Assistant Secretary Post [...] and only 556 of the remainder were upheld and the persons involved ordered deported," which was "a far cry from the 2,720 deportations which the attorney general had prophesied earlier."[74] Since the Department of Labor contained the Bureau of Immigration, it fell to William B. Wilson, Department Secretary, to handle all deportation cases, especially those resulting from the raids. Reluctant from the beginning to even issue warrants of arrest, Secretary Wilson – no relation to President Wilson – and his Assistant Secretary Post, continually dismissed Palmer's accusations of a radical revolution and thereby aided in devaluing the mass hysteria created by the First Red Scare.[75] Despite the fact that at the time of the raids William J. Flynn, Director of

---

69 To the American People: Report Upon the Illegal Practices of the United States, Department of Justice, Washington, D.C. May 1920, 39.
70 "Louis F. Post: Former Assistant Secretary of Labor, Washington, D.C. Speech at Harvard Student's Liberal Club, Harvard University, Cambridge," 3.
71 The New York Times, 5.1.1920.
72 Gordon S. Watkins, "The Present Status of Socialism in the United States." The Atlantic Monthly (December, 1919), 821.
73 Allen, 42.
74 Murray, 251.
75 Ibid., 246-247.

the Department of Justice, maintained that "we have succeeded [...] in breaking the backbone of the radical, revolutionary movement in America," the constant reversing of deportation cases made the Bureau's actions seem rather unfounded.[76]

Faced with losing momentum garnered during the November and January raids, Palmer once again used the media as a means of encouraging national hysteria toward radicalism. By the end of April 1920, headlines announced "May Day Death Plot Is Uncovered," informing readers that Palmer revealed that "plots against the lives of more than a score of federal and state officials have been discovered by the department of justice as part of radical May day demonstrations."[77] Palmer's charges once again put the nation's attention directly on the possibility that a massive assault against the United States was imminent and this time federal and local authorities responded in full. While the scare brought additional security measures to New York City, Boston, Chicago, and Washington D.C. as local newspapers instructed the public to be mindful of the May Day celebrations, in reality, just as it had in 1919, the day came and went without incident in the United States.[78] On 2 May 1920, the *New York Tribune* aptly commented that:

"The Red revolution scheduled to come to America yesterday must have missed the boat. With eleven thousand members of the Police Department, a legion of Secret Service agents and countless volunteer defenders of the nation waiting to receive it in a manner worthy of the best American traditions, the guest from Russia failed to appear. Similarly fortunate conditions prevailed in other large cities of the country."[79]

Though Flynn "intimated that it was because the advance notices had been so widely circulated and so thoroughly drawn that the trouble did not arrive," confidence in both Palmer and the Department of Justice was drastically failing. Amid the backlash from the failed deportations of the January raids, Assistant Secretary Post continued to publicly accuse Palmer and his office of misconduct. Not only had Post "criticized severely the attitude of the Department of Justice in the treatment of aliens arrested as alleged radicals," but he maintained that "efforts had been made [...] to get aliens out of the country regardless of their guilt"

---

76 The Ogden Standard, 3.1.1920.
77 The Morning Daily, 30.4.1920.
78 Murray, 252 - 253.
79 New York Tribune, 2.5.1920.

while "excessive bail had also been demanded [...] to keep men in jail."[80] The department's allegations that large stock piles of weapons had been collected during the raids were dismissed by Post who claimed that "with all these sweeping raids all over the country," including one on 14 February 1920 targeting members of the anarchist group *L'Era Nuova*, "there have been three pistols [...] brought to our attention."[81] Instead of being hailed as a protector of the American public and establishing his campaign for the 1920 Presidential election, Palmer was instead forced to justify his department's actions during an inquiry set by the Committee on Rules of the House of Representatives in June 1920.

By the time Palmer was called to testify, the National Popular Government League had already issued a pamphlet entitled *To the American People: Report upon the Illegal Practices of the United States Department of Justice*. In the 64-page account, twelve lawyers not only charge that "the wholesale arrests of both aliens and citizens during the Department's various raids had been made without justification," but they also acknowledge that "there is no danger of revolution so great as that created by suppression, by ruthlessness, and by deliberate violation of the simple rules of American law and American decency."[82] Despite these charges, Palmer defend his actions, by arguing that while "the department's methods might have appeared arbitrary and hasty, they were undertaken to alleviate a very real and awful danger."[83] Considering the post-war period, especially the influence of bolshevism in Europe after 1917, events like the Spartacist Uprising became cautionary tales in the United States. To men in positions of authority, like Palmer, the "very real and awful danger" was that the new powers granted during the war that allowed for the federal government to denounce outsiders without reproach were set to expire. Bolshevism, as a result, permitted government agencies to not only retain political power, but also to expand as evident with the GID. For the average citizen, however, the constant charge that a radical revolution could explode at any moment and did not, caused public sympathies to wane. Neither the Wall Street bombings in September 1920 nor another congressional investigation into Palmer's actions, led this time by Senator Thomas J. Walsh in January 1921, ignited another surge of mass hysteria. Since bolshevism failed to take hold in Germany following the Spartacist Uprising or indeed overrun any other European nation outside of the Soviet Union, the general attitude in the United States was a desire to return to normalcy as ex-

---

80 To the American People: Report Upon the Illegal Practices of the United States, Department of Justice, 4.
81 Ibid., 5.
82 Ibid., 3 & 8.
83 Murray, 255.

pressed in the Republican platform. As a result, the Department of Justice no longer had an excuse to openly target radical organizations in the United States.

5. CONCLUSION

When the November Revolution erupted in Germany before the armistice was even set, many world leaders took the act to signify that a broader Bolshevik uprising was imminent. Even though Germany, more so than the United States, came closer to facing a Red inspired revolution, leaders of both nations used the potential threat of bolshevism as a means of inflicting state sponsored terror on the public in an effort to preserve the authority of the national executive. As David Mitchell argues, it was in 1919 that "the doors of power swung loose. Iconoclastic bourgeois renegades were rising from slimy depths. It was all most unhealthy, and it was all, somehow, connected with the Bolsheviks."[84] While the United States endured general uprisings and labor disputes, fear that a Bolshevik revolution was going to overthrow the government was far less of a threat considering how removed the nation was from the European continent. Even though President Wilson was noticeably absent for most of 1919, the government as a whole was never truly vulnerable to an attempted overthrow like the uprisings taking place in Germany or elsewhere. In fact, despite the sporadic attacks against the general safety of public officials in the spring and early summer of 1919, Palmer did not launch his raids until 7 November, well over a month after President Wilson became incapacitated. Without the fear of an executive reprimand, Murray explains that those left in positions of power, like Palmer, became "the chief apostles of that false security which it seemed the whole nation was seeking and, burning with personal ambition and trafficking in human weakness and emotion, they [...] fashioned the mood of the 1919 political scene."[85] And so, when Palmer unleashed his first major raids against suspected communist, he was not initially held accountable to other higher office in the United States, being that he too was a member of the Executive Cabinet. With the turbulent events of the post-war period, the general population was still harboring war hostilities toward anything foreign.

Although the Great War was supposed to have been the "War to End all Wars," 1919 is best understood as a period of consecutive uprisings, labor strikes, and political fear mongering both in and outside of Europe. The outcome of the war not only incited revolutions and uprisings, but 1919 also created an

---

84 David Mitchell, 1919. Red Mirage, London 1970, 19.
85 Murray, 11.

atmosphere where fears manifested by the four-year struggle could be redirected by states that were intent on maintaining order and stability. As the heads of government convened in Paris in an attempt to restore some semblance of order in Europe, President Wilson's absence meant that government officials in the United States were left to their own devices. In an effort to promote a political platform based on nativist ideals, officials like Palmer used the events in Germany as a means of not only suppressing labor, but also as justification for targeting and expelling foreign aliens. Whereas Germany and the United States took such divergent paths during the war, 1919 marks a crucial period in the history of both countries, given that newly empowered national leaders used real and clandestine threats against the state as justification for openly attacking all elements of foreign ideals. Incidentally, the reaction of Germany and the United States toward radicalism and especially labor ultimately resulted in the general public acceptance of the fact that in moments of crisis civil liberties could be suspended or even revoked. Such practices in the wake of the Spartacist Uprising and the Palmer Raids ultimately gave rise to the acceptance of a national security state in Germany and the United States, which both nations would continue to capitalize on throughout the twentieth century.

German Defeat in World War I, Influenza and Postwar Memory

OLIVER HALLER

1. INTRODUCTION

World War I ended amidst profound recrimination and accusation in Germany. On 12 November 1918, a day after the armistice that stopped the slaughter of WWI, Field Marshal Paul von Hindenburg proclaimed that "We end the struggle proudly and with our heads held high where we have stood for four years in the face of a world full of enemies".[1] The curtains had closed on imperial Germany. A sense of urgency still prompted the socialist politician Friedrich Ebert to join forces with the German officer class. He interpreted the events of 1918 in a manner that helped hold back the revolutionary tidal wave unleashed by the Kaiser's abdication. Ebert partially lobbied for the support of the military by repeatedly reassuring the returning masses of soldiers that "no enemy has defeated you".[2] This act of political expediency legitimized interpretations of "defeat" that deflected blame away from the warriors. The determination of responsibility for the war's outcome represented an ordinary human search for meaning. Modern academic interpretations of this process, however, categorically reject any credibility of the stab in the back trope. This myth or legend, as it is now universally known, is even decried as a major reason for the ultimate collapse of the Weimar Republic and causally linked to the subsequent horrors of Nazism.

---

1 Paul von Hindenburg quoted in Martin Kitchen, The German Front Experience, 03.10.2011, bbc.co.uk/history/worldwars/wwone/ german_experience_01.shtml.
2 Nationalversammlung, 1. Sitzung. Donnerstag, den 6. Februar 1919, 1919/20, Reichstagsprotokolle, www.reichstagsprotokolle.de.

The characterization of a particular form of remembrance as "toxic" unmasks a perplexing historiographical issue. It is first of all illuminating to emphasize that the legend narrative itself addressed and explained a profoundly emotional moment marked by intense fear, uncertainty, and tremendous political upheaval. Myth creation often originates in this kind of societal context.[3] Military defeat and open rebellion against the old order were unquestioned realities in late 1918. Visibly divided into militant political factions, the vicissitudes of German society forced an immediate confrontation with a series of unpleasant and disturbing facts. In this manner, myth and history fused into a narrative typology and "fertilized" each other.[4] Why, for example, did so many German soldiers, after four years of self-sacrifice and discipline, either surrender to the enemy in large numbers, disobey orders to fight on or even turn their guns against the state itself? Hindenburg and Ebert emphasized in their speeches that the Entente had not defeated the military in the field. These men alluded to other exogenous factors that later wove their way into numerous narratives blaming a treacherous homefront for betraying the army and that espoused a return to the enthusiasm of August 1914 and ultimately a remodulated conservative order.[5] As summarized by Jay Winter, the German army clearly lost on the battlefield against the Entente powers and German leaders deployed this "self-serving narrative, turned into 'memory' by German soldiers like Hitler, to lie about the past".[6]

This chapter questions the absolute certainty with which historians approach this axiomatic stance concerning a stab in the back lie. The central point here is that the specific assumptions advanced by historians represent abstract universals distended backwards through deductive reasoning. Mythical archetypes such as victor and vanquished merge with these particular assumptions.[7] But what are

---

3 Jeffrey Verhey, The Spirit of 1914. Militarism, Myth and Mobilization in Germany, Cambridge 2004, 229.

4 Peter Munz, History and Myth, in: The Philosophical Quarterly 6:22 (1956), 1 and Jay Winter, Remembering War. The Great War and Historical Memory in the Twentieth Century, New Haven 2006, 284.

5 Boris Barth, Dolchstoßlegenden und politische Desintegration. Das Trauma der deutschen Niederlage im Ersten Weltkrieg, 1914-1933, Düsseldorf 2003; Friedrich Freiherr Hiller von Gärtingen, Dolchstoß – Diskussion und Dolchstoßlegende im Wandel von vier Jahrzehnten, in: Waldemar Besson/Friedrich Freiherr von Gärtingen (eds.), Geschichte und Gegenwartsbewustsein, Göttingen 1963, 122-160; and Joachin Petzold, Die Dolchstoßlegende. Eine Geschichtsfälschung im Dienst des deutschen Imperialismus und Militarismus, Berlin 1963.

6 Winter, 284.

7 Munz, 4.

they? The answers to this question can for the sake of clarity be divided into two conceptual schemes. The first advocates a materialist perspective based on specific physical objects or empirical manifestations of human groupings such as the number of machine-guns or an increase in pamphlets protesting societal class structures. Boris Barth, for example, determines that Germany already lost the war after the Battle of Passchendaele in 1917 simply because of the high losses incurred and the growing preponderance of American power on the European continent.[8] Correlation, of course, does not necessarily imply causation and is fraught with a number of potential fallacies.[9] But the act of representing victory or defeat in this cut and dried manner also limits more nuanced investigations of the postwar German type. The politicians and soldiers of the victorious Entente powers hardly required any soul-searching in order to explain the war's outcome in this way. As far as British policymakers were concerned, the raw numbers of men and material at their disposal had always offered a favorable position in this conflict of conflicts.[10] The British explanation implied that abundance would erode their adversary's military discipline.[11] Other materialist interpretations, also advanced by wartime Entente propaganda, infer that the feudal composition of German society itself created a rift between the officers and the ranks that ultimately broke into outright rebellion as conditions inevitably deteriorated.[12] It is not possible here to challenge the persuasive power of the materialist perspective beyond hinting at its rigid determinism. Still, it must be acknowledged that this conceptual scheme today exerts so much influence on the historical discipline that Jeffrey Verhey derides idealistic alternatives as "a mythic approach to truth".[13]

The axiomatic assumption that German military defeat in the field represented the only historically "true" or "real" explanation of the war's outcome betrays an important contradiction inherent in the empirical approach. This denigration of alternative explanations as nothing more than crude lies implies a curiously

---

8   Barth, 144-148.
9   John Aldrich, Correlations Genuine and Spurious in Pearson and Yule, in: Statistical Science 10:4 (1995), 364-376.
10 Thomas Noble, Western Civilization. Beyond Boundaries, Boston 2011, 714.
11 David T. Zabecki, The German 1918 Offensives. A Case Study in the Operational Level of War, New York 2006; and Michael S. Neiburg, Fighting the Great War. A Global History, Cambridge 2005, 317-318.
12 Wilhelm Deist, Verdeckter Militärstreik im Kriegsjahr 1918?, in: Wolfram Wette (ed.), Der Krieg des kleinen Mannes. Eine Militärgeschichte von Unten, Munich 1992, 146-167.
13 Verhey, 221.

normative dismissal of ontological phenomena such as societal depression or other mental afflictions. Was the conservative narrative of a military treacherously struck down by an exogenous agent purely fabrication? Or was it instead a metaphor for something equally "real" but only less tangible than simply calculating ratios of artillery shells? Historians acknowledge that British policymakers tended to view the unfolding of history from the perspective of mechanistic principles and that this stood in stark contrast to the German fixation on human will and the phenomenological archetype of the self.[14] Prewar German psychiatry in particular helped promote a "new emphasis on behavior and personality" that obviously struggled with the illnesses of the human mind.[15] „There is nothing metaphorical in such affliction", it must be emphasized, "and nothing mythical in the construct of psychiatric disease".[16] Even the German portrayal of the war in abstract cultural or metaphysical terms, by attempting to define "the essence" of aspects of the past, "cannot be distinguished one from the other by means of criteria which distinguish metaphysical claims to knowledge from verifiable ones".[17]

Only recently have historians questioned the reliability of an underlying "us vs. them" mentality in the German army. The research of Alexander Watson in particular suggests that German military discipline actually remained intact until the end of the war. For him, the elemental "human resilience" that led to the industrialized slaughter of millions of men only broke down at the end of the conflict.[18] As demonstrated in this chapter, German soldiers in fact surrendered in larger numbers after July 1918 and incidents of insubordination escalated. The aggregate German determination to continue the conflict confronted by the advancing Entente, however, calls older interpretations of German defeat into question. Watson's unique perspective addresses the paradoxical issue of extremely high Entente casualties up until November 1918. If it is true that German military effectiveness fell dramatically during the final months, whether precipi-

---

14 Peter Novick, That Noble Dream. The "Objectivity Question" and the American Historical Profession, Cambridge 1988, 31.

15 Paul Lerner, Hysterical Men. War, Psychiatry, and the Politics of Trauma in Germany, 1890–1930, Ithaca 2003, 23.

16 Ronald W. Pies, Mental Illness Is No Metaphor. Five Uneasy Pieces, http://www.psychiatrictimes.com/articles/mental-illness-no-metaphor-five-uneasy-pieces/page/0/1.

17 Frank R. Ankersmit, History and Tropology. The Rise and Fall of Metaphor, Berkeley 1994, 47.

18 Alexander Watson, Enduring the Great War. Combat, Morale and Collapse in the German and British Armies, 1914-1918, Cambridge 2008, 235.

tated by material disadvantages or societal cleavages, how can historians understand the extremely high Entente losses prior to the armistice? Put another way, how can historians explain the simultaneously high number of German desertions with the maintenance of a cohesive fighting force. This matter is of relevance in determining the revolutionary zeal of German soldiers in 1918.

This chapter builds on Watson's notion of "human resilience" by introducing a largely unexplored phenomenon to the debate surrounding German defeat and the stab in the back legend. The following pages augment the standard causal sequences that draw on evidence derived from the military narrative of the war itself, such as the impact of the British blockade or the Entente learning curve. Relying on evidence collected at the military archives in Freiburg and Munich, this chapter re-evaluates the tendency to dismiss Quartermaster General Erich von Ludendorff's assessment that the influenza pandemic of 1918-1920 seriously complicated combat operations during his great offensives and the final months of the war. "It was a grievous business", Ludendorff wrote in his admittedly self-serving memoirs, "to listen every morning to the chief of staffs' recital of the number of influenza cases, and their complaints about the weakness of their troops".[19] These kinds of comments were hardly limited to Ludendorff or others. The official German military history of the war continually referred to the effects of the viral agent – such as fatigue and depression – without however evaluating the overall impact of influenza.[20] Through the exploration of a phenomenon "outside" the confines of traditional narratives, this chapter widens the ontological complexity of German defeat. The hypothesis that the influenza virus seriously impacted German combat operations helps explain the serious confusion surrounding explanations of defeat that later fed conservative narratives.

2. PRELIMINARY HISTORIOGRAPHICAL OBSERVATIONS

A number of scholars have addressed the fact that influenza itself disappeared from the discourse of the 1920s and beyond. A series of recent influenza outbreaks around the globe have stimulated interest in the "Spanish flu" pandemic of 1918-1920. The contagion that killed as many as 50 million people worldwide, almost five times the number claimed by World War I, was largely forgot-

---

19 Erich von Ludendorff, Concise Ludendorff Memoirs 1914-1918, London 1933.
20 Die Entwicklung der Gesamtlage vom 13.5. - Anfang Aug. 1918, 1943, Bundesarchiv-Militärarchiv Freiburg [Freiburg], RH-61/2012.

ten for much of the last century.[21] These scares have encouraged the medical community in particular to scour the historical record to study the origins and path of the world's most ravenous pandemic.[22] In terms of the historical discipline, recent publications address why influenza disappeared from collective memory in the 1920s by scouring the literature of the postwar period.[23] Additional work examines the phenomenon with the arsenal of tools available to gender studies. These works deepen our understanding of medicalization and the politics of the human body. Unfortunately, however, treatments of influenza's impact on the war itself remain virtually non-existent.

Even though influenza claimed 350,000 lives in Germany between 1918-1919, a recent article by Eckard Michels asserts that the country suffered less than other combatants.[24] Michels' exclusive focus on mortality rates underlines how historians have potentially underestimated the impact of influenza. The postulate that a virus can impede combat operations without significant loss of life hardly requires explication. Another historian, David Stevenson, writes that "During June, up to half a million German soldiers contracted influenza, this being the first of two great waves of 'Spanish flu' during 1918. Both sides suffered but the undernourished Germans earlier and more severely".[25] Other than granting influenza a marginal and unexplained role in German defeat, Stevenson excludes the pandemic from the rest of the narrative. In general, descriptive phrases such as "suffering heavily", "hard hit" or "strained" characterize the historiography.[26] Worse still from a medical point of view, an issue discussed later in the chapter, influenza is linked to nutrition and the debilitating impact of

---

21 Alfred Crosby, America's Forgotten Pandemic. The Influenza of 1918, New York 1989.

22 Wilfried Witte, Die Grippe-Pandemie 1918-20 in der medizinischen Debatte, in: Berichte zur Wissenschaftsgeschichte 29 (2006), 5-20.

23 Catherine Belling, Overwhelming the Medium. Fiction and the Trauma of Pandemic Influenza in 1918, in: Literature and Medicine 28:1 (2009), 55-81; Joshua Doležal, Waste in a Great Enterprise. Influenza, Modernism, and One of Ours, in: Literature and Medicine 28:1 (2009), 82-101; and Caroline Hovanec, Of Bodies, Families, and Communities: Refiguring the 1918 Influenza Pandemic, in: Literature and Medicine, 29:1 (2011), 161-181.

24 Eckard Michels, Die Spanische Grippe 1918/19. Verlauf, Folgen und Deutungen in Deutschland im Kontext des Ersten Weltkriegs, in: Vierteljahrshefte für Zeitgeschichte 58:1 (2010), 1–33.

25 David Stevenson, Cataclysm. The First World War as Political Tragedy, New York 2005, 341; and Noble, 714.

26 Zabecki, 237, 275-276 and 294.

the British naval blockade. It almost seems as if influenza's impact is simply submerged underneath the more traditional military explanations of the war's outcome.

The postwar treatment of influenza's impact in Germany suffered a similar fate. In the days and weeks after 11 November 1918, as the future hardships of occupation and a difficult peace settlement were unveiled by the victors, Germans struggled to explain why the wooden titan and his soldiers had not saved their country from the miseries and disasters of the war. As is commonly understood, this search for answers took various forms that hinged on the organizing principle of the stab in the back legend. The right, as is well-known, carefully crafted the "image of the demobilized hero of the trenches coming home to an unappreciative, disrespectful, scornful home-front" that had been infected by socially dislocative political ideologies culminating in the November Revolution.[27] The left, however, offered the same argument in a different package. In proclaiming that "no enemy has defeated you", Ebert also insisted that only as the "weight of enemy manpower and material became more oppressive, did we suspend the fight".[28] Instead of viewing the overwhelming power of the Entente as the determining reality of the war, however, the future president rebuked the old order for failing to ensure the conditions for a successful outcome and for throwing in the towel. He clearly explained during the first session of the National Assembly on 6 February 1919 why he believed Germany had lost the war. "This fact", Ebert stated, "is not a result of the revolution [...] it was the imperial government of Prince Max von Baden that initiated the armistice that made us defenseless".[29] Subsequently locked into a struggle to maintain order in postwar Germany, both the socialists and the conservatives therefore cultivated the support of what remained of German military muscle in order to maintain order and prevent the defeated state from descending into chaos.

This need to protect the military itself from responsibility for the war's outcome, scholars often postulate, fed a somewhat warped perception of defeat that shifted blame away from the soldiers and generals. More scathing assessments accuse postwar German historians of manipulating the historical record to reflect innocence for the outbreak of war and for blaming civilians or other factors for

---

27 Walter Rauscher, Hindenburg. Feldmarschall und Reichspräsident, Vienna 1997, 211-212; and Richard Bessel, Germany after the First World War, New York 1993, 263.
28 Nationalversammlung. 1. Sitzung. Donnerstag, den 6. Februar 1919, Reichstagsprotokolle, 1919/20.
29 Ibid.

the outcome.[30] The factors in question included a wide variety of largely discredited theories that focused on long term trends such as societal degeneration, miscegenation, and ideological contamination.[31] In terms of the actual military defeat itself, only a handful of German military historians actually focused on what had transpired on the battlefield. Like Ebert, the military historian Hans Delbrück blamed defeat on the collapse of morale after the start of the Entente offensives on 8 August 1918 and more specifically on the failure of the leadership to provide the modern weapons required for total war such as tanks.[32] For all of the insight that Delbrück brought the debate, however, he still framed the argument in a manner reminiscent of the stab in the back narrative. The reasons for this approach seem clear. The collapse of German morale, an understandably sacrosanct tenet of all interpretations spanning nearly a century of analysis, can it seems only be understood using sequential connections that indicate some kind of grave failing on the part of either officers or the ranks. The major problem with these modes of explanation is their politicized nature.

German parliamentary handling of the subject during the 1920s turned to the same political game of assessing guilt. The postwar Constituent National Assembly had immediately thought it prudent to appoint an investigating commission to look into the matter of defeat. One of its subcommittees started work in early 1920 armed with the noble aims of "impartiality and objectivity". Five years later, after sifting through piles of documents and questioning numerous participants, the group confidently proclaimed that they had "exposed the insidious anti-national propaganda of the revolutionary period of 1918" partly responsible for defeat.[33] Civilian propaganda, thrust like a dagger into the military's back, had transformed warriors into useless shirkers and deserters.[34] Morale, once again, represented the dominant reason for defeat. As described by Boris Barth, a variety of differing interpretations emerged during the 1920s that wrestled with complex psychological issues indicative of the fragmented state of

---

30 Holger H. Herwig, Clio Deceived. Patriotic Self-Censorship in Germany after the Great War, in: International Security 12:2 (1987) 5-44.

31 Heeresentziehung (Drückeberger), n.d., Militärarchiv München [Munich], II. Mob. 4, 13 424.

32 Gordon A. Craig, Delbruck. The Military Historian, in: Peter Paret (ed.), Makers of Modern Strategy, Princeton 1986, 326-353.

33 Ralph Haswell Lutz, The Causes of the German Collapse in 1918. Sections of the Officially Authorized Report of the Commission of the German Constituent Assembly Officially Approved by the Commission, North Haven 1969, v-ix.

34 Ibid., 67-68.

Weimar society. The right, expressed another way, sorted facts in such a way as to distend myth backwards into historical events.

Hermann Cron, the chief historian of the Reichsarchiv, offered the only significant departure from this pattern. He wrote a lengthy paper that addressed whether or not the German military could have continued to offer significant resistance after November 1918. Relying on war diary entries and reports from the last months of the war, Cron concluded that a lack of replacements forced German divisions into the frontlines for excessive periods of time and that these formations therefore experienced "extreme bodily exhaustion" that translated into broad psychological tensions intermittently resulting in the breakdown of discipline. Despite desperate and marginally successful attempts at holding back the enemy, he continued, superior Entente artillery and the mass deployment of tanks broke the resolve of the German army. For these reasons, Cron concluded that the German military would not have survived a prolonged continuation of hostilities beyond 11 November 1918. "Heroic self-destruction", in his opinion, was the best that the German military could have offered.[35] Cron's paper therefore foreshadowed the materialist orientation of later historians.

The historiography therefore suggests three dominant interpretative strains in answering why war ended in November 1918. The first and most straightforward points out the undeniable statistical reality that the Entente marshalled superior manpower reserves and economic resources to that of Germany. The defeat of Russia gave Ludendorff only a small window of opportunity in order to concentrate military forces in France prior to an inevitable flood of fresh American troops. Failure to achieve a decisive result in the early months of 1918 foreshadowed mounting difficulties based on increasing numerical disparity. Second, it is often argued that the Entente, more so than the Central Powers, benefitted from a so-called "learning curve" whereby Britain, France and less so the United States learned how to deploy their superior resources in a manner sufficient to deliver a series of disastrous blows to the German military. This argument therefore pits German changes such as the development of infiltration tactics based on combined arms against Entente coalition warfare and on new technologies such as tanks. The third dominant argument combines material advantages, technological improvements and the failure of Ludendorff's offensives to explain the sudden erosion of German morale by mid-summer. This progressive deterioration, it is argued, continued throughout the final "Hundred Days" until Ludendorff and

---

35 Hermann Cron, Konnte das deutsche Heer im November 1918 weiterkämpfen? Untersuchung auf Grund der Kriegsakten der Kommandobehörden?, n. d., Freiburg, RH-61/2247.

the German army fell completely apart.[36] Each of these explanations lay blame directly or indirectly on poor German decision-making.

These arguments, while compelling and necessary components of the enlarged narrative, do not answer why German morale seemed to collapse so suddenly in mid-1918. These explanations instead rest on axiomatic assumptions that "something" had changed in 1918. That "something" appears as a curious statistical shift in overall available German manpower at the front. Whereas the Entente outnumbered the Germans for most of the war, the brief period of German numerical superiority at the outset of 1918 ended with a steadily shrinking manpower pool that did not reflect battlefield losses. Cron's report, steeped in the prewar language of spiritual decay, hinted that something insidious had sapped German strength during 1918. Instead of pointing to political contamination or other psychological explanations, he proposed that something outside of the military "environment" had rapidly undermined the will of certain soldiers to fight on. Cron could not put his finger directly on what it was. He restricted himself to listing general symptoms such as poor discipline. The military historian further pointed to disappointment, helplessness, weakness and most of all depression. Cron's emphasis of depression stood out as a radically different approach at a moment when blame and vitriol inhibited more balanced investigation into why Germany had actually lost the war in 1918. The tendency to reductively frame the outcome of combat as dependent on numerical superiority, technological factors, or military resources indirectly minimizes discussion concerning war-weariness and particularly what is now termed clinical depression.[37] It is the contention of this chapter that historians underestimate the impact of the influenza epidemic on the outcome of the war and on the postwar German revolution.

3. LUDENDORFF'S OPTIONS IN 1918

The morale of the German people sank lower and lower as the war entered the final year. The hardships brought by the British blockade and the strains of armaments production persuaded workers to take to the streets and protest in fantastic numbers. The Spartacists in particular also understood that the defeat of

---

36 James Edmonds, Military Operations in France and Belgium, 1918, London 1939, 215-216.
37 H. Stursberg, Bemerkungen über funktionell-nervöse Störungen im Kriege; and "Bemerkungen über funktionellnervöse Störungen im Kriege", 1917-1918 Freiburg, PH - 7/6.

Russia and the conclusion of a separate peace promised an intensification of the war in France and Belgium. "Any kind of separate peace", they argued in a pamphlet that openly called for revolution, "will only lead to the prolongation and intensification of collective murder". The pamphlet demanded that that the workers seize power in Germany and "transform the separate peace into a general peace".[38] Hundreds of thousands of German workers went on strike in a short-lived expression of dissent that spread from Berlin across all of Germany.

The Spartacist pamphlet correctly predicted the outcome of a debate among German political and military elites concerning the best course of action for 1918. Russian defeat did offer a theoretical chance for a diplomatic end to the conflict. Moderates believed that the transfer of German forces from the eastern theatre might grant a degree of leverage in negotiations leading to a compromise peace. But this diplomatic solution rested on principles that were no longer valid. German leverage disappeared with the failure of the U-boat campaign in 1917. The hawks at OHL therefore more accurately understood the harsh realities of the American entry into the conflict. The presence of millions of "Doughboys" in Europe threatened more than just a serious erosion of morale at home and at the front. American involvement invalidated the need for serious diplomatic negotiation on the part of British or French policymakers. The delusion shared by some moderates that President Woodrow Wilson could somehow mitigate the worst of British or French war aims could not obscure the cold hard truth that time worked against even the most restrained German peace proposals. Ludendorff therefore correctly understood that a successful and devastating offensive push represented the surest method of securing a real seat at any future negotiating table.[39]

Hindenburg advised the Kaiser in January 1918 that the German military had to "defeat the Western Powers in order to secure the political and economic position in the world that we need".[40] The wooden titan's comment masked Ludendorff's real strategic objective in terms more apt to excite Wilhelm than explain the intricate notion of bringing the enemy to battle in a "Vernichtungsschlacht" or "battle of annihilation". Robert Foley quite expertly points out that the historiography, in particular the works of Martin Kitchen and David Zabecki, generally distorts German strategic and operational planning through the prism of Entente military conceptions. Germany's enemies viewed battle as a "step-by-step process" whereby the seizure of critical objectives such as railway nodes act

---

38 Aufruf zum Massenstreik, in: Wolfdieter Bihl (ed.), Deutsche Quellen zur Geschichte des Ersten Weltkrieges, Darmstadt 1991, 367-68.
39 Die Vorbereitung der deutschen Westoffensive 1917/18, 1943, Freiburg, RH-61/2001.
40 Martin Kitchen, The German Offensives of 1918, Stroud 2001, 16.

at punches to throw the enemy off balance for the knockout blow. Instead, Ludendorff and OHL planners aimed exclusively for a return to a war of movement in order to "break the enemy's will to continue the fight". The quartermaster general did not therefore seek total victory over the enemy and certainly not an outcome on the battlefield resulting in "the destruction of his existence".[41] Ludendorff instead sought a repetition of the battles in Russia that forced a political decision in Germany's favour. Historical debates concerning the objections of Crown Prince Rupprecht, namely that the offensives "did not lead in any favourable operational direction", discount the overall limited strategic goal sought by Ludendorff.[42]

Ludendorff and OHL had sufficient grounds for attempting an offensive of this nature. For the first time since 1916, OHL could marshal enough manpower and resources to consider a major offensive against the British and French. The number of men facing the Entente in France and Belgium prior to the Russian collapse rose to over 5 million men in the field and two million in the rear line of communications preceding the start of the Battle of Passchendaele in July 1917. After sustaining heavy losses as a result of Field Marshal Douglas Haig's devastating operations around Ypres, the Germans were still able to replenish the front for 1918. Critically, the flow of replacements and military hardware from Germany retained numerical superiority throughout the first half of the year and only fell drastically in July 1918 after Operation Friedensturm.[43] Zabecki furthermore argues that the "Germans managed to muster the will and the resources to launch four more major offensives, and they were planning and actively preparing yet another one when the Allies finally counterattacked on 18 July".[44] The older notion that the length of the war itself seriously sapped German strength in relation to the Entente rings hollow.

Three German armies were involved in Operation Michael, the first of a series of offensives, from 21 March to 4 April. Ludendorff massed 74 divisions and over 10,000 artillery pieces and mortars for the initial onslaught against two British armies along a 70 km front between Arras, St Quentin and La Fère. The

---

41 Robert T. Foley, Breaking Through. The German Concept of Battle in 1918, https://www.academia.edu/4955175/_Breaking_Through_The_German_Concept_of_Batte_in_1918 and David Stevenson, Cataclysm: The First World War as Political Tragedy, New York 2005, 328.
42 Hew Strachan, The First World War, Toronto 2006, 286.
43 Reichswehrministerium, Sanitätsbericht über das deutsche Heer (Deutsches Feld- und Besatzungsheer) im Weltkriege, 1914-1918, III, Berlin, 1934, 8; Michael Geyer, Deutsche Rüstungspolitik 1860-1980, Frankfurt 1984, 83-96; and Bessel, 5.
44 Zabecki, 160.

opening barrage of the campaign, the most intense of WWI, foreshadowed the later American doctrine of "shock and awe". The five-hour concentration of firepower on selected enemy positions stunned the German enemy. Groups of specially selected and trained "Stoβtruppen" from the 54 "Angriffsdivisionen" leaned into the accompanying rolling barrage and infiltrated line after line of the enemy's defenses. These attack divisions, like the Panzer divisions of the next world war, were composed of young men who had been withdrawn from the frontlines for rest, refitting and retraining. That these young men received higher food rations, the best equipment, and a higher number of horses than other divisions would prove extremely costly later in the summer.[45] Within a few days of the initial March offensive, however, the powerful attack divisions penetrated 60 km of Entente territory and punched a significant gap between the British and French forces by pushing particularly hard on General Hubert Gough's depleted 5th Army.

Historians often note that the German achievement, while spectacular, did not rout the British military. According to Zabecki, the lack of clear operational goals, such as the neutralization of the English marshalling yards at Amiens, meant that Ludendorff failed to exploit a major English logistical weakness. The quartermaster permitted the enemy to recover instead of forcing a major retreat to the safety of the Channel ports. Ludendorff, he explains, needlessly wasted frontline strength by switching the main axis of attack in search of irrelevant tactical successes. Michael reached culmination by 30 March and was called off by OHL a few days later. Inflicting a total of 254,739 causalities on their enemies, the advancing Germans captured 90,000 prisoners of war. The Germans suffered 239,800 casualties. Zabecki oddly disregards the matter of losses for British or French fighting proficiency and argues that these "were [German] losses that could not be replaced for the rest of the war".[46] Zabecki does not explain that the British prisoners of war were marched off to internment camps whereas a large number of German light casualties or lightly ill – including a growing number of influenza cases – returned to the front after doctors quickly tended to their medical issues.[47]

From this misinterpretation of Ludendorff's strategic intentions, based almost exclusively on the projection of the Entente way of war onto German "Kriegführung", it is possible to derive a number of important observations. The

---

45 Der Weltkrieg 1914 bis 1918, XIV, Berlin 1944, 41.
46 Zabecki, 160.
47 See the "Zehntägige Truppen Krankenrapporte" for the Bavarian Army at the archives in Munich; and C. B. Davies (ed.), Military Operations France and Belgium, 1918. The German March Offensive and its Preliminaries, London 1935, 51-56.

quartermaster first of all intended Operation Michael to initiate a series of continuous short and violent frontal assaults by numerically superior forces. The officers all along the military chain of command would assign centres of gravity or "Schwerpunkte" in relation to the continuously changing fortunes of war.[48] Referring to a derisive comment made by Foch and found in the work of Hans Delbruck, Walter Goerlitz termed this policy of short penetrations a "buffalo strategy".[49] This strategy ironically also mirrored the successive hammer blows delivered to the German army during the final months of the war. "Here was a concept of operations", Hew Strachan argues, "which harnessed the Entente's superior resources to the constraints of total war".[50] But what were the ultimate differences between Ludendorff's strategic thinking and that of Haig or Foch? Since the German military inflicted disproportionate losses on their British and French adversaries prior to July 1918, and Germany's enemies suffered from their own difficulties in replenishing their combat formations, only the poorly trained soldiers of the United States could alter combatant ratios after July 1918. It is for this reason that historians continually return to the issue of numbers.

Ludendorff and OHL clearly understood that Germany faced significant future manpower difficulties. Projections of American troops arriving in France fuelled this line of thought. Modern assessments of combatant strength in July 1918, which incidentally rely on French intelligence estimates and clash with the official German military histories, indicate that 3,156,000 German soldiers faced 2,972,000 Entente troops.[51] Two of the major reasons for the Entente inability to attain "overwhelming preponderance" in France and Belgium related to the exhaustion of Britain and France themselves and the extremely high loss rates experienced by the American forces.[52] OHL planners even considered the possibility of failure and fresh plans called for increasing frontline strength for another last-ditch offensive in 1919. While historians sometimes assume that "Germany would be out of reserves by summer",[53] documents from the Bundesarchiv in Freiburg demonstrate that the planners set to work in September and October and prepared for the mobilization of a further 600,000 men as a one-time boost

---

48 Ia/II Nr. 6578, 1918, Freiburg, RH-1986; and Foley, Breaking Through.
49 Walter Görlitz, History of the German General Staff 1657-1945, New York 1953, 193.
50 Strachan, 310.
51 Neiburg, The Second Battle of the Marne, 34.
52 Meleah Ward, The Cost of Inexperience. Americans on the Western Front, 1918, in: Ashley Ekins (ed.), 1918 Year of Victory. The End of the Great War and the Shaping of History, Canberra 2010, 111-130.
53 Noble, 713.

for a final desperate gamble in 1919.[54] These documents reflect the desperate straits of the German military since the transfer depended on denuding industry of critical workers and what remained of the armed forces in Russia. But the documents also indicated a potential for numerical growth unavailable to Britain or France and only marginally offset by waves of Americans whipped forward in suicidal rifle and bayonet charges by the American General John J. Pershing.

In addition to questioning the materialist perspective on the basis of the statistics, it must be pointed out that far too much of the historiography treats the German military in isolation at this critical juncture. The assertion that the German army had been "burned out" by 1918 and that it could not support offensive operations for any protracted period rests on a host of wildly self-serving sources. The assumption of overall Entente material preponderance, even where none existed such as between March-July 1918, leads to a curious dismissal of British and French realities and instead turns to the myopic assessments of certain German officers from the postwar period. The arguments of these men, propelled by Hans Delbruck, typically placed virtually exclusive blame on Ludendorff after 1918. "The Army that stood ready to attack in March of 1918", General Hermann von Kuhl argued after the war, "was no longer the body of troops of 1914". Kuhl goes on to support the counterfactual alternative that Ludendorff should have sought a diplomatic solution or have opted for a defensive posture on the part of the "Westheer" in favour of offensive operations in Italy or elsewhere.[55] Delbruck developed this point of view in his 1922 book entitled "Ludendorffs Selbstporträt". The military historian and long term critic of the OHL therefore incorrectly argued that Ludendorff first of all sought total military victory in 1918. From this assumption, he in turn went to great pains to demonstrate how the resources and capabilities of the German military were insufficient for that end. These postwar assessments, such as those of Cron, clearly demonstrated a strange admixture of incidental observations such as supposed widespread alcohol consumption with an erosion of morale caused by insufficient resources for offensive military operations. "The collapse was not a result of revolution", Delbruck therefore easily concluded, "but rather the revolution was a result of the collapse".[56]

---

54 Kriegsjahr 1918. Korrespondenz, 1921, Freiburg, RH-61/1977.
55 Hermann von Kuhl/ Hans Delbrück, Ursachen des Zusammenbruchs. Entstehung, Durchführung und Zusammenbruch der Offensive von 1918, Berlin 1923.
56 Hans Delbrück, Ludendorffs Selbstporträt, Berlin 1922, 57 and 61.

4. THE INFLUENZA VIRUS

Influenza and illnesses of various kinds have always influenced the outcome of wars in varying degrees.[57] Advances in medicine prior to 1914, however, determined that combat casualties during WWI outnumbered those related to most diseases such as typhus for the first time in history. Influenza, however, represented a departure from this trend for a variety of reasons. Historically, the virus often accompanied armies on the march and was transmitted by domesticated animals such as chickens, pigs and especially the horses on which the soldiers relied.[58] No treatments or vaccines existed for this highly contagious virus that struck humans and animals alike. Utterly dependent on horse drawn transport, the German army required horses for the fluid offensive operations envisioned for early 1918. The disproportionate loss rates of German horses that year, an issue not yet adequately examined by historians, cannot be granted adequate treatment in this chapter.[59] Second, influenza outbreaks in the years leading up to WWI, one such epidemic originating in Russia in 1889, increased in severity owing to higher European population density and the diffusion of the virus along the recently constructed railway lines.[60] The medical services of the combatants could not effectively alter these epidemiological patterns that in fact grew more precarious in 1918.

Much of the literature concerning the outbreak of influenza in 1918 points to the southwestern United States as the point of initial outbreak. Beginning in the early months of 1918, the virus spread from soldiers training at Ft. Funston, Kansas who travelled along the railway routes to the Atlantic seaboard and from these debarkation points onto the troop carriers that crossed the Atlantic to the European theatre. This initial wave was considered "mild" in nature and did not arouse the suspicions of either the medical community or the military authorities. Drowned out in the press coverage devoted to the war itself, this wave of infections only resulted in a handful of deaths from pneumonia. A far larger number suffered from mild cold symptoms and recovered after a short period of convalescence. James E. Hollenbeck points out that the initial outbreak "was not even

---

57 Frank Aker and James C. Cecil, The Influence of Disease upon European History, in: Military Medicine 148 (1983), 441-446.

58 James E. Hollenbeck, The 1918-1919 Influenza Pandemic. A Pale Horse Rides Home from War, in: BIOS 73:1 (2002), 19-26.

59 John Singleton, Britain's Military Use of Horses, 1914-1918, in: Past and Present 139 (1993), 178-203.

60 Hollenbeck, 20.

mentioned in the index in the 1918 volumes of the Journals of the American medical association" owing to its harmless nature.[61]

Ludendorff, as senior proponent and architect of the offensive German strategy of 1918, could not have anticipated the dangers that a virus presented to an army of millions on the move. Medical researchers first isolated viruses during the 1930s and vaccines against influenza emerged a decade later. The wartime German medical services, while trumpeting significant advancements in hygiene and inoculations against bacterial infections such as typhus, were not equipped to deal with a viral enemy.[62] This same state of affairs prevailed throughout the western world. A report prepared by the British Ministry of Health after the war stated that "the epidemiological features of the pandemic are even more complex and puzzling than the clinical characteristics and the present report does little more than present a large body of data which await interpretation".[63] Even the use of the label "Spanish" reinforces this uncertainty. Consistent with the common practice of blaming the origins of illness on others, the name stuck owing to the wartime suppression of newspaper reports among the belligerents.[64] Ludendorff and the German medical services mirrored the same limitations which therefore inhibit analysis of the pandemic owing to wartime realities. Worse still, the tendency in 1918 of classifying influenza as a bacillus led to misdiagnosis and general confusion.

Even though researchers today generally assume that the epidemic originated in the United States in the form of a mild fever that then radiated outwards along the paths travelled by the American "Doughboys",[65] voices of disagreement point to other areas of the globe or more importantly to the genetic evidence that suggests significant mutation on the frontlines in France or the attachment of a bacterial pneumonia strain originating in eastern Europe.[66] The course of the influenza virus, according to the German official medical history or "Sanitätsbe-

---

61 Ibid.
62 Derek S. Linton, War Dysentery and the Limitations of German Military Hygiene during World War I, in: Bulletin of the History of Medicine 84:4 (2010), 607-639.
63 E.W. Kopf, Report on the Pandemic of Influenza, 1918-1919 by Ministry of Health of Great Britain, in: Quarterly Publications of the American Statistical Association, 17:136 (1921), 1038-1040.
64 Beatriz Echeverri, Spanish influenza Seen from Spain, in: Howard Phillips/David Killingray (eds.), The Spanish Influenza Pandemic of 1918-19. New Perspectives, New York 2003, 173.
65 Hollenbeck, 21.
66 Patick Zylberman, A Holocaust in a Holocaust. The Great War and the 1918 Spanish Influenza Epidemic in France, in: Philips/Killingray, 192; and Hollenbeck, 22.

richt", conflicts in one important way with the west-east movement depicted in the orthodox model. In early May, German doctors witnessed a stark increase in influenza cases in all divisions and ancillary formations of 6th Army positioned in the centre of the frontlines in France.[67] For the medical services, this outbreak differed only slightly from the typical patterns seen throughout the war. As in the United States, no alarm bells sounded. Influenza had been a normal irritant for most of the conflict. During all of the previous winters, the onset of cold weather brought with it varying degrees of symptoms that doctors recorded as the common cold or "Grippe". This cyclical spike took place in December and January and impacted roughly 4% of those serving in the army.[68] However, the phenomenon witnessed in May by 6th Army appeared similar to something recorded earlier in the war on the eastern front.

Owing to the more severe cold and damp conditions of Eastern Europe, soldiers stationed in Russia had typically witnessed higher rates of the common cold than those manning the frontlines in warmer regions. In January 1918, as preparations for the transfer of troops to France for the coming offensives were underway, cases of a peculiar "flu-like" illness witnessed earlier in the war rose steadily. In 1916, an unpredictable form of influenza was reported by Prof. Dr. Penzold, the Advisory Internal Medicine Physician, who described an infectious illness that he held for a type of "Grippe" or influenza. This illness started with shivering, leg pains, a low fever and a sudden feeling of general illness that then required 8 to 10 days for recovery. Other than an increase in the severity of pneumonia, the low mortality of the illness led to its characterization as "benign". Sick soldiers returned to the front after a short period of convalescence. In early 1918, the reemergence of this "benign" contagion amidst the preparations for the coming offensives did not initially worry medical officials.[69] This evidence does, however, conflict with orthodox accounts.

Due to the later severity of influenza during the summer months, the "Sanitätsbericht" speculated that the movement of troops to the west offered the "flu-like" illness ideal conditions. "The fourth year of the war", the report argued, "gave the flu contagion a larger concentration of hosts than among the more dispersed troops residing in the east".[70] By March 1918, a first dramatic increase in infection rates, far above the standard 4% figure, warned of things to come. A large segment of the medical staff transferred from the east to support Operation Michael fell ill with influenza and a significant enough number succumbed to

---

67 Reichswehrministerium, II, 782.
68 Reichswehrministerium, III, 121-123.
69 Ibid.
70 Ibid.

the virus during the first week of the offensive. According to the medical records, influenza and pneumonia claimed one-half of all the doctors who died (43 of 86) in 18th, 2nd and 17th Armies during the first week of fighting. At the start of the offensive on 21 March, 1,403 doctors served with the attacking armies. A week later, war-related casualties and illnesses had reduced this number by 260 or nearly 20%.[71] As discussed later, even the loss of medical staff for an 8 to 10 day convalescence period proved an equally serious "friction" for offensive operations.

The hypothesis that one strain of influenza or pneumonia followed the German soldiers from east to west and combined with another brought over by the Americans helps explain a series of important conundrums in the historiography. First of all, the principle problems concerning the movement of German troops from Russia have been attributed to insubordination. Richard Bessel points out that in one particular case 5,000 soldiers refused to board trains to the west and that "bloody confrontations" took place between officers and enlisted men.[72] Part of the reason for rampant insubordination related to the naïve belief that the defeat of Russia meant the war was over.

Another more hard-hitting explanation related to the prevalence of various "fevers" afflicting the soldiers in Russia. The medical history recorded both a serious typhoid outbreak and higher than usual rates of influenza at the end of 1917 and throughout 1918. In order to protect German soldiers and the indigenous population, huge delousing facilities were created though which millions of soldiers and civilians were passed. As a medical transport commissar recorded, the need to transfer men to the delousing stations placed severe strains on the communications network. In some cases, the men who arrived at the newly constructed camps were so covered with lice and other pests, that they were essentially forbidden transport through Germany and housed at makeshift quarters for the rest of the war.[73] Considering the extreme historical fear of typhus, every soldier who appeared feverish was treated as a potential candidate.[74] At one facility near Warsaw, over 700,000 Germans and Poles were forced to submit to a procedure that was both dehumanizing and frightening. The trains pulled up to the facilities, the soldiers and civilians were ordered to strip off their clothing and put all of their belongings into containers for decontamination. After

---

71 Reichswehrministerium, I, 34-35 and II, 758.
72 Bessel, 24.
73 Sanitätstransportkommissare, 25 March 1919, Munich, XI Mob 30/13 838.
74 Oberstabsarzt d. Res. Prof. Dr. Fuelleborn, Über Entlausung und Fleckfieber-Vorbeugung, 1935, Freiburg, RHD-43/1.

being shaven they were then marched straight to the disinfection rooms.[75] Under these conditions, and considering the numbers involved, it is worthwhile asking whether morale suffered because of socialist contamination or the fearful prospects of disease and the associated medical precautions. In any case, substantial rioting erupted in the early months of 1918.

German officers consistently interpreted this dissatisfaction as evidence of an even more perplexing problem. A supposed "lack of morale fibre" was attributed to both psychological and socialist contamination.[76] During the war, physiological explanations for illnesses in the German army were slowly displaced by psychological alternatives that focused on addressing the human will. OHL generally supported methods that promised to return soldiers to the battlefield as quickly as possible. Electrotherapy, for example, aimed at convincing the "shell-shocked" to return to the dangers of the front by making the cure next to unbearable and thereby restoring the will to fight.[77] Even the treatment of the bodily injured followed suit. The Psychiatrist Wilhelm Julius Ruttmann wrote in 1917 that "The helplessness of the victim caused by injuries had to be exploited early in the field hospitals [...][but] they were not to be excessively spoiled or pampered in order to avoid increasing their sense of helplessness [...] in order to waken their iron will".[78] In this environment, medical doctors ultimately transformed illnesses such as influenza into a form of mental infirmity. The morale of the soldiers would further deteriorate as the influenza pandemic raged beyond the control of the medical authorities.

Prior to a more detailed examination of the impact of influenza on the fighting capabilities of the German army in France and Belgium, it must be emphasized that historians typically confront the higher German infection rates with an answer derived from illusory correlation.[79] The implicit assumption that

---

75 Veröffentlichungen auf dem Gebiet des Heeres-Sanitätswesens; and Die Krankentransportanstalten in Metz und Warschau, Freiburg, RHD-43/1.
76 Krankheiten aller Art, Seuche im Kriege 1914/1918, 1 January 1919, Munich, XI Mob 16/13 795 .
77 Ruth Kloocke, Psychological Injury in the Two World Wars. Changing Concepts and Terms in German Psychiatry, in: History of Psychiatry 16:1 (2005), 43-60.
78 Wilhelm Julius Ruttmann, Erblichkeitslehre und Pädagogik. Ausschnitte aus der experimentellen und angewandten Erblichkeitslehre und Individualforschung, Leipzig 1917.
79 The argument that food shortages led inexorably to higher German rates of infection appears as a universal constant in the literature. Three recent examples include Robert T. Foley, From Victory to Defeat. The German Army in 1918, in: Ekins, 69-88; Nick Lloyd, Hundred Days. The Campaign That Ended World War I, New York 2013 and Zabecki, 237.

a reduced diet helps precipitate certain diseases such as typhus lies at the heart of the observation that influenza impacted the Germans "much harder" than the soldiers of the Entente. The British naval blockade certainly subjected their enemy to profound privation at home and an "inferior diet" at the front. But the inferior German diet and the strained medical system, both byproducts of Entente military policy, do not explain increased susceptibility. Instead of striking the weaker members of society, such as the very young and old, the influenza pandemic of 1918 wreaked havoc among the strongest cohorts.[80] The lungs of young adults aged 20-40 filled with fluids more dangerously than those of the virus' usual victims.[81] Virile immune systems reacted more dangerously and eventually led to the suffocation by drowning later witnessed around the globe. In other words, the German concentration of fit young males into the more lavishly supplied "Angriffsdivisionen" ultimately backfired.

The distribution of influenza cases among the various German divisional types explains a curious statistical anomaly concerning prevailing opinion. If an "inferior diet" had increased German susceptibility to the influenza virus, the rates of infection among the combatants would have differed accordingly. When these rates are superficially examined, however, no immediate differences become apparent. Both the German and American medical histories record for example that roughly 1 in 5 soldiers contracted influenza during the final year of the war.[82] These numbers reflect an even distribution across the entirety of both military organizations from the start of the German offensives to the armistice. These data also highlight the incidence of mortality and in particular focus on the final influenza wave of the war that killed a significant number of American soldiers. That number was nearly as large as that of combat deaths or 46,992 to 50,385.[83] Eckard Michels therefore concludes that the impact of influenza on Germany has been exaggerated.[84] The modern medical understanding of this extraordinarily contagious virus, seen in this way, actually suggests that German food shortages and blockade-induced malnutrition should have shielded German

---

80 James E. Hollenbeck, 20.
81 Emily Breidbart, The Forgotten Influenza of 1918. When a Strong Immune System Becomes a Weakness, 23 September 2009, www.clinicalcorrelations.org/?p=1862.
82 Reichswehrministerium, III, 12 and 31 and Milton W. Hall, Inflammatory Diseases of the Respiratory Tract (Bronchitis; Influenza; Bronchopneumonia; Lobar Pneumonia), The Medical Department of the United States Army in the World War, IX, Washington 1923, 67.
83 Hall, 68.
84 Michels, 1-33.

military operations from the worst effects of the virus. Certain data even appear to prove this point.

The following section explores the validity of this supposition in greater detail. A few summary remarks should be kept in mind, however. The singular focus on overall infection rates or the number of fatalities distorts the impact of influenza on Ludendorff's offensives, the subsequent military collapse and how these events were remembered after 1918. The rough statistics do not recognize that the individual influenza waves struck the combatants at different moments in 1918. Nor do the neat tables listed in the medical histories distinguish between formations such as the "Angriffsdivisionen". One of the major dilemmas, from the German perspective, was simply that cases of influenza increased steadily through March, April and May before an exponential rise during June and July. The "Sanitätsbericht" does not cover the period after Operation Friedensturm owing to postwar difficulties in collecting reports from the various branches of the medical services. Historians therefore depend on the surviving "Zehntägige Truppen Krankenrapporte" or 10-day illness reports in order to fill in the holes. These reports indicate that even the staggering numbers listed in the German medical history require revision. In July 1918, for example, the "Sanitätsbericht" recorded that the German field army and lines of communication suffered 165,000 battlefield casualties of all types and an additional 538,052 cases of influenza. The latter number represented roughly 15 to 20% of German forces in France and Belgium. Only 14.9% of these men were treated at military hospitals and roughly 500 men died. A month previously the number of sick was 186,073. The British medical services recorded approximately 50,000 influenza cases over the same two month period and noted that the worst was over by the start of July. The French army followed a similar pattern. The ratio of German to Entente influenza cases was therefore roughly 7:1 and most acute among the German forces participating in Operation Friedensturm.[85] The summer ordeal did have one silver lining. Virologists today postulate that infection with milder forms of influenza such as that witnessed in mid-1918 wave resulted in a high degree of immunity against later lethal mutations of the virus. This observation would explain the subsequent lower German mortality rates indicated by Michels.[86]

---

85 Reichswehrministerium, III, 121-123, William Grant Macpherson, History of the Great War Based on Official Documents. Medical Services. Diseases of the War, I, London 1923, 174; and Lloyd, 36.

86 Yuang Feng, Seasonal H1N1 Influenza Virus Infection Induces Cross-Protective Pandemic H1N1 Virus Immunity through a CD8-Independent, B Cell-Dependent Mechanism, in: Journal of Virology 86:5 (2012), 2229–2238.

5. Influenza and the German Collapse

Operation Friedensturm, the final large German offensive of the war, began on 15 July 1918 and ended two days later with a meticulously planned French counterattack. Foch's divisions had developed deep defensive lines that dissipated the concentrated power of the opening artillery barrage and quickly halted the infiltration of secondary objectives by the German assault troops. Foch's masterstroke lay in the assembly of a large reserve that included 350 Renault FT tanks. Stalled by the French defensive dispositions and the assistance of British and American forces, Foch struck at the German flanks and took his enemy completely by surprise. Although the fighting that followed did not witness the spectacular successes attained by Ludendorff's earlier offensives, Foch's forces ground down what remained of German offensive strength and the battle marked the start of the great retreats that ultimately led to the armistice in November 1918. "In the end", Neiburg concludes, "attrition played an enormous role in deciding Allied victory".[87] This conclusion and the implications of German defeat such as the unleashing of revolutionary forces rest on a confluence of material factors that included German battlefield losses and the increasing numbers of American soldiers on the frontlines. In 1922, the historian Ralph Haswell Lutz, along with Hans Delbruck and others, initiated a long tradition of blaming Ludendorff and OHL planners for a series of critical errors that ultimately destabilized the German state and ushered in the German Revolution.[88]

The force ratios of the belligerents did change dramatically after 15 July 1918. It is the contention of this chapter, however, that the impact of influenza acted as a sort of "deus ex machine" that played a dominant role in final Entente victory. The virus, as pointed out, spread among German soldiers at a disproportionate rate during the summer of 1918. The German 6th Army mentioned previously reported 10,000 new cases per day during the first half of July. It still recorded 1,000-2,000 new cases per day well into August.[89] These kinds of infection rates were witnessed all across the western front. An approximate number of over one million German soldiers fell ill during the period leading up to Friedensturm and the French counteroffensive after 18 July. Army Group Crown Prince was hit particularly hard prior to offensive operations.[90] The virus did not distinguish between frontline soldiers and those responsible for logistics or the

---

87 Neiburg, Marne, 36
88 Ralph Haswell Lutz, The German Revolution 1918-1919, Stanford 1922, 9.
89 Krankheiten (inkl. Grippe) 1914-1918, 1918, Munich, AOK 6/247 Bund 247.
90 Erich von Ludendorff, Meine Kriegserinnerungen, Berlin 1919, 514.

medical services.[91] Influenza slowed preparations for Friedensturm which in turn increased the likelihood of Entente discovery. Things degenerated to such a degree that the head of the German medical services, Otto von Schjerning, tried to calm down his panicking subordinates. He reassured them that the pandemic was "harmless" and would pass in due course. Instead of returning the sick to Germany, as was customary, Schjerning ordered influenza patients to be quarantined near the front. He hoped that special infirmaries would speed their return to the frontlines.[92]

With doctors themselves falling ill, the growing pressures on the medical services led to inevitable shortcuts. Some doctors, later described as incompetent, simply packed the sick onto trains heading for Germany.[93] Other soldiers could not even locate medical staff. The required certificates were forged by their comrades and the sick were sent home. Confusion resulted. A report by the medical transport commissioner in Trier concluded that the hospital trains arriving in Germany were filled with soldiers who apparently "had nothing wrong with them". Instead of understanding that the men had simply recovered from the worst effects of influenza while on route to Germany, the offenders were berated as shirkers and returned to their formations at the front.[94] The number of riots and desertions increased. The example of the 1st Bavarian Infantry Division, which participated in "Friedensturm" as an attack division, demonstrated this complexity in mid-Summer 1918.[95] Between mid-May and the end of July, 2,603 cases of influenza, 407 cases of pneumonia and 968 cases of gastro-intestinal diseases were reported.[96] After the war it was determined that many soldiers afflicted by pneumonia or gastro-intestinal troubles were misdiagnosed and in fact suffered from influenza.[97] This specially selected formation of younger men suffered far more grievously than the older soldiers of the garrison or ersatz divisions.[98]

---

91 Der Juli-Angriff 1918 beiderseits von Reims, n.d. Freiburg, RH-61/2154.
92 v. Schjerning, Chef des Feldsanitätswesens an alle Herren Armee- und Etappenärzte des Westens einschl. Brüssel, 24 July 1918, Munich, AOK 19/25.
93 Verwendung von Sanitätsoffizieren und Ärzten im Kriege 1914/1918, June 1918, Munich, Bund XXXII, M Kr. 13708: XI MOB 1.
94 Reichswehrministerium, II, 757-758.
95 Zehntägige Truppenkrankenrapporte 1918, June-July 1918, Munich, 1.b.I.D./96.
96 Grippe usw., June-July 1918, Munich 1.b.I.D./95
97 Sanitätsberichte im Kriege 1914/18 (Rapporte), 1917-1921, Munich, XI Mob 15/13 790.
98 Ibid.

Owing to the efforts of Schjerning, the official medical history reported that "The state of health was good until the emergence of flu-like illnesses. Other infectious diseases remained localized".[99] Despite that ominous observation, there was initially no reason for Ludendorff to suspect that the "flu" might seriously hamper future operations. In the month leading up to the Second Battle of the Marne, he was generally optimistic and even declared that the Entente could not counterattack in any meaningful sense.[100] Ludendorff informed a group of Austrian officers visiting the Rheims front at the end of June that only one more offensive was necessary prior to Operation Hagen and the ultimate blow against the Entente.[101] The Austrians offered a different perspective. Their German allies noted serious deficiencies in frontline strength and wondered why the gaps had not yet been filled prior to an offensive only weeks away.[102] British intelligence supported these observations and concluded that "the German army was in its poorest condition of the war".[103]

The medical service's optimism that influenza cases would return after a brief period of convalescence clouded Ludendorff's judgment. The German 1st, 3rd, 7th and 9th Armies that participated in "Friedensturm" suffered immensely as a result. The first serious reports of influenza that grabbed the attention of OHL were discussed on 22 June 1918. On 6 July, reports lamented that the majority of the divisions of 3rd Army were now infected. The officers in particular worried that infected soldiers required a convalescence period that threatened to delay the offensive even further.[104] The other armies recorded between 6 and 13 July 1918 that "the number of sick due to influenza is very high in almost all the divisions" and that "their fighting strength has been temporarily reduced". The shortfall represented thousands of soldiers per division. The numbers ranged between 25 and 50%. OHL disregarded the bad news and clung to the hope that the men would recover quickly, but still recognized that the time required for convalescence meant "an acute weakness in view of the already low frontline

---

99 Reichswehrministerium, II, 787.
100 Heeresbefehle an der Westfront, May-July 1918, Freiburg, PH 5-II/640.
101 30.5.1918, Auszüge aus den Berichten des K.u.K. Bevollmächtigten Generals bei der deutschen Obersten Heeresleitung Feldmarschalleutnants Frhr. v. Klepsch-Kloth, April – October 1918, Freiburg, RH-61/1989.
102 23.6.18, ibid.
103 Edmonds, 215-216.
104 Reims-Angriff. Auszug aus dem Kriegstagebuch der 3. Armee, June-July 1918, Freiburg, RH-61/2151.

strength of several divisions".[105] A request for four divisions by 9th Army on 11 July, reinforcements required to alleviate shortages created by the epidemic, were denied by OHL. Even though officers pointed to the very serious levels of exhaustion that accompanied influenza, influenza struck the entire breadth of the field army and lines of communication and tied the hands of OHL. The 9th and 7th Armies therefore represented tantalizing targets for Foch's offensive.[106] It mattered little that the armies issued reports to Ludendorff that the enemy in the area of offensive operations appeared to be mimicking German defensive strategies, establishing a considerable reserve and that tanks were being assembled for a counterthrust.[107] Influenza inhibited the creation of adequate defensive positions by 9th Army and Ludendorff ultimately decided to throw the dice and hope for a miracle.

It is worthwhile to consider the plight of the thousands of Germans bedridden with fever or languishing in open fields that served as rudimentary casualty clearing stations. Those men who only recently regained the ability to stand upright, normally after three to five days, were herded together and driven by their officers towards the frontlines. Those who found their way back to Germany were ordered back without the anticipated furlough. The confusion prior to the attack on Rheims seriously complicated the normal collection of casualty reports and the system largely broke down after mid-July. Schnerning ordered the doctors of the medical services to treat influenza cases with an iron hand and forgo recording them at all.[108]

The final German offensive, launched on 15 July 1918, was an unmitigated disaster for the German military. Influenza had inhibited the movement of men and material owing to the pandemic's spread along the entire breadth and depth of the frontlines and rear lines of communication. These delays completely sacrificed the element of surprise. The routine collection of intelligence through prisoners of war and aerial reconnaissance warned Foch of the impending offensive and he was able to mass a considerable reserve and prepare a pre-emptive artillery bombardment. The Germans who advanced against the Entente defensive positions, particularly the critical "Stoßtruppen", had only recently recovered from influenza or still felt the months-long exhaustion that accompanies it.

---

105 Auszug aus den Aktenstück der OHL. Beurteilung der Lage. Wochenmeldungen der Armeen vom 1.7. bis zum 15.8.1918, June-August 1918, Freiburg, RH-61/1992.

106 Feststellung der OHL über die bis Anfang September 1918 entstandene "ungünstige Lage". Die Ansicht von Hindenburg über die Ursachen (Besprechung am 6.9.1918), 6 October 1918, Freiburg, RH-61/1000.

107 Ibid.

108 Reichswehrministerium, II, 783.

The army weekly reports attempted to dismiss these problems by downplaying the longer term complications of influenza and chose to classify the "Angriffsdivisionen" as "combat effective" even though the 10-day casualty listed up to half of entire divisions as recovering from influenza.[109] Considering these difficulties, it was hardly surprising that the final German offensive operation only lasted three days. When the French and Americans counterattacked on 18 July, they took the Germans completely by surprise despite a high degree of foreknowledge. Considering the preliminary difficulties caused by influenza, and the "iron will" that it took to ignore the implications, Ludendorff and OHL had lost all sense of reality and they paid the price. Pushed onto the defensive, racked by influenza, the German military never recovered.

It was only now that German soldiers began to surrender in large numbers. Niall Ferguson points out that 340,000 Germans surrendered between 18 July and the armistice. That figure dwarfed battlefield losses. In the last three months of fighting 4,225 British officers were killed and 59,311 men, compared with equivalent figures for Germans in the British sector of 1,540 officers and 26,688 men. As Ferguson correctly points out, "it is not enough simply to say that the Germans were 'war-weary', 'demoralized' or, for that matter, cold and hungry".[110] He argues in that the ability to surrender in large numbers (and not be killed) induced the Germans to do so. It is argued here that overall weakness of German soldiers, a weakness based on illness, led them down this path.

Even though Ludendorff and others saw influenza as a serious enough problem, the fact that it did not kill large numbers in mid-summer 1918 led them to underestimate its impact. Soldiers who were bedridden for 4 or 5 days, and who then required another 10 just to walk, lost the will to fight. It is no wonder that morale plummeted during this period. It is also no wonder that defensive lines were not dug. It is also no wonder that the Germans sometimes appeared to simply be waiting to surrender. 1.5 million men contracted influenza in the days prior to Friedensturm and during the Entente counteroffensive. No amount of "willpower" was sufficient to rescue the German army after it had been knocked off balance. After July, when the Entente strongly tested German willpower in a series of short swift blows, the war changed in a dramatic fashion. Ludendorff

---

109 Die Entwicklung der Gesamtlage vom 3.5. - Anfang Aug. 1918, 1943, Freiburg, RH-61/2012; Der Juli-Angriff 1918 beiderseits von Reims, n,d., Freiburg, RH-61/2154; Auszüge aus den Aktenstück der OHL. Beurteilung der Lage. Wochenmeldungen der Armeen vom 1.7. bis zum 15.8.1918, RH-61/1992; and Zehntägige Truppen Krankenrapporte 1918, July 1918, Munich, various.
110 Niall Ferguson, The Pity Of War. Explaining World War I, New York 1998, 368.

famously called 8 August 1918 the "black day of the German Army".[111] English forces broke through German lines using tanks and captured approximately 50,000 soldiers. Although the frontlines were stabilized, a series of small offensives whittled away at what was left of German resolve until collapse appeared imminent in September 1918. Ludendorff had to consider either immediate armistice negotiations or face the near-impossible prospects of some kind of national uprising and a fight to the end.

6. Conclusion

The fatigue and depression brought by influenza added to the miseries suffered by German soldiers following the failure of Friedensturm. Morale steadily declined after July, a moment when the effects of the virus disproportionally hit the "Westheer" by a factor of 7:1. The determined resilience of a few was bested by a profound sense of disillusionment on the part of a majority of officers and soldiers. The decisive turning point therefore came with the failure of Ludendorff's 1918 offensives and the Central Powers collapsed in short order. Even prior to the armistice, German formations melted away and the soldiers marched home. And still, yet another wave of influenza returned to afflict the German people and added to the deprivation brought by a British naval blockade that lasted well into 1919. The German Revolution that erupted as a consequence of defeat and misery was hobbled by the simple reality that the reasons for defeat were so unclear. The politicians and generals of the Entente powers could loudly proclaim victory based on a deterministically-driven appreciation of statistics that translated into a strange sense of murky military superiority. The Germans of all political hues knew and more importantly felt differently. Conservatives, socialists and communist revolutionaries all sought the allegiance of the soldiers and blamed the decisions made by a few men such as Ludendorff whose world had fallen apart.

While German officers understood that the military had been defeated in the field, the perplexing question remained why the military organization broke apart so suddenly in 1918.[112] It is the contention here that the standard causal chain relating to Entente strategy and tactics suffers from serious deficiencies. The crushing effect of the influenza virus on German morale underscores a human component that is obscured by mechanistic explanations. The debate con-

---

111 Ludendorff, 547.
112 Michael Geyer, Insurrectionary Warfare. The German Debate about a Levee en Masse in October 1918, in: Journal of Modern History 73:3 (2001), 459-527.

cerning November 1918, and especially the matter of the stab in the back legend, influenced the 20th Century to such an astounding degree that the current paucity of explanations concerning the war's outcome might in and of itself require serious reflection. It is too easy and convenient to view the legend as a creation of the military in order to blame others for defeat. It is even easier to denigrate memory as myth. As Modris Ecksteins asserted in his examination of "All Quiet on the Western Front", the war itself was submerged in imagination and memory as a way of coping with the more pressing concerns of postwar survival and the myth was not meant as an accurate depiction of reality.[113] The truth is that myth, memory and history all intersected. In 1918, German officers continually refused and indeed could not acknowledge the debilitating effects of the influenza virus. The flu was simply the flu. Instead of explaining defeat in medical terms, officers and even doctors clung to older prejudicial classifications of the rebellious shirker. In an important sense, this view approximated the impact of influenza more closely than the mechanistic explanations that dominate the historiography.

---

113 Modris Ecksteins, Rites of Spring. The Great War and the Birth of the Modern Age, Boston 1989, 297.

Activist Subjectivities and the Charisma of World Revolution
Soviet Communists Encounter Revolutionary Germany, 1918/19

GLEB J. ALBERT

1. INTRODUCTION*

In his recent analysis of the German Revolution of 1918/19, Michael Geyer speaks of its „blocked transnationality" in a twofold sense – firstly that the event itself was fragmented and cut off from international events, and secondly that its historiography has in the past too quickly debunked its transnationality.[1] However, in its international emanation, the revolutionary events in Germany – from the November Revolution to the January Uprising, the murder of Karl Liebknecht and Rosa Luxemburg, and finally, the short-lived Munich council republic – were anything other than blocked. The events in Germany were part of the post-war social upheaval that pulled Europe into a stream of revolutionary and counterrevolutionary violence between 1917 and 1923.[2] In other countries, "rev-

---

* I thank the volume editors and Brendan McGeever for their useful comments, suggestions, and critique.
1 Michael Geyer, Zwischen Krieg und Nachkrieg. Die deutsche Revolution 1918/19 im Zeichen blockierter Transnationalität, in: Alexander Gallus (ed.), Die vergessene Revolution von 1918/19, Göttingen 2010, 187-222.
2 On the period of upheaval in Europe: Chris Wrigley (ed.), Challenges of Labour. Central and Western Europe, 1917-1920, London 1993. On violence: Robert Gerwarth/John Horne (eds.), War in Peace. Paramilitary Violence in Europe after the Great War, Oxford 2012.

olutionaries" and "reactionaries" watched the German revolution with hope and awe.[3] This was particularly true for Soviet Russia – a state that had a revolutionary government already for over a year when the German revolution set in.

When it comes to the historiography of early Soviet society, we are confronted with two paradoxes. Firstly, on the one hand we know what an immense role the ideas of world revolution and revolutionary internationalism played for the early Soviet leadership.[4] The perception of the German revolution from 1918 to 1923 by the Bolshevik leaders has been particularly well explored in this literature.[5] On the other hand, though, we know only very little about how foreign revolutionary events were portrayed and perceived in early Soviet society apart from the Bolshevik elites.[6] The second paradox concerns revolutionary agency in the early Soviet state. We know that committed Bolshevik cadres below the level of national leadership played a central role in establishing Bolshevik rule on a regional and local level. As Robert McKean pointed out, it was the local "revolu-

---

3 On the mutual perceptions of the council republics in Munich and Budapest as well as of both by conservative contemporaries, see: Martin Schulze Wessel, Avantgarde der Weltrevolution. Die Räterepubliken in München und Budapest, in: Alois Schmid/ Katharina Weigand (eds.), Bayern mitten in Europa. Vom Frühmittelalter bis ins 20. Jahrhundert, Munich 2005, 372-384.

4 See e.g. Stanley W. Page, Lenin and World Revolution, New York 1959; Neil Harding, Lenin's Political Thought. Theory and Practice in the Democratic and Socialist Revolutions, Vol. 2, London 1983.

5 In general: Dietrich Geyer, Sowjetrussland und die deutsche Arbeiterbewegung 1918-1932, in: Vierteljahrshefte für Zeitgeschichte 24:1 (1976), 2-37. For 1918: Abraham Ascher, Russian Marxism and the German Revolution, 1917-1920, in: Archiv für Sozialgeschichte 6/7 (1967), 391-439; Alexander Vatlin, Deutschland im weltpolitischen Kalkül der Bolschewiki 1918, in: Wladislaw Hedeler/Klaus Kinner (eds.), "Die Wache ist müde." Neue Sichten auf die russische Revolution 1917 und ihre Wirkungen, Berlin 2008, 102-12. For 1923: Bernhard H. Bayerlein, The Abortive 'German October' 1923. New Light on the Revolutionary Plans of the Russian Communist Party, the Comintern and the German Communist Party, in: Kevin McDermott/John Morison (eds.), Politics and Society Under the Bolsheviks. Selected Papers From the Fifth World Congress for Central and East European Studies Warsaw 1995, Basingstoke 1999, 251-62; Leonid G. Babichenko, Politbiuro TsK RKP(b), Komintern i sobytiia v Germanii v 1923 g. Novye arkhivnye materialy, in: Novaia i noveishaia istoriia (1994), no. 2, 125-57.

6 For 1923, see recently: Gleb J. Albert, 'German October is Approaching'. Internationalism, Activists, and the Soviet State in 1923, in: Revolutionary Russia 24:2 (2011), 111-42.

tionary sub-élite", not the exiled intellectuals, who kept Bolshevik organisations going in Russia during World War I.[7] It was these activists, often young, skilled and literate workers, who "served as the conduit through which ideas of class and socialism passed to the wider workforce,"[8] and who played a crucial role in the establishment of the Bolshevik regime as well as in its defence during the Civil War.[9] However, we know very little about the daily lives and motivations of these Bolshevik protagonists, dubbed by Boris Kolonitskii as "functionary enthusiasts" – individuals "formally linked with the regime and [who] felt a personal tie with it".[10]

This chapter attempts to address both lacunae in the historiography. It will examine the impact that the revolutionary events of 1918-1919 in Germany had on Bolshevik activists at the regional and local level. By resorting to their diaries as well as internal correspondence and the provincial party press, it shall be argued that these events were crucial for their authors' subjectivisation as Bolshevik activists. Subjectivisation is understood as a process in which an individual assumes a particular social identity that is intelligible as such for him- or herself as well as for others.[11] Subjectivisation is, as sociologist Thomas Alkemeyer stresses, a process that is active as well as it is perpetual: Individuals pursue subjectivisation through participation in social practices, and they have to pursue it again and again.[12] As I will show, activists pursued their subjectivisation as "true" Bolsheviks by assuming a stance of active solidarity towards revolutionary movements abroad, performed in manifold ways.

---

7   Robert B. McKean, St Petersburg Between the Revolutions. Workers and Revolutionaries, June 1907 – February 1917, New Haven 1990, XIV.
8   S. A. Smith, The Russian Revolution. A Very Short Introduction, Oxford/New York 2002, 31. See also: Robert Service, The Bolshevik Party in Revolution. A Study in Organisational Change 1917-1923, London 1979, 46-47.
9   Eduard M. Dune, Notes of a Red Guard, ed. by Diane P. Koenker and S. A. Smith, Urbana etc. 1993.
10 Boris I. Kolonitskii, 'Revolutionary Names'. Russian Personal Names and Political Consciousness in the 1920s and 1930s, in: Revolutionary Russia 6:2 (1993), 210-228, here 219.
11 Gesa Lindemann, Subjektivierung in Relationen. Ein Versuch über die relationistische Explikation von Sinn, in: Thomas Alkemeyer/Gunilla Budde/Dagmar Freist (eds.), Selbst-Bildungen. Soziale und kulturelle Praktiken der Subjektivierung, Bielefeld 2013, 101-124, here 101.
12 Thomas Alkemeyer, Subjektivierung in sozialen Praktiken. Umrisse einer praxeologischen Analytik, in: Alkemeyer/Budde/ Freist, 33–68, here 61.

The belief in an imminent world revolution, for which the events in Germany were seen as a starting point, was so strong that one can speak of world revolution as a charismatic idea that had power over Bolshevik activists. Charisma in a Weberian sense is understood as a force that is ascribed to persons, objects and ideas.[13] What counts is not an objective validation of charismatic qualities as such, but rather, whether those subject to charismatic authority, the "followers" or "disciples", recognise these qualities.[14] As a social relation, charismatic authority is described by Max Weber as a "matter of complete personal devotion [...], arising out of enthusiasm, or of despair and hope."[15] Although in studies of revolutionary movements charisma has usually been analysed as something embodied by individuals,[16] ideas can also have charismatic qualities. Weber (as well as more recent sociologists) pointed out that with the growing rationalisation and differentiation of society, ideas can appear as a charismatic force independently of their bearers. Even though a movement based on charisma of ideas is often spearheaded by individuals, a dedication to an idea is still a dedication not so much to a leader as such, but to a "common cause".[17]

The fact that internationalism constitutes a super-rational, faith-like element of the socialist movement has already been noted by Werner Sombart. Internationalism, he remarks, "does not appeal to the intellect alone, it also appeals to the heart. Socialists become enthusiastic about it because it stands for a noble idea, for the idea of the Brotherhood of Mankind."[18] Modern studies of the la-

---

13 Winfried Gebhardt, Charisma und Ordnung. Formen des institutionalisierten Charisma. Überlegungen im Anschluß an Max Weber, in: Winfried Gebhardt/ Arnold Zingerle/ Michael N. Ebertz (eds.), Charisma. Theorie – Religion – Politik, Berlin etc. 1993, 47-68, here 50.

14 Max Weber, Economy and Society. An Outline of Interpretative Sociology, New York 1968, 241-242.

15 Ibid., 242.

16 Jan Willem Stutje (ed.), Charismatic Leadership and Social Movements. The Revolutionary Power of Ordinary Men and Women, New York 2012; Thomas Welskopp, Amerikas große Ernüchterung. Eine Kulturgeschichte der Prohibition, Paderborn 2010, 399-426; Id., Das Banner der Brüderlichkeit. Die deutsche Sozialdemokratie vom Vormärz bis zum Sozialistengesetz, Bonn 2000, 384-418.

17 Gebhardt, Charisma und Ordnung, 57; Id., Charisma als Lebensform. Zur Soziologie des alternativen Lebens, Berlin 1994, 36-37; Weber, 1209.

18 Werner Sombart, Socialism and the Social Movement, London 1909, 194. For internationalism in the labour movement, see e.g.: Frits van Holthoon/Marcel van der Linden (eds.), Internationalism in the Labour Movement, 1830-1940, 2 Vols., Leiden etc. 1988.

bour movement have focused their attention on internationalism as the "international faith" of socialism.[19] The faith of Bolshevik activists in world revolution was, however, not purely irrational. World-revolutionary charisma was anything but a mysterious force or a craze that took hold of provincial revolutionaries. On the contrary, as it is to be shown here, the activists' subjection to world-revolutionary charisma had firm roots within their everyday life and social position.

2. THE GERMAN REVOLUTION AND BOLSHEVIK RUSSIA

The revolutionary events in Germany that unfolded in November 1918 were of utmost importance for the victorious revolutionaries in Soviet Russia. The Bolsheviks took power in 1917 under the premise that their revolution will not remain isolated.[20] As Marxists, the Bolshevik leaders were convinced that proletarian revolutions were to happen first and foremost in developed, industrialised countries; the fact that a revolution took place in "backward" Russia was for them an anomaly in historical development that was to be straightened out by forthcoming revolutions in the industrialised West.[21] The revolution that broke out in Germany with its traditionally strong labour movement and its high grade of industrialisation seemed to fulfil their expectations.[22] The Bolshevik leadership's enthusiasm made itself noticeable in their internal communication: When Lenin wrote to his closes associates, Lev Trotsky and Iakov Sverdlov, on 1 October 1918 upon hearing the news of the first signs of revolutionary turmoil in Germany, he made clear that "[w]e may all die in order to help the German workers to push forward the revolution begun in Germany."[23] However, the

---

19 Christine Collette, The International Faith. Labour's Attitudes to European Socialism 1918-39, Aldershot 1998.
20 Rex A. Wade, The Russian Revolution, 1917, Cambridge 2000, 221-227.
21 Gleb J. Albert, From 'World Soviet' to 'Fatherland of All Proletarians.' Anticipated World Society and Global Thinking in Early Soviet Russia, in: InterDisciplines. Journal of History and Sociology 3:1 (2012), 85–119. For the theoretical discussions on this question within Bolshevism, see most recently: Neil Davidson, How Revolutionary Were the Bourgeois Revolutions? Chicago 2012, chapter 12.
22 Ascher; Geyer; Vatlin.
23 Vladimir I. Lenin, Polnoe sobranie sochinenii, Vol. 50, Moscow 1965, 185-186. For more documents on the Soviet and Comintern leaders' passion for the German revolution, see most recently: Hermann Weber/Jakov Drabkin/Bernhard H. Bayerlein (eds.), Deutschland, Russland, Komintern. Dokumente 1918-1943, Berlin 2014, 50-91.

Bolshevik leadership had overly optimistic expectations about the prospect of a victorious revolution in Germany, in part due to their faulty and unstable communication channels with the West.[24]

It was, however, not only the fact that it seemingly confirmed the leadership's Marxist convictions that made the German revolution so crucial for the Bolsheviks. It was also a powerful propaganda tool in addressing the party rank and file and the general population. From their ascension to power in 1917, the Bolsheviks never ceased to proclaim that all hardship and violence was just temporary until the revolution in the West had succeeded and would free Soviet Russia from its misery. Naturally, such arguments proved less and less convincing the longer the revolution in the West remained absent. Already in March 1918, Lenin warned his party comrades against putting too much hopes on the imminence of a revolution in Germany:

"[I]f you tell the people that civil war will break out in Germany and also guarantee that instead of a clash with imperialism we shall have a field revolution on a world-wide scale, the people will say you are deceiving them. [...] If the revolution breaks out, everything is saved. Of course! But if it does not turn out as we desire, [...] the masses will say to you, you acted like gamblers – you staked everything on a fortunate turn of events that did not take place [...]."[25]

When, half a year later, the German revolution finally did set in, it meant for the Bolsheviks that they could conduct their world-revolutionary propaganda far more convincingly. For party members, it meant the overturning of the shameful peace treaty of Brest-Litovsk that had caused major dissent within the Bolshevik ranks.[26] And for sceptics outside the party, the events in Germany could pursue them to revise their anti-Bolshevik position, as can be seen in the diary of the

---

24 For Bolshevik expectations not corresponding to German revolutionary reality, see their teleprinter conversation with the new German government: Richard K. Debo, The 14 November 1918 Teleprinter Conversation of Hugo Haase with Georgii Chicherin and Karl Radek. Document and Commentary, in: Canadian-American Slavic Studies 14:4 (1980), 513-534.

25 Vladimir I. Lenin, Collected Works, Vol. 27, Moscow 1965, 102.

26 Yoshiro Ikeda, The Reintegration of the Russian Empire and the Bolshevik Views of 'Russia'. The Case of the Moscow Party Organization, in: Acta Slavica Iaponica 22 (2005), 124–125. For party rank and file expectations about the German revolution as an antidote against the Brest-Litovsk treaty, see: Dune, 122. For the opposition against Brest-Litovsk within the party, see: Ronald I. Kowalski, The Bolshevik Party in Conflict. The Left Communist Opposition of 1918, Houndmills 1991.

Petrograd historian Georgii Kniazev, who on 11 November 1918 reflected on the malicious joy with which people like himself had rebutted the Bolshevik hopes for world revolution. Now, however, "[t]he events have turned out not like we 'clever ones' have expected them, but how they were anticipated by the 'crazy ones'."[27]

Given the belief of the Bolsheviks in the necessity of a German revolution as well as its potential for propaganda within the country, the party leadership launched a large-scale campaign of solidarity with revolutionary Germany. The aforementioned letter by Lenin demanded not only preparing grain shipments to Germany, but also public assemblies and demonstrations all over the country to enlighten the population on the revolutionary events.[28] These plans did not just remain on paper: Grain was (presumably forcefully) collected by the party authorities to be sent by train to Berlin,[29] and German revolution-themed rallies were held even in the most remote provincial towns.[30]

Very soon, however, it became clear that the German revolution was nothing like the Bolshevik leaders had expected it to be: Not only did the Germans not proclaim a Soviet republic, but the revolutionary government declined to accept Soviet grain shipments,[31] and, most importantly, Karl Liebknecht and Rosa Luxemburg, the German revolutionary leaders in which the Bolsheviks had put their highest hopes, were murdered in January 1919 by counter-revolutionary troops with the consent of the new government. Both events caused indignation in the Bolshevik media, and the murder of the German left leaders, which the

---

27 G. A. Kniazev, Iz zapisnoi knizhki russkogo intelligenta za vremia voiny i revoliutsii 1914-1922 gg. 1918 g., in: Russkoe proshloe 4 (1993), 35-149, here 127.
28 Lenin, Polnoe sobranie, 185-186.
29 The Soviet government ordered the provinces to collect grain on 12 November: Il'ia I. Mints, Sovetskaia Rossiia i Noiabr'skaia revoliutsiia v Germanii, in: Voprosy istorii (1974), no. 11, 3-22, here 20. See Gosudarstvennyi arkhiv Rossiiskoi Federatsii [State Archive of the Russian Federation, in the following: GARF], 1235/93/555, for the correspondence between the government and the state organs in Tula province, which have put together a train named after Karl Liebknecht and sent it to Moscow.
30 For the solidarity campaign, see the document compilation: V. A. Kondrat'ev, Otkliki na noiabr'skuiu revoliutsiiu v Sovetskoi Rossii, in: V. D. Kul'bakin (ed.), Noiabr'skaia revoliutsiia v Germanii. Sbornik statei i materialov, Moscow 1960, 439-454. For the penetration of the countryside by rallies on the German revolution, see the diary of a provincial peasant: V. V. Morozov/N. I. Reshetnikov (eds.), Dnevnik totemskogo krest'ianina A.A.Zamaraeva. 1906-1922 gody, Moskva 1995, 201.
31 I. N. Zemskov etc. (eds.), Dokumenty vneshnei politiki SSSR, Vol. 1, Moscow, 1959, 571.

Bolsheviks were quick to accuse the SPD of, was the subject of a large-scale protest campaign.[32] The unfolding of the German events, especially the murder of Liebknecht and Luxemburg, contributed to the consolidation of Bolshevik hatred towards Western social democracy in general and the SPD in particular.[33] However, on 7 April 1919, when a council republic was proclaimed in Munich, Bolshevik hopes of revolution in Germany were again raised. The Communist regime lasted only a few weeks before being bloodily suppressed by government troops.[34] In the short time span of its existence, the Bolshevik leadership failed, despite several attempts by Lenin himself, to make proper contact with the Munich revolutionaries.[35] However, together with the slightly longer-lived council republic in Hungary, the events in Munich received much attention in Soviet Russia – not only in the state media, but from Bolshevik activists in the provinces.[36]

3. ACTIVISTS AND THE CHARISMA OF WORLD REVOLUTION

The group within the party that shall be referred to as "activists" here is hard to grasp with "hard" social criteria. What defines and unites them is rather their self-perception as dedicated revolutionaries. Ol'ga Morozova in her prosopographical work on Soviet Civil War veterans defines such Bolshevik activists as "half-intelligentsia" *(polu-intelligentsiia)*. These were former skilled factory workers and craftsmen, peasant sons who had risen on the social ladder, former

---

32 Ascher, 407-408. For the protest campaign: "Vsem komitetam, organizatsiiam Rossiiskoi Kommunisticheskoi Partii i vsem sovdepam", Pravda, 18.1.1919.

33 Ascher, 439.

34 For an overview, see Schulze Wessel; Martin H. Geyer, Munich in Turmoil. Social Protest and the Revolutionary Movement 1918-19, in: Wrigley, 51-71. Most illuminating on terms of the relationship between the Munich council republic and Soviet Russia: Helmut Neubauer, München und Moskau 1918/1919. Zur Geschichte der Rätebewegung in Bayern, Munich 1958.

35 Neubauer, 54-88.

36 See the short-hand reports of regional Bolshevik speeches: Shorthand report of the 14th Moscow *guberniia* party conference, 12.4.1919, Rossiiskii gosudarstvennyi arkhiv sotsial'no-politicheskoi istorii [Russian State Archive of Social and Political History, in the following: RGASPI], 17/6/151, 10; Resolution of a citizens' rally in the Spassko-Maretskii *raion* (Arkhangel'sk *guberniia*), 21.4.1919, RGASPI, 17/6/1, 149-150.

clerks or grammar school teachers. While they did not yet completely escape their milieus of origin, in their habitus these members of the revolutionary movement attempted to adopt the lifestyle of the higher classes not only in attire and manner of speech, but also in their striving to educate themselves, in the regular reading of newspapers and the habit of self-reflection by producing autobiographical texts.[37] Such self-manifestation in writing, mostly through diaries, could be "part of a distinctive lifestyle" for such social climbers.[38] For activists, writing a diary could be a practice of subjectivisation. Unlike other, well-researched Bolshevik rank and file diarists from the 1930s, they were not merely inscribing themselves into an established "Soviet self",[39] but were reassuring themselves as revolutionary subjects – the definition of which was much more in flux in these transitional years between the 1917 revolutions and early Stalinism.

The social position of such Bolshevik activists in the first years after the revolution was defined by a threefold isolation. First of all, it was a geographical one. The communication networks during revolution and civil war were faulty and unstable. In remote areas, party members were at times completely cut off from the Central Committee in Moscow. Even as relatively near to the capital as in the Volgograd province, local party activists complained that newspapers and letters from Moscow took a month to reach them.[40] In other, more remote regions it was even worse.

Secondly, they had to face social isolation. Party members outside bigger towns were completely lost within the non-party population. In December 1917 the Bolsheviks had only 4122 members working in the countryside among a rural population of some 100 million, and the ratio became only slightly better during the Civil War.[41] Also, many of these rural party members were not even peasants themselves, and thus had a hard time building relationships with those

---

37 Ol'ga N. Morozova, Dva akta dramy. Boevoe proshloe i poslevoennaia povsednevnost' veteranov Grazhdanskoi voiny, Rostov-on-Don 2010, 293ff.

38 Cf. Julia Herzberg, Autobiographik als historische Quelle in 'Ost' und 'West', in: Julia Herzberg/Christoph Schmidt (eds.), Vom Wir zum Ich. Individuum und Autobiographik im Zarenreich, Cologne 2007, 15-62, here 61.

39 Cf. Jochen Hellbeck, Revolution on my Mind. Writing a Diary under Stalin, Cambridge MA 2006.

40 Letter of the party committee of Mikhailovka (Tsaritsyn guberniia) to the Central Committee (CC) of the RCP(b), 25.3.1919, RGASPI, 17/65/81, 89. Quoted from: V. V. Anikeev (ed.), Perepiska Sekretariata TsK RKP(b) s mestnymi partiinymi organizatsiiami, Vol. 6, Moscow 1971, 424-425.

41 Samuel Farber, Before Stalinism. The Rise and Fall of Soviet Democracy, Cambridge 1990, 50–51.

who actually stood behind the plough.[42] Even the Bolshevik elite had to recognise as early as 1919 that the majority of the peasantry had a hostile attitude to their programme and saw the party as a despotic elite.[43] Among the workers, the Bolsheviks' self-proclaimed major social force of support, the situation was not much different. Since party cells on the shop floor increasingly took over administrative tasks, workers came to perceive Bolsheviks in the factories not as a force that stood in for their interests, but rather one that stood on the same side as the "bosses" and "exploiters".[44] What is more, just as in the countryside, the party was not particularly well-represented at the shop floor: Even in 1922, only 1,5 % of the industrial workforce claimed party membership, and about one third of all factories and plants did not even have party cells.[45]

Finally, the third type of isolation revolutionary activists had to face was the one within the party itself. The Bolshevik party underwent major transformations in the wake of the October revolution. While the party had about 23,600 members in early 1917 when it was still illegal, it grew substantially under the conditions of a pluralistic political landscape: the disintegration of the political system under Kerensky and the party's consequent stand against the ongoing war provided it with a mass followership. By the October revolution, it came to consist of 100,000 to 400,000 members.[46] Now that the Bolsheviks claimed sole power in the new Soviet state, they needed cadres in abundance to fill positions of power throughout the huge country. Despite the rise in membership in the previ-

---

42 Helmut Altrichter, Die Bauern von Tver. Vom Leben auf dem russischen Dorfe zwischen Revolution und Kollektivierung, Munich 1984, 146-147.

43 Smith, 91.

44 Richard Sakwa, Soviet Communists in Power. A Study of Moscow During the Civil War, 1918-21, Basingstoke 1988, 129; Sergei V. Iarov, Gorozhanin kak politik. Revoliutsiia, voennyi kommunizm i NEP glazami petrogradtsev, Saint Peterburg 1999, 49–53; V. S. Tiazhel'nikova, Leninskii prizyv 1924-1925 gg. Novye liudi, novye modeli politicheskogo povedeniia, in: Sotsial'naia istoriia 8 (2008), 113–136, here 120; Aleksandr V. Gogolevskii, Revoliutsiia i psikhologiia. Politicheskie nastroeniia rabochikh Petrograda v usloviiakh bol'shevistskoi monopolii na vlast' 1918-1920, Saint Peterburg 2005.

45 Hans-Henning Schröder, Arbeiterschaft, Wirtschaftsführung und Parteibürokratie während der Neuen Ökonomischen Politik. Eine Sozialgeschichte der bolschewistischen Partei 1920-1928, Wiesbaden 1982, 265.

46 T. H. Rigby, Communist Party Membership in the U.S.S.R., 1917-1967, Princeton NJ 1968, 59-61. For the party's rise in popularity in Moscow between February and October, see Diane Koenker, Moscow Workers and the 1917 Revolution, Princeton NJ 1981, 187-227.

ous months, the party still lacked enough cadres for this task, which led it to loosen its membership criteria.[47] As a result, the party grew twofold within the first few year of Soviet power.[48] The prospect of being a member of the party in power was highly attractive, and many of those who joined after the October revolution did so no doubt out of careerist aspirations. The party experienced an influx of individuals who had no previous relation whatsoever to the revolutionary movement. Party membership came to be the main mechanism of upward social mobility in early Soviet society.[49] Already by 1922, the percentage of members who joined before 1917, when the party was still an underground revolutionary organisation, amounted to a mere 2,7%, while still 9,1% of the membership had joined the party in the revolutionary year of 1917. For the majority of the post-revolutionary cadres, party activism was "merely a role to play to gain promotion [and] a necessary initiation rite to be dispensed with once one made it to the top."[50]

The influx of careerists into the party led to internal conflicts at rank and file level already in the first years after the revolution.[51] The provincial party journalist Aleksandr Voronskii reflected upon the problem in an editorial article written for a regional Bolshevik newspaper in late 1918:

"Together with the broad masses of workers and peasants, some individuals managed to squeeze themselves into the party, for whom world revolution is not any more interesting

---

47 Schröder, 57ff.
48 Rigby, 69; Jonathan R. Adelman, The Development of the Soviet Party Apparat in the Civil War. Center, Localities, and Nationality Areas, in: Russian History 9:1 (1982), 86-110.
49 Sergej A. Golovin, Chlenstvo v RKP(b)-VKP(b) kak osnovnoi put' povysheniia sotsial'nogo statusa. 1920-1930-e gg., in: Otechestvennaia istoriia (2008), no. 3, 33-44; Igor' V. Narskii, Zhizn' v katastrofe. Budni naseleniia Urala v 1917-1922 gg., Moscow 2001, 452-467; Schröder, 235ff; Vladimir N. Brovkin, Russia after Lenin. Politics, Culture and Society, 1921-1929, London 1998, 37-44.
50 Brovkin, 42.
51 Carmen Scheide, Kinder, Küche, Kommunismus. Das Wechselverhältnis zwischen sowjetischem Frauenalltag und Frauenpolitik von 1921 bis 1930 am Beispiel Moskauer Arbeiterinnen, Zürich 2002, 311; Donald J. Raleigh, Experiencing Russia's Civil War. Politics, Society, and Revolutionary Culture in Saratov, 1917-1922, Princeton NJ 2002, 132-133.

than yesteryear's snow. [...] They hate the real communists and at best take them for fools who don't know how to make use of their position."[52]

As a true Bolshevik, Voronskii remained faithful to the dominant Bolshevik narratives of class, otherwise he would have realised that it was particularly the "workers and peasants" for whom party membership was the main mechanism of upward social mobility.[53] What is more striking, however, is the role that "world revolution" plays in his diatribe. A keen interest in revolutionary events abroad is perceived here as a key feature of "real" communists that distinguished them from the careerists within the party. And the particular time of the article's publication – 30 November 1918, when the German revolution was in full swing – only strengthens this point.

In the texts produced by Bolshevik activists below the level of national leadership, world revolution indeed presents itself as anything but "yesteryear's snow ". The dedication to revolutionary events abroad manifests itself in numerous pleas by provincial activists directed to the party leadership in Moscow, such as this letter written in mid-1918 by a Siberian Bolshevik:

"We wait for news from the West. It cannot be that our [...] comrades leave their younger brothers, the Russian proletariat, to fight alone against the international bourgeoisie. No! I believe so strongly that the comrades from the West will soon come to our aid, I am already counting the hours."[54]

Of course, such a letter, directed at the party leadership, can serve to display mastery in "speaking Bolshevik" just as much as attesting to individual enthusiasm.[55] When, however, another provincial Bolshevik speaks in his diary entry, written at about the same time, of world revolution as a "marvellous thing" *(pre-*

---

52 A. Voronskii, "To, chego ne dolzhno byt'", in: Rabochii krai, 30.11.1918. Quoted from: Aleksandr K. Voronskii, Sbornik statei, opublikovannykh v gazete "Rabochii krai" 1918-1920 gg., Moscow 2010, 125–126.
53 Golovin, 40; Brovkin, 41.
54 Letter from the Omsk RCP(b) committee to the CC of the RCP(b), [after 1.5.1918], RGASPI, 17/4/23, 81. Quoted from: V. V. Anikeev (ed.), Perepiska Sekretariata TsK RSDRP(b)-RKP(b) s mestnymi partiinymi organizatsiiami, Vol. 3, Moscow 1967, 213-214.
55 On the concept of "speaking Bolshevik" see Stephen Kotkin, Magnetic Mountain. Stalinism as a Civilisation, Berkeley CA 1995.

lestnaia veshch),[56] he does not have to prove anything to anyone but himself. Instead, he is reassuring himself of his revolutionary subjectivity a core part of which consists of the firm belief in world revolution.

An identification with revolutionary events abroad could help activists to cope with their threefold isolation. By internalising the concept of world revolution, they could be sure that their political struggle in the provinces was interconnected with what they perceived to be similar struggles worldwide. As Mikhail Voronkov, a young Bolshevik revolutionary and party functionary in the provincial town of Riazan', put it in a public speech in July 1919:

"[E]ven the most insignificant tailor, who sits in a sleepy village near Riazan' and sews a shirt for our Red Army soldiers, supports by this the struggle against global imperialism, and at the same time the smallest upheaval of workers in the mountains of far-away Scotland has a great influence for the stability of our position."[57]

Whether Voronkov had any particular class struggles in the Scottish Highlands in mind, is unlikely.[58] The main point is that Scotland comes to symbolise a location on the world's periphery, just like the "sleepy village" in Soviet Russia – both peripheries are rhetorically united by their struggle for world revolution, and by this they gain importance contrary to their peripheral status.

Also, activists could attenuate their isolation from the populace by putting their hopes on revolution abroad. The notion of world revolution overcoming the problems of domestic society is a predominant topos in activists' letters and autobiographical documents. As Eduard Dune, a Latvian worker and Bolshevik militant in 1917, noted in his memoirs:

---

56 I. V. Bukina/L. A. Kyz'iurov/N. G. Lisevič (eds.), 'V avguste nemnogo sochuvstvoval ia Kornilovu i ego zheleznoi distsipline, teper' ia – bol'shevik'. Iz dnevnika pervogo predsedatelia Soveta krest'ianskikh deputatov s. Mokhcha Pechorskogo uezda N.I. Zykova. 1918 g., in: Otechestvennye arkhivy (2007), no. 6, 91–117, here 104 (diary entry from 20.2.1918).

57 Michail Voronkov, speech "On the interior situation of the Soviet Republic" at the 5th Soviet Congress of the Riazan' *guberniia*, 1.7.1919. Published in: Mikhail I. Voronkov, Intelligent i epokha. Dnevniki, vospominaniia, stat'i. 1911-1941 gg., ed. by A. O. Nikitin, Riazan' 2013, 590–593, here 590.

58 The reference to Scotland might stem from the immense popularity that the Scottish socialist leader John Maclean enjoyed in early Soviet Russia: Ian D. Thatcher, John Maclean. Soviet Versions, in: History 77 (1992), 421–429.

"We saw the October revolution as a first stage, a first attempt, and of course mistakes were inevitable. The 'world revolution' would teach us how to govern a country and how to organize the economy so that it would satisfy the millions for whose sake revolutions were made. And the more difficulty we encountered on our path, the more hope we placed in the 'world' proletariat."[59]

Obviously, the "lessons" offered by "world revolution" were also expected to fix the relationship between Bolsheviks and the populace – an expectation that activists were able to directly connect to their everyday lives. Voronkov complained in an early 1919 diary entry about countless petitioners from the population straining his nerves, and in the next sentence expressed hope for deliverance from outside: "Only if the workers' revolution in Germany and France would set in faster! How painful it is to wait!"[60]

Even more telling in this regard is the diary fragment of Nikolai Zykov, first chairman of the village Soviet of Mokhcha (north-western Russia). The son of a peasant, he took part in the revolution of 1905 and was banished by the authorities to this remote area. In early 1918 he teamed up with soldiers returning from the front and proclaimed Soviet power in the village. Thus he nominally became the highest representative of state power in the locality, but local peasant society viewed him as a disturber of peace and traditional life, and thus confronted him with ongoing hostility and numerous assassination attempts. These circumstances make Zykovs diary extraordinary gloomy, full of complaints about peasant ignorance, the remoteness of the village and unrealistic party politics. The only "positive" diary entries refer not to local or domestic politics, but to the inherent worldwide transformations. In February 1918, he noted: "I've received a few newspapers. Got to know that the revolution is stabilising, and that revolutions in other countries are ripening. That means that there are still reasons to be joyful!"[61]

4. THE GERMAN REVOLUTION AND BOLSHEVIK ACTIVISTS

In May 1918, fellow peasants assaulted Zykov and killed him with rifle butts.[62] Thus, he heard nothing of the news of the November Revolution, which would surely have given him even more reason "to be joyful". The revolutionary events

---

59 Dune, 122.
60 Voronkov, 135 (diary entry from 5.4.1919).
61 Bukina/Kyz'iurov/Lisevich, 100.
62 Ibid., 97.

in Germany did not only cause the party leadership to launch an extensive campaign, but they also evoked massive response "from below". One indicator of this eruption of activity is the amount of solidarity telegrams reaching the Soviet government from provincial party and trade union organisations, hailing Karl Liebknecht and the German workers and asking that their greetings be forwarded to revolutionary Berlin.[63] Soliciting such letters was not part of the campaign launched by the Bolshevik leadership, so one can suggest that the initiative in sending these telegrams surfaced "from below" – be it for conformist reasons to display acclamation for the current agitprop line, be it for genuine enthusiasm with the events in Germany. Other manifestations of solidarity with revolutionary Germany "from below" were recorded in the provinces – such as demonstration banners inscribed in letters that resembled the German Gothic print.[64]

The German revolution provoked such enthusiasm for several reasons. Firstly, it was the first significant revolutionary event abroad since the Bolshevik revolution of 1917. The fact that revolutionary sailors in Kiel rose just a few days before the first October anniversary, and the republic in Berlin was proclaimed only two days after the jubilee, granted the events even more symbolic power in Russia. Secondly, the impact was even stronger because it was the Germans, the former arch enemy, who were making this revolution. Tsarist state propaganda during World War 1 was predominantly built on anti-German sentiments, which were shared by large strata of the population.[65] The Bolsheviks, however, gained power throughout 1917 predominantly as an anti-war movement.[66] A revolution in Germany meant obtaining the German "working masses" as allies – a powerful fact that symbolised a radical break with the politics of the "imperialist war". And finally, Germany was not a country somewhere far away – German events had influence on activists' everyday lives. Some had fought on the front against German troops, some had spent time (and were politicised) in German POW camps, and for some, the ongoing German occupation of the Western borderlands had direct consequences for friends and relatives.

All three factors are reflected in the diary of Iosif Golubev. A skilled worker "from the bench", employed as a cabinet maker in a wagon factory during the war, Golubev joined the Social Democrats in Minsk in March 1917, and aligned with the Bolshevik faction after the split that occurred shortly after.[67] His politi-

---

63 See GARF, 1235/93/2 and 1235/93/8.
64 Narskii, 431.
65 See Hubertus F. Jahn, Patriotic Culture in Russia During World War I, Ithaca 1995.
66 Cf. Wade, 177ff.
67 Like many social-democratic party organisations inside Russia, the Minsk Social Democrats did not follow the Bolshevik-Menshevik split of 1903 because, unlike for

cisation, as reflected in his diary, was strongly connected to his growing weariness of the war: while patriotic entries predominated in 1914-1915, soon afterwards laments about the senseless bloodshed set in. His understanding of social democracy was first and foremost one of international unity against the ongoing strife. Shortly after joining the party, he wrote down in May 1917: "Our brotherly suggestion for the whole of Europe is the International, the slogan of love and brotherhood, a social life on a democratic basis."[68] After October 1917, Golubev became a rank and file party organiser and spent most of the Civil War years travelling through the countryside, heading a party cell of railroad workers in the second half of 1918. As a literate, self-reflective worker and self-styled revolutionary activist he felt isolated among his careerist and opportunistic comrades. Furthermore, he suffered from being separated from his wife and children who stayed behind in German-occupied Minsk. It is striking and logical at the same time that the few positive entries in his diary relate to revolution abroad.

In late October 1918, after being confronted by his party comrades with claims of party funds embezzlement which he considered unjust, he cooled down his anger and disappointment by calling upon his hopes in world revolution:

"And after that I'm supposed to work for the party still? I receive nothing but deepest ungratefulness. The only thing that calms me down is that the European proletariat is on the rise, and the all-encompassing international flame *[vsenarodnoe plame]* can fire up at any moment. That's what makes it worth working for the sake of the toiling people. It will be the best reward."[69]

Needless to say, the news of unrest in Germany on 8 October 1918 meant a great deal to Golubev:

"Only one thing makes me happy right now – that finally there is a real revolution going on in Germany. That means that soon we will have no frontline, and then I can go back to Minsk, fix my affairs a bit, calm down the kids and stay at one place. That would be quite nice. The German proletariat has started to get conscious – well, it was about time to erect a new order, topple the Bourgeoisie and free the people from century-old slavery. This is necessary."[70]

---

the party intellectuals abroad, it was not relevant for their everyday work. See also Vatslav Solskii, 1917 god v Zapadnoi oblasti i na Zapadnom fronte, Minsk 2004.

68 Iosif Golubev, 'Schast'e moe...'. Dnevniki Iosifa Golubeva 1916-1923 gg., ed. by Ales' A. Klyshka, Minsk 2002, 69 (diary entry from 11.5.1917).

69 Ibid., 175 (diary entry from 21.10.1918).

70 Ibid., 171 (diary entry from 8.10.1918).

Golubev intertwines his superficial usage of Marxist terminology with concrete hopes that profoundly touch upon his private life. The imminent German revolution meant for him not only fulfilment of his dreams on an ideological level, and not only being able to leave the local party bickering behind for the sake of higher goals, but also a fulfilled private life, namely being able to reunite with his wife and children. When the November revolution finally took place, he celebrated it as "our hope, the pillar and stronghold of the proletariat"[71] – the "we" did not just refer to Golubev's collective identity as a Bolshevik, but also to his comrades and family members.

Writing diaries was not the only practice of subjectivisation that the German revolution provided Bolshevik activists with. The events of 1918-1919 caused a major emergence of internationalist motives in the provincial party press. In these first years of Bolshevik power, party newspapers were far from as uniform as they would soon become under Stalinism.[72] After the February revolution eradicated the restrictive press laws of Tsarist Russia, revolutionary organisations in particular made extensive use of the new freedom. Every provincial soviet, every army unit, every party organisation strove to have its own press organ. When the Bolsheviks came to power, they cracked down on those organs that did not align to their political line, but the production of regional and local newspapers of the regime's political organisations remained abundant, despite their poor outreach and low print run. For the local organisations, having their own newspaper was a status symbol.[73] Moreover, it was their mouthpiece. Provincial party newspapers were often staffed by a handful of enthusiasts who rarely possessed any journalistic training but were eager to spread the revolutionary message.[74] And if we resort to the ideal-type dichotomy of "activists"

---

71 Ibid., 183-184 (diary entry from 22.11.1918).

72 On the character of Stalinist provincial newspapers, see: Jan C. Behrends, Repräsentation und Mobilisierung. Eine Skizze zur Geschichte der Öffentlichkeit in der Sowjetunion und in Osteuropa, 1917-1991, in: Ute Daniel/Axel Schildt (eds.), Massenmedien im Europa des 20. Jahrhunderts, Cologne 2010, 229-254, here 242; Sheila Fitzpatrick, Newspapers and Journals, in: Sheila Fitzpatrick/Lynne Viola (eds.), A Researcher's Guide to Sources on Soviet Social History in the 1930s, Armonk etc. 1990, 176-188.

73 Peter Kenez, The Birth of the Propaganda State. Soviet Methods of Mass Mobilization, 1917-1929, Cambridge 1985, 46; Charles Sargent Sampson, The Formative Years of the Soviet Press. An Institutional History 1917-1924, PhD diss. Amherst 1970, 99-101.

74 See e.g.: Efim A. Dinershtein, A.K.Voronskii. V poiskakh zhivoi vody, Moscow 2001, 42-53; Elena Kiseleva, Rannesovetskaia provintsial'naia pechat'. Vyzhivanie i

versus "careerists", it is logical to assume that the former tended to be found staffing the newspapers, while the latter would make use of their power in more rewarding ways.

In the first months of Bolshevik rule, however, local newspapers were rather busy focussing on their task of being organs of state power. Official proclamations and decrees filled the pages, making the newspapers a dull and uniform read.[75] International news coverage only consisted of reprints of telegrams from ROSTA, the governmental news agency – the local press organs showed little effort in covering international affairs on their own.[76] This changed radically in the second half of 1918, when the revolutions in Central Europe, most importantly in Germany, set in.[77] The development can be traced on the example of "Izvestiia Vologodskogo gubispolkoma" (later renamed to "Krasnyi Sever"), the soviet and party newspaper in the north-Russian provincial town of Vologda. Before the autumn of 1918, the paper mostly consisted of official decrees and classified ads; international news coverage had a random character, consisting of ROSTA reprints and having no special focus on revolutionary movements abroad. This picture changed with the November Revolution, which was declared the "eve of the German October" in headline news.[78] Throughout the following months the focus on the European and mostly German revolutionary events remained predominant, and the staff did not limit itself to reprinting news telegrams from Moscow, but also published their own editorials on world revolution, proclaiming the "dawn of world communism".[79] The November revolution in Germany thus changed the outlook and content of this provincial press organ completely. The same can be observed in another provincial newspaper,

---

bor'ba za soznanie mass. Na primere Orlovskoi i Brianskoi gubernii RSFSR, in: Aktual'nye problemy otechestvennoi i vsemirnoi istorii [Khar'kov] (2010), no. 13, 61-68, here 64; S. A. Zhadovskaia, Rol' mestnoi periodiki v literaturnom protsesse na Russkom Severe. Uezdnyi gorod Vel'sk v 1910-1920-e gg., in: A. A. Kozhanov/V. V. Volochova/ A. V. Golubev (eds.), Provintsial'naia zhurnalistika i zhizn' Rossiiskoi imperii v XIX - nachale XX v., Petrozavodsk 2008, 95-113, here 105–106.

75 Kenez, 46; Sampson, 94.

76 There is, however, some evidence that the treaty of Brest-Litovsk was controversially discussed in some local party press organs: Aleksei N. Kharin, Vneshniaia politika sovetskogo pravitel'stva v vospriiatii rukovodstva i naseleniia Viatskoi gubernii. 1917-1925 gg. Kand. diss. Kirov 2000, 32-36.

77 Kharin makes this observation for the Viatka province: Ibid., 38.

78 Pr., "Pered nemeckim oktiabrem", Izvestiia Vologodskogo gubernskogo ispolnitel'nogo komiteta, 8.12.1918.

79 V-kij, "Kanun mirovogo kommunizma", Krasnyi Sever, 16.11.1919.

"Derevenskaia Kommuna", the mouthpiece of the rural party organisation of the "North Commune" province.[80] Consisting solely of decrees and classified ads during the first half of 1918, it began to take a keen interest in international revolution in October and introduced the front-page column "It is beginning...", where it reported on revolutionary events abroad. From late October onwards, the newspaper began carrying the regular column "World Revolution" (sometimes "World Bolshevism"), carrying revolutionary news reports from all over the world, obviously with a predominance of the developments in Germany. The column continued to be part of the newspaper well into 1919.[81]

It is important to note that the attention given to the German revolution in these and other such provincial Bolshevik newspapers was not a consequence of any set of directives from Moscow. The Central Committee's grip on the local press was very weak in these first years, a fact that changed only gradually after it formed its own press supervision structures in the early 1920s.[82] Given this circumstances and the composition of the local party newspapers' staff, it is more likely that by hailing world revolution from the front-pages, provincial activists were exercising themselves as "true" communists and expressing and mutually reassuring their hopes for international revolution to come to their aid. This is even more likely given the fact that the excessive world-revolutionary news coverage was not in the interest of the party leadership, which saw the primary function of the provincial newspapers in addressing the local populace and not in being a mouthpiece of activists and their enthusiasm. Already the 8th Party Congress in March 1919 reprimanded local newspapers for the negligence of local affairs,[83] but their excessive focus on world revolution remained a thorn in the central party authorities' side throughout the following years.[84]

Another way that provincial activists practiced their commitment to the German revolution was their attempt to partake in the events themselves in a direct way – namely by going to Germany. While there were no coordinated efforts by the party to send its militants abroad, its position on this question was still ambiguous. The party press reported on 12 November 1918 about a session of the Moscow soviet which had decided to send "special representatives and

---

80 The "North Commune" was a territorial formation between 1918 and 1919, encompassing Petrograd and the aligning North-Russian provinces.
81 I thank Brendan McGeever for information on "Derevenskaia Kommuna".
82 See: Ingo Grabowsky, Agitprop in der Sowjetunion. Die Abteilung für Agitation und Propaganda 1920-1928, Bochum etc. 2004.
83 P. N. Fedoseev/ K. U. Chernenko (eds.), KPSS v rezoliutsiiakh i resheniiakh s''ezdov, konferentsii i plenumov TsK, 1898-1970, Vol. 2, Moscow 1970, 84.
84 See e.g.: Albert, German October, 118-120.

agitators" to Germany.⁸⁵ Such reports could nourish the hopes of those activists wishing to be sent abroad. The party organisation in the Saratov province wrote to the Central Committee's Secretariat in Moscow on 23 November that they had comrades at their disposal that could speak German, English and French who were willing to be sent across the border. The provincial functionaries were so certain about the party's need to do so that they already asked where to send them to.⁸⁶ Indeed, the Secretariat in Moscow seemed to leave this possibility open: They wrote back to Saratov and inquired about the qualifications of the foreign-language-speaking comrades.⁸⁷ However, when another provincial party committee wrote to the Secretariat a few days later offering to send communists to Germany and Austria, the reply was negative: Only after being appointed by the central party apparatus, were individuals to be sent abroad.⁸⁸

Apart from the very small circle of top-ranking Bolshevik emissaries such as Karl Radek and Peteris Stučka,⁸⁹ no Soviet communists were sent to assist revolutionary Germany. However, individual activists still dreamt of a world-revolutionary mission. The aforementioned Voronkov began to learn German shortly after the November revolution, taking lessons from an Austrian POW. Upon embarking on his studies Voronkov noted down in his diary: "How I long to master the language and go abroad! *Nach Österreich oder Deutschland!*"⁹⁰ Some weeks later, after having made progress, he noted, making use of his freshly acquired German: "*Ich danke [sic], dass [ich] in dem Frühling nach Deutschland fahren werde. Es ist sehr angenehm.*"⁹¹ Given the revolutionary events that unfolded in Germany and Austria in the preceding months, it is unlikely that Voronkov longed to go abroad just to enjoy the spring. Furthermore, the fact that

---

85 "Otklik Germanskoi revoliutsii", Bednota, 12.11.1918.
86 Letter from the Satarov RCP(b) committee to the CC of the RCP(b), 23.11.1918, RGASPI, 17/4/64, 13. Quoted from: V. V. Anikeev (ed.), Perepiska Sekretariata TsK RKP(b) s mestnymi partiinymi organizatsiiami, Vol. 5, Moscow 1969, 170.
87 Letter of the Secretariat of the CC of the RCP(b) to the Saratov committee of the RCP(b), 20.11.1918, RGASPI, 17/4/5, 303. Published in: Ibid, 30.
88 Letter of the RCP(b) committee of Kamyshin (Satarov guberniia) to the CC of the RCP(b), 29.11.1918, RGASPI, 17/4/64, 92. Published in: Ibid., 197.
89 On their mission to Germany in 1918/19, see: Ottokar Luban, Russische Bolschewiki und deutsche Linkssozialisten am Vorabend der deutschen Novemberrevolution. Beziehungen und Einflussnahmen, in: Jahrbuch für Historische Kommunismusforschung (2009), 283-298.
90 Voronkov, 88. The German phrase translates "To Austria or Germany!".
91 Ibid., 99 (diary entry from 21.12.1918). The German phrase translates: "I thank [sic, means: think] that [I] will go to Germany in the spring. It is very nice."

Voronkov was practicing his German on the pages of his diary shows how he strove to subjectivise himself as a dedicated world-revolutionary: Not only was the German revolution anything but "yesteryear's snow" for him, he displayed the highest dedication by preparing personally to take part in it.

Voronkov was far from the only Bolshevik wishing to travel westwards during these months. For example, Aleksandr Spunde, deputy director of the People's Bank in 1918, also tried to find ways through private correspondence to go to Germany and join the revolutionary movement there directly after the outbreak of the revolution.[92] Both Voronkov and Spunde were dedicated Bolsheviks and held functions in the party-state apparatus; they neither had a desire to escape Soviet Russia nor to obtain material privileges by going abroad. There are no "rational" reasons for their desire to partake in the German revolution other than to exercise their activist subjectivities by showing their utmost dedication to revolutionary events abroad, and by extension, to break through the aforementioned threefold isolation that they were subject to in Russia. Neither Voronkov nor Spunde, however, were sent to their dream destination.

5. CONCLUSIONS

The German revolution was not just a topic of propaganda within Soviet Russia launched by the party leadership – on the contrary, it meant a lot for Bolshevik activists below the level of party elites, and particularly on the country's peripheries. This was the case for several reasons. Firstly, the dedication to world revolution was considered part of being an ideal Bolshevik activist. Thus, displaying such dedication was part of Bolshevik practices of subjectivisation, and the events in Germany provided a perfect occasion for such practices. However, this was not just a way to adapt to a ruling discourse or a way to learn to "speak Bolshevik". International revolution – and the German revolution in particular – meant a lot for activists for concrete and tangible reasons: Activists could see direct positive consequences from the victory of revolutions abroad in relation to their everyday lives. This extremely powerful combination of high ideals and concrete hopes allows us to consider world revolution as a charismatic idea that exercised its authority over Bolshevik activists who were willing to dedicate themselves to this cause – in some cases, even up to the point that they were willing to go abroad.

---

92 Malte Griesse, Communiquer, juger et agir sous Staline. La personne prise entre ses liens avec les proches et son rapport au système politico-idéologique, Frankfurt 2011, 393-394.

Charismatic authority, however, is known to be unstable and deficient.[93] It tends to weaken and ultimately fail if constant validation of its charismatic power remains absent.[94] In the case of world revolution this validation was particularly unstable since its source were events abroad on which neither the Bolshevik leadership nor the rank and file activists had any considerable influence. The German revolution in particular failed again and again from the Bolshevik perspective – not only through the suppressions of the January Uprising and the Bavarian council republic in 1919, but also through the catastrophic outcome of the "March Action" in 1921 and finally the "German October" of 1923, onto which the Bolsheviks placed immense hopes and which ultimately turned out to be a non-event – an outcome which led to immense disappointment throughout the whole party.[95]

The fact that internationalist convictions and Bolshevik subjectivisation went hand in hand becomes apparent when both disappear simultaneously from the sources, as can be observed in diaries of Bolshevik activists who terminated their Bolshevik engagement altogether. Both of the diarists cited here, Iosif Golubev and Mikhail Voronkov, distanced themselves from Bolshevik politics while continuing to maintain their diaries. For the former, whose published notes go up to early 1923, the affairs of world revolution stop playing any role already in 1920, after socialist revolutions abroad failed to materialise and problems of everyday life came to the fore instead. In August 1921, the disappointed Golubev quit the party – from about the same time onwards, his diary entries are mostly preoccupied with everyday hardships and quarrels with his former comrades, while his judgements even become antisemitic at times.[96] In the construction of the diarist's new self, internationalism – either in the form of belief in world revolution, or of an anti-chauvinistic stance – has no place anymore. The second diarist, Voronkov, quits the party in March 1923, being tired of political intrigues and having given up hope for building a better society. Already in the late 1920s, while acting as a seemingly apolitical but loyal bystander of the regime, he positions himself on his diary pages as a pronounced anticommunist, developing political arguments against the very same Soviet system he helped to build up in the first years after the revolution.[97] Already in late 1923, while reacting to the supposedly impending revolutionary crisis in Germany, Voronkov reflects upon the situation in his diary without any hint of world-revolutionary

---

93 Gebhardt, Charisma und Ordnung, 51.
94 Weber, 242.
95 See Albert, German October.
96 See e.g. Golubev, 384-386.
97 Voronkov, 53-57.

enthusiasm – instead he is worried, just like the majority of the population, that a possible Soviet involvement in Germany would lead to a new war.[98]

This is not to say that enthusiasm over world revolution among Bolshevik activists ceased to exist altogether in 1923 or afterwards. Memoirs just as contemporary sources testify to revolutionary internationalism remaining a possible mechanism of activist subjectivisation for individual Soviet enthusiasts, particularly young communists who, just like their elder comrades in 1918, strove to go abroad to fight for international revolution during the second half of the 1920s.[99] In the long run, however, the failure of the German revolution to live up to Bolshevik expectations, and thus the absence of a source for validation of the charisma of world revolution, led to the fact that for new generations of party cadres, coming onto the stage of politics in the course of the 1920s, world revolution came to be more and more irrelevant. "[W]hilst parroting the language of class and internationalism, [they] deeply resented the notion that Russia was inferior to the West",[100] and thus proved wilful supporters for Stalin's new course of "building socialism in one single country" from 1925 onwards, which led to a new discourse of isolationism and "Soviet patriotism".[101]

Ultimately, the impact of the German revolution on the Bolshevik party beyond its leadership highlights the need for an integrated history of the post-World War I revolutions that includes Soviet Russia – not just as a power structure that tried to take influence on the international revolutionary movements via the Comintern, but as a society on which the other European revolutions had a profound impact.

---

98 Ibid., 244-245 (diary entry from 3.9.1923). For the war scare of late 1923, see Albert, German October; David R. Stone, The Prospect of War? Lev Trotskii, the Soviet Army, and the German Revolution in 1923, in: The International History Review 25:4 (2003), 799-817.

99 Lew Kopelew, Und schuf mir einen Götzen. Lehrjahre eines Kommunisten, München 1981; Corinna Kuhr-Korolev, Gezähmte Helden. Die Formierung der Sowjetjugend 1917-1932, Essen 2005, 75-77.

100 Smith, 114.

101 See: David Brandenberger, Proletarian Internationalism, 'Soviet Patriotism' and the Rise of Russocentric Etatism During the Stalinist 1930s, in: Left History 6:2 (2000), 80-100.

'Moral Power' and Cultural Revolution
Räte geistiger Arbeiter in Central Europe, 1918/19

IAN GRIMMER

1. INTRODUCTION

On November 11, 1918, the *Berliner Tageblatt* announced that a *Rat geistiger Arbeiter*, or council of intellectual workers, had organized itself alongside the workers' and soldiers' councils that had taken control of the Reichstag at the beginning of the 1918–19 German Revolution. "It acts for the cultural political radicals on the ground of the new republic," the paper stated, and listed its members as follows: Dr. Kurt Hiller, Siegfried Jacobsohn, Rudolf Leonhard, Dr. Leo Matthias, Dr. Helene Stöcker, Dr. Frank Thieß, and Armin T. Wegner.[1] All who wanted to support the council's activities were encouraged to contact it. Within days, similarly named councils then formed in over a dozen German cities, and as revolution spread to the collapsing Habsburg Empire, additional councils appeared in Vienna and Salzburg.[2] The formation of these institutions during the revolutionary period in Central Europe was an unusual development, for while workers and soldiers organized *Räte* not unlike the soviets created by similar groups during the previous year in revolutionary Russia, the councils of "intellectual workers" lacked a recent precedent, contributing to an ambiguity surrounding their role in the revolution. Nearly a century later, questions still persist about what it meant for intellectuals to organize themselves in this way and how this self-understanding informed their concrete practices.

---

1 Ein 'Rat geistiger Arbeiter,' Berliner Tageblatt Abendausgabe, 11.11.1918.
2 These cities in Germany included Breslau, Chemnitz, Darmstadt, Dresden, Göttingen, Hamburg, Hanover, Karlsruhe, Cologne, Königsberg, Leipzig, Magdeburg, Marburg, Munich, Oldenburg, and Stuttgart.

In view of Kurt Hiller's efforts to politicize German intellectuals during the war years and his leading role in the Berlin council, many historians have interpreted these *Räte* as manifestations of *Aktivismus*.[3] This is a term that Hiller coined together with the expressionist writers Rudolf Kayser and Alfred Wolfenstein in the fall of 1914 to designate a shift among German authors toward active political engagement, and it subsequently became associated with a pacifist, non-Marxian socialist, and neo-aristocratic worldview that Hiller personally espoused.[4] More recent research complicates this picture, however, by highlighting the heterogeneity of the councils in Germany, arguing that they stemmed instead primarily from local initiatives.[5] Evidence can certainly be found in support of both of these claims. Yet in considering this phenomenon in relation to its broader Central European context, and in view of some of the more peripheral councils in Germany, it is possible to see that although these *Räte* failed to cohere as an organized movement and cannot be reduced to a singular philosophy, they did share a common aim. Intellectuals established these councils as a way extend the revolution beyond the demands of the traditional labor movement in the hope of advancing a cultural revolution that would fundamentally change many aspects of subjective experience. A new polity and economy, they believed, also required a new people, and this was something that men and women of letters now had a distinct responsibility in helping to cultivate in the aftermath of the war. The significance of these councils was that they created a space for

---

3   See, for example, Istvan Deak, Weimar Germany's Left-wing Intellectuals, Berkeley 1968; Eva Kolinsky, Engagierter Expressionismus. Politik und Literatur zwischen Weltkrieg und Weimarer Republik. Eine Analyse expressionistischer Zeitschriften, Stuttgart 1970; George Mosse, Left-wing Intellectuals in the Weimar Republic, in: Germans and Jews: The Right, the Left, and the Search for a "Third Force" in Pre-Nazi Germany, New York 1970, 171-225; and Rolf von Bockel, Weimarer Profile: Kurt Hiller und der "Rat geistiger Arbeiter", in: Neue Gesellschaft, Frankfurter Hefte 38:10 (1991), 946-948. For a more recent account of Hiller and the Berlin council, see Harald Lützenkirchen, Kurt Hiller und der Politische Rat geistiger Arbeiter in der Novemberrevolution, in: Heidi Beutin/Wolfgang Beutin/Ralph Müller-Beck (eds.), Das Waren Wintermonate voller Arbeit, Hoffen und Glück . . ., Frankfurt 2010, 83-109.

4   Kurt Hiller, Leben gegen die Zeit, vol. 1, Logos, Reinbek 1969, 98. See also Kurt Hiller, Ortsbestimmung des Aktivismus, in: Die Erhebung 1 (1919), 360-377. For a discussion of Hiller's idiosyncratic view of aristocracy, see Alexandra Gerstner, Neuer Adel: Aristokratische Elitekonzeptionen zwischen Jahrhundertwende und Nationalsozialismus, Darmstadt 2008.

5   Hans-Joachim Bieber, Bürgertum in der Revolution: Bürgerräte und Bürgerstreiks in Deutschland 1918-1920, Hamburg 1992, 126.

intellectuals to pursue these cultural-revolutionary aims while simultaneously allowing them to preserve their independence – the source, as Pierre Bourdieu suggests, of their power to influence public life.

2. THE PRECEDENT OF BERLIN

What was perhaps most notable about Berlin's *Rat geistiger Arbeiter* (RGA) is that it grew out of an already existing organization. Hiller had attempted to bring together intellectuals around a broad agenda of cultural reform already during the time of the First World War, soliciting essays that he personally considered to exemplify this new perspective in his yearbook, *Das Ziel*. Inspired by both Plato and Friedrich Nietzsche, Hiller envisioned these contributors as future twentieth-century philosopher kings, an elite of cultural radicals who he described as *die Geistigen*.[6] *"Die Geistigen* – what does that mean?" he asks in a programmatic essay from 1915, "It means (with twenty-three letters) those who feel responsible."[7] It was out of a sense of duty to the public, especially in view of the catastrophic destruction of the war, that Hiller hoped writers would finally enter German political life – ultimately to lead it.[8] Members of this circle met for the first time in August 1917, initially calling themselves the *Bund zum Ziel*, and later following a second conference held in Berlin from November 7-8, 1918, they renamed themselves the *Aktivistenbund*.[9]

Thus when the revolution began on the following day, the Berlin group was already well organized – including having drafted a program – and was able to effectively insert itself into the provisional structure of the new revolutionary government. Due to the support of Hans-Georg von Beerfelde, a former military officer and the second chair of the *Vollzugsrat* of the combined workers' and

---

6 The word intellectual, by contrast, had a more negative connotation for Hiller, which he associated with those who were simply in possession of technical knowledge. See Dietz Bering, Die Epoch der Intellektuellen 1898-2001. Geburt, Begriff, Grabmal, Berlin 2010, 72-78.

7 Kurt Hiller, Philosophie des Ziels, in: Das Ziel 1 (1915), 206. See also Kurt Hiller, Bund der Geistigen, in: Die Schaubühne 11:24 (17 June 1915), 559.

8 See, for example, Kurt Hiller, Ein Deutsches Herrenhaus, in: Das Ziel 2 (1917/1918), 379-425.

9 For documents related to the *Bund zum Ziel*, see Bund zum Ziel: Leitsätze, in: Das Ziel 3 (1919), 218-19; and der ersten Vorbesprechung des (erweiterten) "Ziel"-Kreises, in: Juliane Habereder, Kurt Hiller und der literarische Aktivismus: zur Geistesgeschichte des politischen Dichters im frühen 20. Jahrhundert, Frankfurt 1981, 312-319.

soldiers' councils, the group was briefly able to secure a place for itself as a "third power" in the Reichstag dedicated to cultural policy.[10] According to Hiller's recollection, von Beerfelde had only one stipulation: the group should rename itself the "*Rat geistiger Arbeiter*," so that it would be consistent with the names of the other revolutionary institutions.[11] Hiller accepted this with great reluctance, later remarking that this was not their language, and that the term *geistiger Arbeiter* had nothing in common with their understanding of *Geist*.[12] For members of this intellectual milieu, the political language of "*Geist*" and "*geistige Politik*" had a deeper connotation that Hiller later defined as "the embodiment of all efforts to improve the lot of humanity (the physical and the metaphysical)."[13] It suggested nothing less than the collective efforts to realize the utopian ideal of "paradise."[14] The term *geistiger Arbeiter* for this reason "would be misunderstood, even by supporters," Hiller feared, "and it was simply kitsch."[15]

This concern with the council's name later proved to be correct for a number of reasons. As Hans-Joachim Bieber observes, the term "*geistiger Arbeiter*" scarcely existed prior to the revolution, contributing to uncertainties about the group's composition, intentions, and relationship to the working class.[16] Indeed, the Berlin council soon found it necessary to include the adjective "political" in its name – now calling itself the *Politischer Rat geistiger Arbeiter* (PRGA) after mid-December 1918 – in order to distinguish itself from the politically neutral associations of the intellectual professions that had also organized councils as a means to protect and advance their interests.

The polysemy associated with this term thus brings us to one of the key distinctions to be made in relation to the councils of intellectual workers: despite often sharing a similar name and organizational form, only approximately half of these *Räte* had an explicitly political self-understanding, and it is the specificity of this latter form of engagement that will be our concern here. Additional com-

---

10 Hiller, Logos, 128.
11 Ibid.
12 Ibid., 128-129. The German word *Geist* used in this context lacks an identical English equivalent. It is best translated as spirit, mind, or the intellect.
13 Kurt Hiller, Der Aufbruch zum Paradies, Munich 1922, 102.
14 Hiller describes his idea of paradise as follows: "It is utopian, but not fantasy. For paradise is not a Garden of Eden; it is more likely to look like a big, beautiful city. But it is a place, where all of its inhabitants are allowed to be vital, and to vitality belongs more than the animalistic." See Hiller, Philosophie des Ziels, 196.
15 Hiller, Logos, 128-129.
16 Bieber, 124.

plications came from more widespread confusion about the purpose of the RGA. In the course of the revolution hundreds of Germans contacted the Berlin council with the mistaken belief that it might assist them in finding employment, as Hiller later regretted.[17]

In the end, the period of the council's activity in the Reichstag was extremely short lived. After only three days, a conflict between von Beerfelde and the Majority Social Democratic faction over his attempt to have the Prussian Minister of War, Heinrich von Scheüch, arrested led to von Beerfelde's dismissal from the *Vollzugsrat*, and the subsequent removal of all non-party based groups from the Reichstag such as the pacifist *Bund Neues Vaterland*, the *Sozialistische Studenten*, and the RGA. The RGA was able to continue its activities independently, however, due to an anonymous donation of 10,000 marks from a former military officer, who sympathized with the council's aims.[18] With this funding, the RGA was able to rent a room in Charlottenberg to serve as its new office.

As Hiller made clear in his speech "Who are we? What do we want?" delivered in the council's first public assembly held on December 2, 1918 in the Berlin Blüthnersaal, the purpose of the RGA was to extend the revolutionary upheaval in politics into the sphere of culture. "We have seen the political revolution; the proletariat, whose interests are covered with the promise of justice, will ensure that the social revolution will follow the political, but the true revolution is first realized where the cultural revolution is successful."[19] Only a deep and thoroughgoing transformation of culture, he believed, could secure the changes already brought about and constitute a new beginning for Germany. Nothing was more important toward this end for members of the Berlin council than an emphatic rejection of the mass killing that had transpired during the last four years: "The guiding star for all future politics must be the inviolability of life," its program began.[20] The seven articles that followed extended from this position, attempting to unite many of the late-Wilhelmine oppositional movements behind a common agenda of cultural change. These included the ideas of sexual reform advocated by Helene Stöcker's *Bund für Mutterschutz*, the pacifist activities of the *Zentralstelle Völkerrecht*, and the left wing of the German youth movement inspired by the writings of the reform pedagogue Gustav Wyneken.[21]

---

17 Hiller, Logos, 129.
18 Ibid., 132.
19 Kurt Hiller, Wer sind wir? Was wollen wir? in: Geist werde Herr: Kundgebungen eines Aktivisten vor, in und nach dem Kriege, Berlin 1920, 73.
20 Rat geistiger Arbeiter, in: Die Weltbühne 14:47 (21 November 1918), 473.
21 Kurt Hiller, Der ersten Vorbesprechung des (erweiterten) "Ziel"-Kreises, 312. Robert Müller noted similar sources of *Aktivismus* in Austria including: "pacifism, the youth

"We do not want to become a new sect next to the many old ones," Hiller explained.[22]

"We want to be the great arc above all of the serious individual movements that aspire to change the world: those concerned with human rights and constitutional law, sexual reform and pedagogy, economic and artistic movements; we want to be the comprehensive representation of the cultural political radicals."[23]

The RGA consequently demanded pacifist measures such as the abolition of military conscription alongside the progressive shortening of the working day and a restructuring of the capitalist economy into one based on workers' cooperatives.[24] It called for sexual freedom and the limitation of criminal law to allow individuals the right to control their bodies. The remaining four points included: the abolition of the death penalty, a "radical reform of public education," the separation of church and state, and the "safeguarding and consolidation of the greater German social republic."[25]

Specifically with regard to the last of these points, the RGA called for itself to be directly incorporated in the structure of the new government alongside a democratically elected Reichstag that was inclusive of women representatives. The criteria through which the council of intellectual workers would be established were conspicuously vague, however: "The *Rat der Geistigen*. It will be created neither by nomination nor by election, but by intrinsic right, which derives from the duty of *Geist* to help. It will renew itself according to its own law."[26] Not all members of the literary avant-garde were convinced by this claim to power. A leaflet circulated in advance of the council's December 2 meeting under the heading of Franz Pfemfert's expressionist paper, *Die Aktion*, for ex-

---

movement, education, the struggle for sexual freedom [...] , land reform, the settlement movement [...] , criminal law reform [...] , the formation of economic experiments and model farms. Many are in all areas of socialism, the radicals in particular, however, are *Aktivisten*." Robert Müller, Thomas Mann, Frankreich, Aktivismus, in: Der Neue Merkur 5:10 (1921/22), 719.

22 Hiller, Wer sind wir? Was wollen wir?, 77.
23 Ibid.
24 Hiller, Logos, 112.
25 Ibid., 230.
26 Ibid., 231.

ample, urged the working class to not be deceived by these "parasites of capitalist dictatorship," and decried the council as "counter-revolutionary."[27]

Siegfried Jacobsohn published the Berlin program in his journal, *die Weltbühne*, on November 21, 1918, and when Hiller later reprinted the document in the third volume of *Das Ziel* in 1919, it was followed by the names of sixty prominent intellectuals, as well as the endorsement of the political councils in Munich and Vienna.[28] On first impression, then, it would appear that the Berlin program had overwhelming support among the politically engaged intelligentsia in Germany, Austria, and among expatriates in Switzerland. Yet the degree of consensus surrounding the ideas of Berlin group was weaker than historians have previously assumed. A memo from Hiller to the Göttingen council of intellectual workers, for example, suggests that Hiller attempted to gloss over individual differences in order to win the endorsement of as many people as possible. Fearing that these councils might go unnoticed if they did not speak with a unified voice, Hiller encouraged all to sign the program "even when they had misgivings about individual points."[29] "Chaos must be prevented," he declared.[30] The question remains, then, just how representative the Berlin group was for this larger circle of intellectuals. In order to understand the significance of these councils, discerning their exact relationship to Berlin's RGA and its attempt to create a unified movement thus needs to serve as our initial point of departure.

One of the first things to observe here is that even within the Berlin council not all members were entirely in agreement with the program. What united them above all was opposition to military conscription, a controversial demand at this time even for many pacifist organizations. The writer Arthur Holitscher, for example, later recalled that this was the only issue that Hiller asked him about to determine his admission to the council.[31] Although attending meetings of the *Aktivistenbund* prior to the revolution, Jacobsohn was also surprised to find his name included in the announcement in the *Berliner Tageblatt*, and publically

---

27 Proletarier! Soldaten! Parteigenossen! Friedrich Ebert Stiftung/Archiv der sozialen Demokratie (AdsD), Sammlung Flugblätter und Flugscriften, 6/FLBL005490. On the political differences within the expressionist movement, see Lothar Peter, Literarische Intelligenz und Klassenkampf: Die Aktion 1911-1932, Cologne 1972.

28 Rat geistiger Arbeiter, in: Die Weltbühne, 14:47 (21 November 1918): 473-475. Politischer Rat geistiger Arbeiter, in: Das Ziel 3 (1919), 219-223.

29 In Namen des Rats geistiger Arbeiter! Bundesarchiv Berlin-Licherfelde (BArch), Nachlass Leonard Nelson, 2210/45, 12.

30 Ibid.

31 Arthur Holitscher, Mein Leben in dieser Zeit. Der "Lebensgeschichte eines Rebellen" Zweiter Band (1907-1925), Potsdam 1928, 161.

resigned after the December 2 meeting, as did Thieß and Holitscher, in response to Hiller's polemic at the meeting against the *Berliner Tageblatt* feuilltonist, Paul Block, and the liberal politician, pastor Friedrich Naumann.[32] Armin T. Wegner for his part was in complete agreement with the group's pacifist aims, yet he also did not hesitate to publically voice his opposition to Hiller's idea of rule by intellectuals.[33] Thus the real influence of the Berlin program was not so much in the specificity of its demands as it was in its precedent of advancing a platform of issues that were either deemphasized or neglected by both wings of the socialist movement. This is precisely what the other politically oriented councils drew on as they attempted to emulate the same organizational form.

3. *AKTIVISMUS* IN VIENNA

While it is common for historians to fold all of the councils in Germany under the aegis of Hiller's *Aktivismus*, the strongest case for this argument is actually best found outside of Germany in the example of the Viennese council. Here, intellectuals formed a group called the *"Bund der geistig Tätigen,"* which met for the first time as a preparatory committee on November 16, 1918, later to formally constitute itself as an organization on January 13, 1919 under the leadership of Dr. Franz Kobler, the group's founder and chair.[34] Kobler had first come to politics in his youth as a member of the Zionist movement while a student in Prague, but it was his commitment to pacifism that most directly motivated his interest in forming this council. Robert Müller, the coeditor of the group's journal, similarly arrived at the *Bund* after his involvement in a secret society called *Die Katakombe*, which he organized with other expressionist writers after his

---

32 Siegfried Jacobsohn, Antworten, in: Die Weltbühne 14:50 (12 December 1918), 566-568. See also Kurt Hiller, Erinnerungen an Alfons Goldschmidt (1879–1940), in: Köpfe und Tröpfe. Profile aus einem Vierteljahrhundert, Hamburg 1950, 277-278.

33 Armin T. Wegner, Brief an Kurt Hiller, in: Der Osten 1:9/11 (January/March 1919), 113-118.

34 According to Kobler's recollection, the key participants in this council were the expressionist author Robert Müller, the art historian Dr. Franz Ottmann, the sculptor Ernst Wagner, the subsequent founder of the pan-European movement, Dr. Richard Nikolaus von Coudenhove-Kalergi, the art historian Dr. Max Ermer, and the philosopher Dr. Ernst Müller. Curriculum Vitae, Leo Baeck Institute (LBI), Franz Kobler Collection 1909 - 1965, box 1, folder 3, 6.

experience of shellshock while serving at the front and his subsequent rejection of the war.[35]

Initially, the first activities of the *Bund* involved a series of public lectures, beginning with a talk by Kobler on "The Organization of the *Geistigen*," followed by one two weeks later by Max Ermer on "*Geistige Bunde* and their Programs." The *Bund* then drafted its own program at the end of December 1918 in a document that was quite similar to the one the Berlin council had initially circulated. It began by declaring that the end of the war had also brought to a close the era of *Realpolitik*, stating its opposition to violence and emphasizing the need for cultural renewal: "Burdened with an abundance of problems, that were foreign to the Enlightenment, but like it driven by an overwhelming force toward realization, the *Geist* wants to once again restore a world that has been turned upside down."[36] The program of the *Bund* thus called for wide array of changes ranging from the abolition of compulsory military service to the establishment of garden cities as the basis of future urban development.[37] Its predominant emphasis, however, was on issues of cultural reform outside of the demands of the organized socialist movement. Evoking the same language as Hiller, Müller summarized his vision for uniting the intellectuals as follows: "for those who live and act for the *Geist* [...] they are their own party, looking beyond contemporary programs, the politicians of utopia. They are the corrective to socialism."[38]

Following the publication of its program, the *Bund* continued to hold public lectures, and on February 8, 1919 its members participated in a public demonstration against the new *Wehrgesetz* in Vienna's *Konzerthaus*. The Viennese council was also notable for its efforts to forge ties internationally.[39] It was able to establish contact with the *Clarté* movement in France, which was similarly attempting to unite European intellectuals in support of socialist and pacifist

---

35 Müller briefly describes Die Katakombe in his essay, Literaria. Keine Geschichte mit beschränkter Haftung, in: Robert Müller (ed.), Literaria-Almanach, Vienna 1921, 105-110. On Müller's biography, see Stephanie Heckner, Die Tropen als Tropus: Zur Dichtungstheorie Robert Müllers, Vienna 1991.
36 This document was published in the first volume of the group's paper, Der Strahl. See Unser erster Aufruf. An die Kulturmenschen aller Länder! in: Der Strahl. Mitteilungen des Bundes der Geistig Tätigen 1:1 (April 1919), 2-3.
37 Ibid.
38 Robert Müller, Sozialistische Vereinigung geistiger Arbeiter, in: Die Neue Wirtschaft 1:1 (30 November 1918), 7.
39 Der Strahl 1:1 (April 1919), 26.

aims.[40] It also collaborated with the Berlin council on the planning of a congress of all the councils of intellectual workers, which they hoped Heinrich Mann, the leader of Munich's PRGA, would host in Munich, but was ultimately held in Berlin.[41] The *Bund* discussed additional projects including forming a library, an academy, and it sponsored what Kobler described as the first public exhibition of expressionist art at the *Künstlerhaus* in Vienna.[42]

The close relationship between the Berlin and Viennese councils can finally be seen in the way that the Viennese group adopted the same term *Aktivismus* to describe its activities.[43] Hiller found in Müller an especially close ally with his neo-aristocratic worldview, and both councils understood themselves as belonging to common movement. These parallels certainly help to support the interpretation of the councils of intellectual workers as a unified phenomenon. A closer examination of the councils in Germany, however, complicates this picture, which one can already see in the example of the second council to endorse the Berlin program: the *Politischer Rat geistiger Arbeiter* in Munich.

4. MUNICH'S DEMOCRATIC ALTERNATIVE

Hiller later described Munich's PRGA was the most important of these various *Räte* in Germany during the revolutionary period next to the Berlin council.[44] He himself had played somewhat of a role in initially fostering its development, insofar as he had planned to deliver a series of public lectures in Munich in the

---

40 See An Henri Barbusse und seine Mitstreiter! in: Der Strahl 1:1 (April 1919), 8-9; and Unser zweiter Aufruf an Henri Barbusse und seine Freunde, in: Der Strahl 1:2 (January 1920), 62–63. These letters were reprinted in France under the heading of "Clarté a l'Estranger" Clarté 1:2 (25 October 1919). On the *Clarté* movement, see Nicole Racine, The Clarté Movement in France, 1919-21, in: Journal of Contemporary History 2:2 (April 1967), 195-208.

41 Robert Müller and Franz Kobler to Heinrich Mann and the Münchener "Politischen Rat geistiger Arbeiter," 20.2.1919, Stiftung Archiv der Akademie der Künste, Berlin (AdK), Heinrich Mann Archiv, 2781.

42 Mitteilungen, in: Der Strahl 1:1 (April 1919): 25-26. For a review of the exhibit, see Bruno Adler, Expressionistische Kunstaustellungen (Neue Vereinigung – Bund der geistig Tätigen), in: Die Wage 22:21 (23 May 1919), 518-522.

43 See, for example, Robert Müller, Aus Deutschösterreich, in: Der Neue Merkur 3:4 (1919), 236-243; and Robert Müller, Bilanz des Aktivismus, in: Der Strahl 1:2 (January 1920), 9-10.

44 Hiller, Logos, 132.

month prior to the revolutionary unrest, and it was here that he found local support from a reform-minded lawyer named Dr. Eugen Neuberger.[45] Yet when the revolution began, not one, but two councils of intellectual workers appeared in the city. The economist Lujo Brentano led the first of these *Räte* alongside sixteen of his colleagues, who were concerned with protecting the interests of the university against the danger of its politicization by the revolution.[46] Declaring that the new republic could not do without the assistance of the intellectual workers, the council stated its goal as: "promoting the good of the entire people by making intellectual work legitimate and to secure within this framework its conditions of existence."[47] This council essentially became a professional association, which claimed a considerable number of members and issued its own publication titled *Der geistiger Arbeiter*. Similar apolitical councils appeared in several other cities including Stuttgart, Hamburg, and Königsberg.[48]

The writer Heinrich Mann led the second council of intellectuals in Munich. Recognizing the possible confusion of the two, this group adopted the name *Politischer Rat geistiger Arbeiter* (PRGA), inspiring the Berlin council to later do the same. The engagement of German intellectuals in politics was something Mann had advocated well before the revolution, most notably in his influential essay from 1911, "*Geist und Tat*," which urged German authors to speak out against injustices similar to the role of writers during the Dreyfus Affair in France.[49] Now, in its first public proclamation, the PRGA stated its support for the overthrow of the Wittelsbach dynasty. It further declared their commitment to democracy, evoking the memory of the revolutions of 1848, and stated their desire to help promote the development of a "social republic."[50] Certainly, this

---

45 Eugen Neuberger, Aktivismus, Münchener Neueste Nachrichten, 17.10.1918. Hiller ultimately had to cancel the full lecture series due to his catching the flu.

46 See Lujo Brentano, Mein Leben im Kampf um die soziale Entwicklung Deutschlands, Jena 1931, 353.

47 Organization der geistigen Arbeit, Münchener Neueste Nachrichten, 15.11.1918.

48 For the programs of these apolitical councils in Munich and Stuttgart, see the documents Satzungen des Vereinigung "Rat geistiger Arbeiter" for Munich, and Leitgedanken des Bundes geistiger Arbeiter, and Der Bund geistiger Arbeiter und Arbeiterinnen, for Stuttgart, all of which are held in the Bayerische Staatsbibliothek.

49 Heinrich Mann, Geist und Tat, in: Das Ziel 1 (1916), 7-8. Hiller had found this call to action so compelling that he used it as the leading essay in the first volume of his yearbook. Mann originally published his essay in the expressionist journal Pan. See Heinrich Mann, Geist und Tat, in: Pan 1:5 (January 1911), 137-143.

50 Organization der geistigen Arbeit, Münchener Neueste Nachrichten, 15.11.1918. This program lists the following members of Munich's PRGA: „Edwin Scharf, sculptor, uni-

adherence to the democratic tradition in Germany differentiated Munich's PRGA from the council in Berlin. If Hiller wanted to introduce rule by intellectuals – those he considered the *aristoi*, or the best – Mann, in particular, was far more sympathetic to Kurt Eisner's vision of using the council system as a whole for "schools of democracy."[51] Nevertheless, both shared an ethical understanding of socialism and an emphasis on subjectivity that was common to nearly all of these councils. In a speech before the provisional national assembly, a Herr Kaufmann summarized his understanding of the purpose of Munich's PRGA as follows:

"We ourselves are not a party-political organization, but what unifies us is our declaration of belief in democracy, our declared belief in socialism. Key to this is not the state or economic form, but much more the disposition. We want to become new people, not just people living under a different form of state or economy."[52]

For Mann, who addressed the PRGA on December 1, 1918, in a speech titled "The Meaning and Idea of the Revolution," this subjective aspect to the revolutionary changes also involved a new moral beginning. "One should not pretend that the socialization of even the last aspect of human activity is the most radical thing to be done," he explained.[53] "There is a radicalism that surpasses all eco-

---

versity professor; Wilhelm Specht, doctor; Heinrich Mann, writer; Paul Graener, composer, Kurt Stieler, actor, professor; Willi Geiger, painter; Dr. Eugen Neuberger, lawyer; Dr. Hierl, Reallehrer, Dr. Bruno Frank, writer, Dr. Röggerath, private instructor."

51 On Eisner's view of the councils, see Kurt Eisner, Aufgaben der Räte. Rede auf der ersten Sitzung des Münchener Arbeiterrats am 5.12.1918, in: Freya Eisner (ed.), Sozialismus als Aktion. Ausgewählte Aufsätze und Reden, Frankfurt 1975, 78-80. For Eisner's use of the expression "schools of democracy," see Tagung der Landes-Arbeiter, Soldaten- und Bauernräte, Münchener Post, 17.2.1919. In his speech at Eisner's funeral on 16.3.1919, Mann declared "the one hundred days of the Eisner government brought forth more ideas, more joys of reason, more vitalization of the spirits than the fifty previous years." Heinrich Mann, Kurt Eisner, in: Macht und Mensch, Munich 1919, 170. See also Waltraud Berle, Heinrich Mann und die Weimarer Republik. Zur Entwicklung eines politischen Schriftstellers in Deutschland, Bonn 1983, 80.

52 Verhandlungen des provisorischen Nationalrats des Volksstaates Bayern im Jahre 1918/1919. Stenographische Bericht, no. 5, 106. Quoted in William Ludwig Bischoff, Artists, Intellectuals, and Revolution: Munich, 1918-19, Diss. phil. Harvard 1970, 163. Translation amended.

53 Heinrich Mann, Sinn und Idee der Revolution in: Macht und Mensch, Munich 1919, 163. This speech was originally printed in Münchener Neueste Nachrichten, 1.12.1918.

nomic changes. It is the radicalism of the *Geist*."[54] This meant for Mann that intellectuals needed to play a leading role in facilitating the reconciliation of Germany with the rest of the world, something that could only be brought about, he believed, in the name of "eternal ideals."[55]

Munich's PRGA met repeatedly throughout the revolutionary period up until at least May of 1919, focusing its activities on holding public lectures by its members.[56] Examples include a talk by Bruno Frank on December 10, 1918, titled "*Von der Menschenliebe*," in which he argued that the humanistic sensibility of intellectuals placed them in a position to see beyond class-based interests and promote the general good.[57] Later on January 8, 1918, Neuberger delivered a speech on "Socialism as a Human Necessity," followed by a talk by Fritz Saenger titled "Socialism, a World Economic Demand."[58] Whereas Neuberger's talk premised the necessity of socialism on the ethical principles of Immanuel Kant and Johann Gottlieb Fichte, Saenger's talk focused on the problem of overproduction in the global capitalist economy.[59] A subsequent meeting on February 6, 1919 included a discussion on the council system and the theme of "organic and representative democracy."[60] Already within the councils that endorsed the Berlin program one can see significant differences, most notably around forms of governance. Some of the more peripheral councils in Germany reinforce this perspective.

5. REGIONAL VARIATION

In considering the relationship of the other councils in Germany to Berlin's RGA, the *Rat geistiger Arbeiter* in Göttingen is an especially important example to consider. Here, a lawyer named Carl Garms was the key figure behind its

---

54 Ibid.
55 Ibid., 165.
56 George Mosse writes that Munich's PRGA met only once, and when it learned of the existence of a similar council in Berlin, it decided to disband. This is inaccurate, however. The agendas of many of the council's meetings can be found in the Heinrich Mann Archiv held in the Archiv der Akademie der Künste, Berlin. See Mosse, Left-wing Intellectuals, 189.
57 Bruno Frank, Von der Menschenliebe, Munich 1919, 8.
58 Einladung zur 2. öffentlichen Versammlung, AdK, Heinrich Mann Archiv, 365.
59 Sozialismus als menschliche Notwendigten in: Der geistige Arbeiter 2 (17 January 1919), 4.
60 Politischer Rat Geistiger Arbeiter, AdK, Heinrich Mann Archiv, 366.

initial formation, later to be joined by the neo-Kantian philosopher and youth movement leader, Leonard Nelson, along with three of Nelson's followers from the *Internationaler Jugendbund* (IJB): Klara Deppe, Max Hodann, and Hans Mühlestein.[61] In the case of Göttingen, like Berlin, continuity with a group that existed prior to the revolution was once again significant. Göttingen's RGA was not an entirely spontaneous creation. Rather, establishing a council gave its members a platform with which they could independently enter the public sphere in order to promote their ideas about cultural reform.

As Garms explained in a letter to Nelson from November 12, 1918, Mühlestein's previous efforts to influence the local soldiers' and peoples' councils [*Volksrat*] could only be regarded as a failure to date.[62] Yet Garms still believed it was possible to play a leading role in the revolution. "In Berlin," he remarked, "the beginning has already been established," and he pointed to the announcement about the *Rat geistiger Arbeiter* that had appeared on the previous day in the *Berliner Tageblatt*.[63] Garms informed Nelson that he had already contacted the Berlin council to express his interest in forming a local group, under the unstated precondition, however, that Nelson would join and assume a leadership position, which Nelson agreed to.[64]

Nelson's subsequent involvement in this council would suggest a great deal of congruence between Berlin and Göttingen, especially considering that Nelson had agreed to Hiller's request that he contribute essays to the first two volumes of *Das Ziel*. This was not the case, however. The program of the Göttingen council was unique, containing only four points that were principally aimed at a reform of education. It declared: "We are opposed to the monopoly on education, that the means and rise to *Bildung* is reserved for a specific class and tied to material wealth and external accomplishments."[65] The second point declared the council's opposition to every form of dogmatism in the sciences, art, and religion, whereas the third called for the necessity of political engagement: "We entirely reject all forms of cultural-political neutrality that serve as a way of

---

61 Additional council members included Kurt Baumann and Johannes Lochner. There were seven members in total including Garms and Nelson. For essays by Deppe and Mühlestein, along with documents from the IJB, see Bertha Gysin (ed.), Der Völker-Bund der Jugend, Leipzig 1920.

62 Carl Garms to Leonard Nelson, 12.11.1918, BArch, Nachlass Leonard Nelson, N2210/45.

63 Ibid.

64 Ibid.

65 Gründung eines Rates geistiger Arbeiter, BArch, Nachlass Leonard Nelson, N2210/45, 5.

forgetting social responsibility [...]."⁶⁶ Finally, the program concluded with a demand for a new era of law and reason in international relations.

This, together with the absence of Nelson's name among those who later endorsed the Berlin program, expressed the fact that Nelson intentionally wanted to distance the council's activities from Hiller and his circle. In an unsigned letter from the Nelson *Nachlaß* dated November 16, 1918, Nelson's personal secretary clearly expressed his feelings about the Berlin council:

"He [Nelson] wants to say to you in strict confidentiality that he does not want to enter into the public with personalities such as Hiller. He assumes that you also do not take seriously the intellectual and moral dilettantes, who have founded and lead the Berlin *Rat der geistigen Arbeiter*, and see themselves as the representatives of the German spirit."⁶⁷

The Göttingen council thus steered an independent course that primarily focused on negotiations with the Prussian Minister of Culture, Konrad Haenisch, about the formation of a new school for political leaders. Nelson considered the greatest threat that Germany was facing in the transition to a parliamentary democracy was a question of *Kulturpolitik*: with the separation of church and state, it would no longer be possible to curtail the influence of the churches in matters of *Bildung*.⁶⁸ He thus proposed the formation of a single school, "a *Führerschule*," dedicated to the cultivation of leaders, who would later be capable of reforming the entirety of public education.⁶⁹ Although receiving an audience with Haenish on January 8, 1919, while fighting from the Spartacist Uprising was taking place in the streets of Berlin, these negotiations ultimately proved to be unsuccessful. Nelson's vision of a school for leaders was only realized several years later with his establishment of the *Landerziehungsheim Walkemühle* in 1923.⁷⁰

The disparate quality of these councils is also suggested by the example of Leipzig. The *Berliner Tageblatt* announced the organization of this council on November 23, 1918. Its founding call repeated the theme of extending the revolution into the realm of culture and the specific role of intellectuals in this task:

---

66 Ibid.
67 Leonard Nelson to Herr Scheffler, 16.11.1918, BArch, Nachlass Leonard Nelson, N2210/45, 15, 1-2.
68 Ibid., See also Rede des Herrn Dr. Nelson gehalten am 8. January 1919 im Kultusministerium, BArch, Nachlass Leonard Nelson, N2210/44, 45.
69 Rede des Herrn Dr. Nelson gehalten am 8. January 1919 im Kultusministerium, BArch, Nachlass Leonard Nelson, N2210/44, 46.
70 Leonard Nelson, Über das Landerziehungsheim Walkemühle, in: Die Tat 17:11 (February 1926), 869.

"Parallel with the political and economic transformations, a radical '*geistige*' reformation also must be demanded. Only the gathering together of intellectual workers guarantees the unbounded development of cultural and artistic creation. So, too, can an ethical politics only be realized though the strong influence of the cultural powers on the entirety of our public life."[71]

While this council was similarly organized around the theme of cultural renewal and the assumption that intellectuals needed to play a leading role in facilitating it, it also did not fit neatly under the rubric of Hiller's *Aktivismus*.

As Hans Natonek, a member of the Leipzig council who personally endorsed the Berlin program, later reflected in his essay "*Räte geistiger Arbeiter und Aktivismus*," despite Hiller's efforts, the councils of intellectual workers were never able to form a unified movement. "The centralization that those in Berlin had in mind proved to be unfeasible," he observed.[72] Although sharing a common goal of influencing Germany's cultural and political life, Natonek believed that these councils were ultimately powerless to do so. Additional problems presented themselves in Leipzig. Here, the council eventually split into two groups over the question of its relationship to socialist party doctrine. "Instead of being a great collection and representation of the cultural interests we had in Leipzig a socialist *Rat geistiger Arbeiter* and a political partyless working group of the intellectual professions."[73] This ultimately led Natonek to the conclusion that the councils of intellectual workers failed precisely because they were not more closely aligned with Hiller's *Aktivismus*.

In the case of Hamburg, the Berlin program served as a template for drafting a more moderate agenda. The judge and art collector Gustav Schiefler played a leading role in forming the politically oriented council in Hamburg. According to Schiefler's account from 1921, Dr. Hans Fischer had contacted him at the beginning of the revolution, encouraging him to lead a local council like the RGA in Berlin, and together they were able to able to unite a small group that met for the first time on November 15. Presented with the question of whether the purpose of their association should be based on the interests of the intellectual professions or "the representation of the demands of the *Geist* in the regulation

---

71 Ein Rat geistiger Arbeiter in Leipzig, Berliner Tageblatt Morgenausgabe, 23.11.1918, 3.
72 Hans Natonek, Räte geistiger Arbeiter und Aktivismus, in: Akademische Rundschau 7:8 (May 1919), 190.
73 Ibid., 191.

of public affairs," those assembled decided unanimously in favor of the latter.[74] Yet when the neo-Kantian philosopher Albert Görland read the program of Berlin's RGA out loud, encouraging those in Hamburg to adopt it as their own, the group was immediately split between radicals such as Görland, and a more moderate faction grouped around the architect and urban planner, Fritz Schumacher, who wanted to substantially revise the Berlin program. Personal affinities between Görland and Schumacher, however, eventually allowed for a compromise around a document that Schumacher drafted. Görland, in turn, suggested the name *Werkbund geistiger Arbeiter* to distinguish their group from another *Rat geistiger Arbeiter* formed in Hamburg on November 24 based on the professional interests of its members.

The *Werkbund* first published its program in Schiefler's journal, *Die Literarische Gesellschaft*, at the end of November 1918.[75] Although this document shared similarities with the Berlin program, it also avoided many of its concrete demands in favor of those that were more abstract. In the place of the Berlin RGA's call for the abolition of the death penalty, for example, the *Werkbund* demanded a more a "more humane criminal law."[76] While declaring its opposition to the violation of the individual, be it "political, military, or economic," it also fell short of calling for an end to military conscription. In the end, the *Werkbund* ultimately focused its activities on advocating for a university and *Volkshochschule* in Hamburg, in response to not only the large numbers of students returning from the demobilized army but also more importantly as a way of cultivating what Görland described as "a new people."[77]

This rewriting of the Berlin program from a more moderate perspective was also true in the case of Breslau. Here the physicist Otto Lummer led efforts to form a local council. As he explained in a letter to Gerhart Hauptmann in reference to his ideas for a program, "I have also not included the destructive, damaging, and foolish points of the Berlin RGA. I pursue only *Realpolitik*, and subsequently only such goals that cannot do harm [...] when they are brought into

---

74 Gustav Schiefler, Eine Hamburgische Kulturgeschichte 1890-1920: Beobachtungen eines Zeitgenossen, in: Gerhard Ahrens/Hans Wilhelm Eckhardt/ Renate Hauschild-Thiessen (eds.), Hamburg 1985, 552.
75 Der Werkbund geistiger Arbeiter, in: Die Literarische Gesellschaft 4:12 (1918), 381-382. See also Fritz Schumacher, Ein Werkbund geistiger Arbeiter, Die Tat 10:2 (1918/19), 786.
76 Der Werkbund geistiger Arbeiter, 381
77 Albert Görland, Der Mensch der neuen Zeit und seine Schule, Hamburg 1920, 7.

reality by true democrats and enthusiastic supporters of a republic."[78] Lummer similarly rejected Hiller's ideas about intellectuals leading their own branch of government. "We do not want to want to form a parallel parliament like the RGA or to expropriate money or land like those in Berlin."[79] Yet despite these notable differences, Lummer also hoped the council could serve as a means to initiate a broad series of cultural and political reforms, ranging from changes in criminal law to the educational system.[80]

Finally, in the case of Dresden, preparations for a council of intellectual workers began when a group of nine men gathered around the publisher Heinar Schilling distributed leaflets calling for a public meeting of the *Revolutionären Rates der Geistesarbeiter* to be held on November 21, 1918. This council soon differentiated itself from the others in Germany, however, by defining its main task as winning the support of the middle class for socialism. The former leader from the left wing of the German youth movement and Wyneken follower, Alexander Schwab, gave the council's opening address in which he spoke of the precedent in Berlin and the need to form a local council, not as a trade union of the intellectual professions, but as a grouping of intellectuals committed to the realization of socialism.[81] At the conclusion of the meeting, those in attendance decided to rename the group the *Sozialistische Gruppe der Geistesarbeiter* (SGG), as a way of making clear their political commitments, and passed a resolution that endorsed the formation of a socialist republic. Debates about the meaning of socialism, its ethical or proletarian basis, and how it should be realized shaped nearly all of the council's remaining public assemblies.[82]

---

78 Otto Lummer to Gerhart Hauptmann, 16.11.1918, Staatsbibliothek zu Berlin Preußischer Kulturbesitz, Handschriftenabteilung, Nachlass Gerhard Hauptmann, GH Br Nl Lummer, Otto, Bl. 8.

79 Ibid.

80 For more on Lummer's efforts in Breslau, see Reimund Torge, Der Physiker Otto Lummer in Breslau: Kulturelle und politische Aktivitäten von 1918 bis 1920, in: Berichte und Forschungen 6 (1998), 165-174.

81 Sozialistische Gruppe der Geistesarbeiter, Menschen Montagsblatt 21.1.1919, 3.

82 For a discussion of the council's relationship to the expressionist movement in Dresden, see Frank Almai, Expressionismus in Dresden. Zentrenbildung der literarischen Avantgarde zu Beginn des 20. Jahrhunderts in Deutschland, Dresden 2005.

6. FAILURE TO UNITE

By May 1919, the radical phase of the German Revolution had come to an end with the overthrow of the *Räterepublik* in Munich by the *Freikorps*. It was against this backdrop that the Berlin and Viennese councils attempted to unite all of the councils of intellectual workers behind a common program at a weeklong congress in Berlin from June 15–21, 1919. As members of the Berlin council explained in a letter to Heinrich Mann in which they hoped to secure his participation, they saw this as the moment to now update the program that Hiller had originally circulated in November 1918.[83]

This letter explains that despite the need to revise elements of the old program in view of changes that had come about in the revolution, most of the original cultural-political demands were just as relevant now as they were at the end of the war: "The official parties conspicuously neglect these demands, and our main axiom, the inviolability of life, isn't merely disregarded, it's not even recognized. That even the independent socialists have not yet included the abolition of military conscription in their program, this alone should suffice as evidence that the 'revolution' has far from made our movement superfluous."[84]

Hiller's report, later printed in the fourth volume of *Das Ziel*, left no doubt about his disappointment with the outcome of the *Aktivistenkongress*, however. Over the course of the week, the gathering witnessed no more than 150 participants at its high point, and although its organizers had great hopes about drawing intellectuals from throughout Europe, the vast majority only came from Berlin.[85] The Viennese council later cited problems with the transportation networks that prevented Müller from attending as its representative. In his place, they sent a telegram in support of the congress restating the council's emphasis on anti-militarism and belief in leadership by *die Geistigen*.[86] Mann was also conspicuously absent, and with the signing of the Treaty of Versailles taking up much of Europe's attention, there was no public acknowledgement of what took place at the meeting.

Debate at the congress focused on four main themes: the problem of violence, individual freedom, radical educational reform, and the uniting of *die Geistigen*.[87] In the revised version of the program, the congress maintained once

---

83 Kurt Hiller, Erich Bielschowsky, and Rudolf Leonhard to Heinrich Mann, 7.5.1919, AdK, Heinrich Mann Archiv, 3112.
84 Ibid.
85 Kurt Hiller, Kongressbericht, in: Das Ziel 4 (1920), 211.
86 Der Strahl 1:2 (January 1920), 74.
87 Hiller, Kongressbericht, 211.

again that its first and ultimately unconditional demand remained the "inviolability of life." Yet despite this shared commitment, Hiller noted that three factions clashed with each other, without any one of them claiming a majority: a "quakerish-Tolstoyan, anarchistic faction in favor of absolute non-violence, a libertarian-socialist, Left-pacifistic (sanctioning violence in certain cases) tendency of our inner circle, and a Lenin-fascinated tendency of aggressive red violence."[88] Its second clause endorsed all means of social change except those that violate the first principle. The congress endorsed an anti-capitalist position in the third, and in its fourth, it combined an idiosyncratic interpretation of aristocracy with its other two pillars of pacifism and socialism. Purportedly situating its critique of parliamentary democracy within the framework of the council tradition, Hiller now introduced the idea of a "double dictatorship" in this section:

"[W]e demand the political-economic dictatorship of those who create material wealth through their labor, and the cultural-political dictatorship of those whose revolutionary creation establishes cultural values – without consideration of whether it is a majority or minority that has dictatorial means at their disposal."[89]

The program thus called for the introduction of the pure council system and the propagation of parallel economic and cultural councils. Finally, in the remaining fifth and sixth clauses, the congress adopted an international outlook and rejected the idea of forming a political party.

Although most of these principles reaffirmed the positions outlined in the various articulations of Hiller's *Aktivismus* from 1915 on, it became clear at the congress that substantial differences existed among those in attendance. Despite endorsing councils of intellectual workers as the primary means for achieving of their goals, the Berlin PRGA recognized that the collapse of the broader council movement in Germany had also sealed the fate of these cultural-revolutionary institutions, and it finally agreed at the end of congress to disband.[90]

88 Hiller, Logos, 136–137.
89 Ibid., 213.
90 Hiller, Logos, 138.

7. INTELLECTUALS AND THE POLITICS OF CULTURE

What this survey indicates is that the council idea was capable of captivating the imagination of many intellectuals throughout German-speaking Central Europe in the revolutionary period. In this respect, the activities of the PRGA in Berlin served as a powerful example, inspiring the formation of councils elsewhere. Despite a shared emphasis on cultural renewal, however, the political solutions these intellectuals arrived at were often quite different. This meant that Hiller's neo-aristocratic politics were by no means the only position advanced by these groups, and it is certainly questionable whether a majority of those who actually signed onto the Berlin program embraced all of the positions Hiller personally advocated.

If, as I am suggesting, the councils of intellectual workers should not be wholly subsumed under Hiller's political philosophy, what then did it mean for intellectuals to organize themselves in this way? What I believe these councils made possible was the creation of an institutional space in which men and women of letters could advance cultural reforms outside the parameters of the traditional labor movement and its parties. This had a correlate in the distinctly anti-materialist variant of socialism that many of the individuals active in these councils adhered to despite their differences in perspective about how it should be institutionalized. They understood socialism as much more than just a socio-economic system, and did not consider class conflict the primary means through which it could be achieved. "If economic socialism is the watchword of our time," Hiller explained in reference to the Berlin group, "the council of intellectual workers gives it a cultural-political accent."[91] The Viennese council similarly noted that it understood the primary purpose of uniting intellectuals was as a means to "preserve the cultural revolution amidst the overturning of just the material conditions."[92] Neuberger echoed these same sentiments in Munich in an essay written in memory of Eisner in which he described these new kinds of socialists: "They transform the economic movement of socialism into one of culture; indeed, they see in the socialist movement the one possibility of a cultural and humanistic politics, as opposed to horse-trading and economics, in this time of degeneration."[93]

---

91 Hiller, Wer sind Wir?, 89-90.
92 Dr. Franz Kobler and Robert Müller to Heinrich Mann and the Munich "Political Council of Intellectual Workers," 20.2.1919, AdK, Heinrich Mann Archiv, 2781.
93 Eugen Neuberger, Geistiger Sozialismus, Der Revolutionär 3 (5 and 12 March 1919), 2.

Both this organizational form and the distinct variety of socialism articulated within it exemplify something Bourdieu describes as the "paradoxical synthesis of the contraries of autonomy and political engagement," shaping the role of the modern intellectual.[94] For Bourdieu, the power of intellectuals stems precisely from their independence from political affairs, i.e., their autonomy, such that in moments of crisis their entrance into the public sphere carries particular symbolic weight. This impact is actually derived from their otherwise non-involvement in politics, as illustrated by the example of the role of writers during the Dreyfus Affair in France.

The significance of the politically oriented councils of intellectual workers, then, is that they created a space that allowed intellectuals to preserve their independence, while also serving as a locus for cultural political engagement during the revolutionary period. This is consistent with what motivated Nelson's participation in the Göttingen council, for example. In contrast with Hiller's attempt to create a mass organization of intellectuals and demand for power, Nelson believed that there was a better way to enter the public sphere. As his personal secretary relayed, "With a small circle of personalities, Nelson thinks that one could gain the necessary moral power by influencing public opinion, which is necessary in order to achieve something reasonable."[95] With this "moral power," members of these councils hoped to initiate dramatic changes in cultural policy ultimately aimed at creating a new people, who were capable of moving beyond a past discredited by war and military defeat. It is in this sense that we should understand Mann's hopes about the "radicalism of the *Geist*," and this also allows us to explain the significant emphasis placed on ideas of educational reform in nearly all of these *Räte*.

But if this independence from traditional politics served as the source of their authority, it also meant their marginalization from many of the institutions through which these reforms might have been realized, bringing to an end the dream of uniting the *Geist* and political power, and relegating them to the position of outsiders and the role of social critics – one that we now commonly associate with intellectuals today. As Natonek concluded, one saw the same pattern repeat itself time and time again in these various *Räte*: "The so-called intellectuals in a city gathered together, established themselves as a council of intellectual workers, composed declarations and programs, created subcommittees [...] and

---

94 Pierre Bourdieu, Fourth Lecture. Universal Corporatism. The Role of Intellectuals in the Modern World, in: Poetics Today 12:4 (Winter 1991), 658.
95 Leonard Nelson to Scheffler, 16.11.1918, BArch, Nachlass Leonard Nelson, N2210/45, 15.

then everything was eerily quiet again."[96] The contrast between the hopes and realities of November 1918, illustrated by these numerous programs and their limited implementation, reminds us that in the search for Germany's revolution of 1918–19, one must also listen for its silences.

---

96 Natonek, Räte geistiger Arbeiter, 191.

Simultaneity of the Un-simultaneous

German Social Revolution and Polish National Revolution in the Prussian East, 1918/19

JENS BOYSEN

1. INTRODUCTION

After decades of research, it is still not easy to decide when and why exactly things began to slide towards revolution in Imperial Germany at the end of the First World War. One certainty is that the revolution that overthrew the Imperial order was the consequence of defeat in 1918 and not *vice versa*. Before the war, and even very late into it, there was no "revolutionary situation" in Germany in the sense of Marxist (or other) theory. Even though this was to a considerable degree owed to manipulated official information on the actual state of the war that broke only in autumn 1918, the German people had until then shown great discipline and loyalty. Complaints and demands, e.g. by the workers, were made mostly *within* the semi-participatory structures that had been established during the war in a peculiar kind of 'popular authoritarianism', notably under the Law for Patriotic Auxiliary Work (*Hilfsdienstgesetz*) of 5th December 1916.[1]

Moreover, precisely the allegedly 'unreliable' Social Democrats, generally little inclined towards revolution, had been loyal to the state throughout the war at the price of no small moral sacrifice. In the final phase of the war when the German Army began to dissolve, and the civilian and military authorities lost control of public life, the majority of the Social Democrats (MSPD) did their

---

1 Petra Weber, Gescheiterte Sozialpartnerschaft – gefährdete Republik? Industrielle Beziehungen, Arbeitskämpfe und der Sozialstaat. Deutschland und Frankreich im Vergleich (1918-1933/39), Munich 2010, 127-129.

utmost to preserve a – reformed, parliamentary – monarchy as the only apparent means to maintain national cohesion in the face of Allied pressure, as well as to avoid a Bolshevik revolution in Germany.

This led to choices, interpreted by some – leftist or liberal – historians as a "betrayal" of an unfolding social revolution, or at least a "failure" to grasp that apparent opportunity.[2] What followed was cooperation with the Imperial elites, and the decision to fight the more radical left-wing forces refuting parliamentary democracy and aiming toward a (more or less) Soviet-styled "republic of councils".

The decision was made against the background of politico-ideological as well as strategic considerations in late 1918. Actually, it was not born out of the blue. On the one hand, the Ebert-Groener Agreement, in a way, continued cooperation under the *Hilfsdienstgesetz*. On the other, the separation of MSPD and USPD[3] in 1917 had created bitter enmity between the two socialist parties. While, nevertheless, the USPD joined the Council of People's Deputies in November 1918 (despite leaving by December of that year), more radical forces that sought to push developments further, attracted the MSPD leaders' wrath since they jeopardised the standing, if modest, achievements of the revolution, and moreover threatened to provoke Allied intervention.

In any case, in Berlin and the other large German cities, i.e. at the centre stage of political events, the Majority Social Democrats finally resorted to force against an identified political enemy. At the same time, they widely failed to recognise another force that, while it seemed to be part of the revolutionary process, turned out to be merely a free-rider with goals effectively detrimental to the German national interest: the politicised Polish national movement in the eastern parts of Prussia, principally the widely rural provinces of West Prussia and Posen.[4]

---

2 One of the protagonists of this view was Sebastian Haffner in his Die verratene Revolution – Deutschland 1918/19, Hamburg 1969. Similarly, if less radically: Eberhard Kolb, 1918/19. Die steckengebliebene Revolution, in: Carola Stern/ Heinrich August Winkler (eds.), Wendepunkte deutscher Geschichte 1848-1945, Frankfurt 1979, 87-109. Reinhard Rürup, Friedrich Ebert und das Problem der Handlungsspielräume in der deutschen Revolution 1918/19, in: Rudolf König/Hartmut Soell/Hermann Weber (eds.), Friedrich Ebert und seine Zeit. Bilanz und Perspektiven der Forschung, Munich 1990, 69-87.

3 Mehrheitssozialdemokratische Partei (MSPD) and Unabhängige Sozialdemokratische Partei (USPD).

4 To some degree, a similar situation existed in Upper Silesia. But there, social life was greatly shaped by industrial relations. Moreover, the Silesians had their own regional identity that often defied clear assignments of "Germanness" or "Polishness". For this

As will be argued in this essay, the drawn-out war, and the accompanying political changes, created a situation in the Prussian east by which a long-term, but rather inactive tension between the ethnic Polish population and the German-Prussian state was gradually heated, and turned into a sort of post-war 'front'. Indeed, that 'national' dimension had been present throughout Imperial German history, but only now, in an unprecedented systemic crisis, it generated a disruptive potential.[5] Thus, the German revolution of 1918 created conditions for a drifting apart of the political goals of the majority population on the one hand, and those of a national minority on the other. This also belied (as would the Paris peace treaties) the idea of a 'transnational' movement towards progress in the international order, and quickly shifted the major parameters of political positioning back to the principle of national competition.

As to *when* this conflict materialised, there is some contradiction here with of the accepted views in Polish historiography.[6] There, the events that began in 1918 – notably the final secession of territory from Germany to the new Polish state – are often interpreted as merely the continuation of a deliberate and active policy aimed towards national independence on the part of all "Poles", as the next step following a permanent cultural and political resistance against "Germanisation"[7]. This position is based on an essentialist insistence on national continuity beginning with the final partition of Poland in 1795 throughout the "long" 19th century. One major factor leading to this questionable view lies in a

---

reason, Upper Silesia, on which region already exists an abundant literature, is not covered in this article. For example, see James E. Bjork, Neither German nor Pole. Catholicism and National Indifference in a Central European Borderland, Ann Arbor 2008.

5 ‚Classic' accounts of Imperial Germany such as Hans-Ulrich Wehler, Krisenherde des Kaiserreichs 1871-1914. Studien zur deutschen Sozial- und Verfassungsgeschichte, Göttingen 1970, tend to exaggerate the peace-time significance of ethnic/national issues.

6 For example, see Janusz Pajewski, Odbudowa państwa polskiego 1914-1918 [The reconstruction of the Polish state, 1914-1918], Warszawa 1978. Likewise, see the many unreflecting nationalist premises in Janusz Karwat, Od idei do czynu. Myśli i organizacje niepodległościowe w Poznańskiem w latach 1887-1919 [From idea to deed. Independence-related thoughts and organisations in the Poznań province, 1887-1919], Poznań 2002.

7 On the difficulty of this term, see Witold Molik, Procesy akulturacyjne i asymilacyjne w stosunkach polsko-niemieckich w XIX i na początku XX wieku. Stan i postulaty badań [Processes of acculturation and assimilation in Polish-German relations in the 19th and early 20th centuries. State of the art and challenges], in: idem/Robert Traba (eds.), Procesy akulturacji/asymilacji na pograniczu polsko-niemieckim w XIX i XX wieku, Poznań 2000, 65-96.

lack of consistency regarding the considerable changes to the social and cultural fabric of the Polish population during that period, in the context of 'alien' imperial states and the onset of modernisation. While these processes are well known to historians, the fairly obvious conclusion is that this rather excludes the idea of an unchanged Polish nationhood, and is difficult to acknowledge by a society that during most of the 20th century was reared on national myths rather than critical reflection.[8] Another shortcoming, more of a methodological nature, is the generalisation of 'patriotic' attitudes held in the 19th century by Polish noble and grand bourgeois families, suggesting the same attitude for all ethnic Poles.[9] Of this, however, there is little empirical evidence.

Actually, precisely in the Polish case – given the backwardness of the old *Nobles' Republic* – the emergence of a modern nation could only happen through a fundamental modernisation of the societal and civilizational fabric. This was initiated notably in Prussia by the protagonists of "Organic Work", such as Karol Marcińkowski and Hipolyt Cegielski. Their concept saw self-modernisation as a precondition for a possible political restart. The result of these efforts was a better education and economic development of the Poles in Prussia enabling them to stand up to German competition.[10] But this did not imply any militant separatism or even secessionism; rather, it was part of a Europeanization process.

In my view, this topic is a useful example to discuss "Subjectivities and Social Movements". Social/political activity is generally driven by individual and/or group interests. When the final phase of the First World War created a situation in which the essential political framework changed in an earth shattering manner, a new pattern of those interests and of political power distribution emerged that was characterised by a national/ethnic definition of interests, in addition to the war-time confrontation between the military alliances and domestic societal tensions.

---

8 This phenomenon still pervades political culture in Poland; on the „politics of remembrance" cf. Agnieszka Pufelska, Raub der Clio – die polnische Geschichtspolitik und ihre Exekutoren, in: Thomas Flierl/Elfriede Müller (eds.), Osteuropa – Schlachtfeld der Erinnerungen, Berlin 2010, 33-56.

9 For examples see cf. Tadeusz Gustaw Jackowski, W walce o polskość [In the fight for Polishness], Kraków 1972; Piotr Krzysztof Kuty, Schedlin-Czarlińscy w walce o polskość Prus Zachodnich 1860-1920 [The Schedlin-Czarliński family in the fight for the Polishness of West Prussia 1860-1920], Lublin 1996.

10 Cf. William W. Hagen, National Solidarity and Organic Work in Prussian Poland, 1815-1914, in: The Journal of Modern History 44:1 (1972), 38-64.

In autumn 1918, the political and societal actors in Germany were confused as to the likely future of the country and possible constellations of domestic power. Under the armistice, foreign and domestic decisions of utmost importance had to be taken and kept in a delicate balance. Given the situation, the Council of People's Deputies was little prepared to deal with yet another major 'front', much less with one that did not correspond to the dominant confrontation along societal lines.

A related problem in this context was a sort of structural incapacity on the part of the former opposition forces of the Imperial era – Social Democrats, left Liberals and political Catholics – to adapt their perception of 'friend and foe' to the changed circumstances. Ever since Bismarck, the representatives of societal and national opposition – i.e., the aforementioned parties as (mostly) ethnic Germans and the non-German parties – had often been lumped together by the conservatives as "enemies of the Reich" (*Reichsfeinde*). And indeed, as a reaction to such hostility, on many occasions those various groups had cooperated, notably during sessions of the German *Reichstag* and the Prussian Diet (*Landtag*).

In any case, despite their cooperation with the military, in November 1918 the new civilian leaders had difficulty switching their perception to help them understand the emerging new frontline in the east.

2. THE PRUSSIAN POLES BEFORE AND DURING THE FIRST WORLD WAR

Essentially, the ethnically Polish citizens of the Reich (or, as Bismarck had called them, "Polish-speaking Prussians") had throughout the war fulfilled their duties no less correctly than the ethnic Germans, both at the battle fronts and at the home front. True, there was little enthusiasm among them for the war since did not then belong to the privileged 'core' of Wilhelminian society for whom the German Reich was dear and worth defending: in the first place Protestant, especially upper or middle class, German-speakers. Here one has to be aware that by this definition, there were large groups also among the ethnic Germans that hardly shared the proverbial "August experience" of 1914, notably – but not only – if they were Catholics as e.g. in (southern) Bavaria.[11] In Prussia, the Ministry of War maintained the right, until the eve of the World War, of a selective

---

11 Benjamin Ziemann, Front und Heimat. Ländliche Kriegserfahrungen im südlichen Bayern 1914-1923, Essen 1997; Wilfried Loth, Katholiken im Kaiserreich. Der politische Katholizismus in der Krise des wilhelminischen Deutschlands, Düsseldorf 1984.

recruitment policy giving preference to conservative, Protestant, rural and – except for the officer corps – lower class individuals.[12] Still, by 1914, Catholics – the same as the Social Democrats – had become widely integrated, and would withstand the hardships of the war, even if they could not fully grasp its meaning, as did most "ordinary" people anywhere in Europe.

According to the military authorities, ethnically Polish conscripts, just as the Germans, joined the ranks without any serious problems. Likely, this was principally an effect not of fear or force but of their century-long integration into the German, and in particular Prussian, administrative and military system.[13] Ludwig Bernhard raised another issue during the first days of the war. Bernard was a known author, supportive of an active "Eastern Marches policy" who sought to strengthen the German position in the ethnically mixed eastern provinces. In a report to the Deputy Chief of the General Staff in Berlin, dated 16th August 1914, he stated that the mobilisation and generally the loyalty of the Poles had been facilitated by the "infiltration of the Polish populace with German settlers". Both these groups had been controlling each other, which had created an "atmosphere of vigilance, thrift and energy".[14]

In fact, in the pre-war decades, tensions had been growing between Germans and Poles, or rather, between the Polish population and the Prussian authorities due to the latter's so-called *Polenpolitik* – measures that aimed at limiting Polish economic and cultural advancement since Germany was perceived as a nation state.[15] The most important result of these – mostly non-violent – struggles, had been an inner distancing of many Poles from the Prussian-German state that had increasingly disappointed their expectations of equal treatment as citizens and, not least, as serving members of the Prussian Army.[16] Accordingly, they had

---

12 Christoph Jahr, Gewöhnliche Soldaten. Desertion und Deserteure im deutschen und britischen Heer 1914-1918, Göttingen 1998, 63-65.

13 On the 'borussification' of the military organisation after 1871, see Manfred Messerschmidt, Das preußische Militärwesen, in: Wolfgang Neugebauer (ed.), Handbuch der preußischen Geschichte, Vol. 3: Vom Kaiserreich zum 20. Jahrhundert und Große Themen der Geschichte Preußens, Berlin etc. 2001, 319-546, esp. 397-408.

14 Geheimes Staatsarchiv Preußischer Kulturbesitz (GStAPK), Titel 863a: Weltkrieg, besonders Polenfrage, Nr. 2b: Preußische Polenpolitik. Verhalten der Polen im Kriege 1914/18, f. 252-256.

15 For a still useful overview – though rather outdated on many details – see Martin Broszat, 200 Jahre deutsche Polenpolitik, Munich 1963, 129-172.

16 For an example see Wolfgang Hofmann, Das *Ansiedlungsgesetz* von 1904 und die preußische Polenpolitik, in: Jahrbuch für die Geschichte Mittel- und Ostdeutschlands 38 (1989), 251-285.

built separate cultural and economic networks to become more independent of the German majority.[17] However, these associations, though pronouncedly "national", were as a rule not of a secessionist character. Indeed, there is little evidence – in contrast with claims made by traditional Polish historiography[18] – that the Polish-speaking population as a whole had become disloyal to the Prussian-German state before the war, and had been waiting for an opportunity to break away from it. Rather, it is likely that the ethnically and denominationally mixed rural population of Prussia's eastern provinces continued to have a lot in common in terms of lifestyle, work relations and mindset. Elderly Poles who had fought in the Wars of Unification, often were members of veterans' organisations, regardless of criticisms spewed by nationalist circles.[19]

Thus, before 1914, secessionism was the fringe position of a small number of Polish nationalists and academic youth who mirrored their peers in other nations by longing for a major war to "air" the stifling atmosphere of Europe and – possibly, but very unlikely – help create a new Polish state.[20] Thus, the (in)famous prayer by the Polish national poet Adam Mickiewicz for a "general war for the freedom of the peoples"[21], most certainly did not mirror the wishes of the majority of Polish-speakers in Germany (or in Austria or Russia, for that matter). Rather, what probably all Poles indeed feared during the "war fever" before 1914 was the prospect of having to fight their relatives wearing the enemy's uniform. In that respect, it may have been a relief to those Poles under military duty that according to the Schlieffen Plan most military units in the Prussian east were sent to the Western Front in August 1914. Only after 1915,

---

17 Rudolf Jaworski, Handel und Gewerbe im Nationalitätenkampf. Studien zur Wirtschaftsgesinnung der Polen in der Provinz Posen 1871-1914, Göttingen 1986.

18 For this position, see e.g. Marceli Kosman, Powstanie Wielkopolskie na tle walk o przetrwanie narodowe pod zaborem pruskim [The Greater Polish Uprising in the context of the battle for national survival under Prussian rule], Poznań 1993, 46.

19 Jens Boysen, Zwischen Königstreue und nationaler Standortbestimmung. Zur Bedeutung der Kriegervereine in den deutsch-polnischen Ostprovinzen Preußens während des Kaiserreichs (1871-1914), in: Studia Historica Slavo-Germanica (Poznań), 143-165.

20 Jens Boysen, Preußische Armee und polnische Minderheit. Royalistische Streitkräfte im Kontext der Nationalitätenfrage des 19. Jahrhunderts (1815-1914), Marburg 2008, 279-282.

21 This phrase stems from Mickiewicz's poem "Pilgrims' litany" (Litania pielgrzymska), a part of his "Books of the Polish people and Polish pilgrimage" (Księgi narodu polskiego i pielgrzymstwa polskiego) published in Paris in 1832; quoted after Dorota Siwicka, Romantyzm 1822-1863, Warszawa 1997, 104.

would some Prussian Poles come to serve in the German administration of the occupied Russian Imperial territories, including "Congress Poland".

So, the Prussian Poles *did* fight for Germany, if often with little enthusiasm. True, in some places during the first days of August 1914, the military authorities had carried out prophylactic arrests of leading persons whom they suspected might possibly sabotage or hamper the mobilization: not only Polish nationalists, but also Social Democrats, "anarchists" and other perceived "enemies of the Reich". [22] However, these measures were repealed shortly thereafter since no evidence of any treacherous activities could be found, and because the government was interested in having the minority leaders' – at least tacit – support for a war that was universally expected to be short.[23] As in other respects, the unexpected length of the war changed the situation at home, and relations between the state and national minorities.

3. LIMITS OF POLISH LOYALTY

In the home front, the Prussian Poles, especially their leading circles – politicians, journalists and most of all priests – showed a somewhat restrained attitude. Obviously, the Catholic clergy duly prayed for the Kaiser and his armies' victory, and called upon the Poles to fulfil their civic duties.[24] Polish enterprises joined the Reich's war economy and were given governmental commissions.[25] Since the provinces of Posen and West Prussia (as well as Silesia) narrowly escaped a Russian invasion in the summer of 1914 , and for the rest of the war were not touched by armed hostilities, these regions were relatively safe and continued their peacetime function of securing foodstuff for the Army and the urban populations. However, the local and regional authorities soon realised that Polish loyalty was a matter of the given situation rather than an expression of positive identification. A Prussian *Landrat* (county administrator) said as early

---

22 Again, I ignore here Upper Silesia that was situated in the substitution district of the VIth Army Corps with headquarters in Breslau.

23 Report by the Oberpräsident of the province of West Prussia in Danzig of 03.09.1914 to the Prussian Minister of the Interior, in: Geheimes Staatsarchiv Preußischer Kulturbesitz (GStAPK), Titel 863a: Weltkrieg, besonders Polenfrage, Nr. 12: Verhaftung von Polen (1914-1917), f. 45-49.

24 Jerzy Kozłowski, Wielkopolska pod pruskim zaborem w latach 1815-1918, Poznań 2004, 279.

25 Friedrich Swart, Die Stadt Posen im Deutschen Reich (1871-1918), in: Gotthold Rhode (ed.), Geschichte der Stadt Posen, Neuendettelsau 1953, 127-154.

as 1915 that although the Poles were not hostile to the German cause, they were only conditionally loyal to it.[26]

In particular, Polish-language newspapers, being the Prussian Poles' main source of information, took an almost neutral (equidistant) position when reporting on the state of the war, in this way avoiding any identification with the German cause even though tens of thousands of Poles fought in the German ranks. Since reprimands by the Prussian authorities did not help to change the Polish editors' attitude, Polish newspapers remained under special censorship even when in late 1914, control of German newspapers was partly lifted.[27]

In a similar way to the journalists, many Polish associations and the (lower) Catholic clergy, fostered an attitude of "minimal loyalty" and a distanced attitude towards the "German" war. Characteristically, Poles tended not to fly the German flag upon news of German victories, and subscribed much less than ethnic Germans to war loan schemes;[28] neither did they support (much) the German Red Cross. One might say that while the whole population of Germany had to face human and material losses, the ethnic Germans sought to give a patriotic sense to the war, an attitude difficult for many Poles to share. Indeed, Polish associations had been providing support to the Poles in the German-occupied part of Russian (Congress) Poland since 1915; in this way, they identified with their ethnic brethren and also nourished a self-image as an innocent victim nation. Although this comportment testified to a quite unwanted attitude from the point of view of the German authorities, the latter came to see it as the second best option to make at least indirect use of the Polish community's economic and moral resources for the war. Therefore, they allowed the setting up of a privately funded *Support Committee for the Kingdom of Poland* (*Komitet niesienia pomocy w Królestwie Polskim*)[29] under the protectorate of the archbishop of Gnesen (Polish: Gniezno) and Posen (aPoznań). In March 1915, the Prussian

---

26 Letter by Landrat of Schwetz county of 10.01.1915, in: GStAPK , Titel 863a: Weltkrieg, besonders Polenfrage, Nr. 12: Verhaftung von Polen (1914-1917), f. 274-279.

27 Copy of an order issued by the Deputy Commanding General of Army Corps No. XVII (Danzig) of 14.08.1914, ibidem, f. 53.

28 Piotr Kosiński, Prusy Zachodnie 1914 – Pomorze 1920. Ludność regionu wobec przemian politycznych okresu I wojny światowej, Warszawa 2002, 144-145. I thank my colleague Piotr Szlanta, Warsaw, for additional information confirming this finding.

29 Throughout the 19th century, the Poles called the Russian part of Poland the "Kingdom" according to its original constitution of 1815, even though Tsar Alexander II had in 1864 abolished its autonomy and incorporated the territory into the Russian Empire, in response to the Polish Uprising of 1863.

military command even provided a car and fuel for a delegation of that Committee sent to Russian Poland.[30]

In spite of all these indicators for a less than full-fledged support to the German cause, until 1916/17 there was no sign of disloyalty among by far most Polish speakers in Germany. True, groups of Polish-German deserters roamed some parts of the Prussian countryside, but this was without greater meaning to the general situation.[31] To be sure, nationalist elite groups clearly did consider a German defeat as an opportunity to gain more political freedom, if not independence. Although the leading Polish party in Prussia was the anti-German *National Democrats* (Endecy), their local leaders did not share the preference for an alliance with Russia as initially proposed by their Warsaw-based leader Roman Dmowski. In fact, they welcomed Dmowski's change of heart in late 1916 when he began to woo the Entente powers to recognize the Poles as allies in the alleged "war for democracy". When the US entry into the war in 1917 began to favour the Allied side, Polish activists enhanced their efforts to gain, not only an independent Polish state, but even a leading position in Central Europe by way of bringing forward imperialist concepts that envisioned the Poles as a leading nation ruling over Lithuanians, Byelorussians and Ukrainians, as had been the case until 1795.[32] With regard to the envisaged western border of Poland, as both the Tsarist and the provisional Government in Russia had done until the October Revolution of 1917, now the Western allies could offer the Poles all those territories claimed to be Polish, thus questioning German territorial integrity.

4. THE PRUSSIAN POLES AND RUSSIAN POLAND

While these considerations, however, until the end of 1918 were the matter only of abstract discussions among small circles of exiled Polish politicians, another

---

30 Supplement of the Polish daily Dziennik Kujawski of 04.04.1915, Nr. 78, in: State Archive Poznań, Inventory 294 – Polizeipräsidium Posen, Sign. 81: Wiadomosci wojenne (wycinki z gazet) 1914-1917, Bl. 13.
31 Piotr Kosiński, Prusy Zachodnie 1914 – Pomorze 1920, 41-42.
32 The border of the area claimed for the new Polish state by Roman Dmowski and which comprised large areas of German, Lithuanian and East Slavic territory, was referred to as "Dmowski's Line". Later, he reduced his claims in the east in favour of a more ethnic nation state with a strong anti-German and pro-French foreign policy. At the same time, though himself strongly anti-Socialist, he was opposed to Pilsudski's anti-Soviet policy. Margaret Macmillan, Paris 1919. Six months that changed the world, New York 2003, 212-213.

factor turned out to have a growing effect on the consciousness and political attitudes of the Prussian Poles: the pro-Polish policy executed by the German administration in occupied Russian Poland. Among a whole range of measures aiming to re-Polonize public life, the reopening of the University of Warsaw figured prominently as a genuinely Polish institution.[33] The temporary 'peak' of this development was the proclamation of a "Kingdom of Poland" on 5 November 1916 on behalf of the two Emperors Wilhelm II and Franz Josef I. However, the hoped-for recognition for this move – that meant a breach of international law since Congress Poland formally still belonged to Russia – on behalf of the Poles had not manifested itself (notably, a planned Polish Army to support the Central Powers for all intents and purposes never materialised), but rather fuelled further Polish claims to full sovereignty.

Even worse, the on the whole benevolent German policy in Russian Poland not only met with little success there, but in addition proved to have a detrimental effect on domestic relations in the Reich since there was a visible gap between this policy and the still restrictive policies on the ethnic Polish population in Prussia. The inherent logic of the Prussian *raison d'état* was to keep the Prussian Poles strictly separate from the Poles in Russian Poland (and even Austrian Galicia), but practical policy could ever less maintain this separation the longer the war lasted. One characteristic issue to illustrate this was a drawn-out dispute between German and Austrian authorities over the question of whether, and under what conditions, to open the borders between Germany, Austria and occupied Russian Poland for private Polish-language postal service. While the Austrians – on whose side a large number of Galician Poles were active – favoured a quick decision, the Germans were much more hesitant with a view to the need for censorship for which, however, they lacked personnel. Finally, in mid-1916, the Germans gave way despite their worries, mainly in order to limit tensions with their Austrian ally.[34]

This visible lack of consistency and unity on part of the Central Powers, together with Allied declarations in 1918 about the stateless nations' "right to self-determination", made Polish national activists in Prussia stage nationalist manifestations on occasions such as the death of the anti-German minded Noble Prize winner for literature Henryk Sienkiewicz in 1916, and on the 100th anni-

---

33 After the Polish Uprising of 1863, the University had been closed down and later re-opened as a Russian-language institution.
34 Bundesarchiv Berlin (Federal Archives) Berlin, Inventory R 1501: Reichsamt des Innern, Rechtsabteilung – Militaria, Generalia, Nr. 14, Adh. 5: Postverkehr mit den besetzten Gebieten Russlands (Gouv. Warschau).

versary of the death of General Tadeusz Kościuszko[35] in 1917. The strategic priority of the Reich leadership was to build a chain of client states in the east out of the Russian Empire's periphery, and thus given their good relations with the Poles, they often disregarded and overrode the Prussian administration's need to maintain state authority on the home front. In effect, the latter were increasingly urged by the Reich leadership to tolerate Polish nationalist manifestations, a fact that was (quite aptly) interpreted by Polish nationalists as a weakness, and further encouraged agitatation in the Polish population.[36] Nevertheless, until mid-1918, the German occupation of vast territories in Eastern Europe, and the stalemate in the west, left the outcome of the war open, and so far, the Prussian east had not experienced any significant impact either military or political. Moreover, most Prussian Poles, even then still displayed an essentially loyal attitude towards the King's government.

5. THE END OF WAR AND THE BEGINNINGS OF ORGANISED POLISH SEPARATISM IN GERMANY

Accordingly, Polish separatist groups were still small in early 1918. A secret local branch of Józef Piłsudski's Warsaw-based *Polish Military Organization* (Polska Organizacja Wojskowa) was founded in February in Posen;[37] but it remained without much influence in the National Democrats' stronghold given Piłsudski's and Dmowski's personal and political rivalry. The National Democrats came to control the *Central Citizens' Committee* (Centralny Komitet Obywatelski) that was set up in July 1918 as a clandestine structure uniting the Polish right-wing parties, which were by far in the majority. But only after the failure of the German offensive of spring 1918, and the subsequent breakdown of the Western front in summer 1918, and especially in light of the recognition by the Western powers of Poland as an allied nation, Polish politicians in Germany began to organise themselves openly. In October 1918, the Polish deputies in the German Reichstag and the Prussian diet declared themselves representa-

---

35 Kościuszko had fought in the American War of Independence, and in 1794 had been the liberal leader of the Polish Uprising against the Russians.

36 Cf. a report by the Deputy Supreme Command of the Vth Army Corps in Posen of 01.11.1917 to the Prussian Ministry of War, in Bundearchiv (Federal Archives) Berlin, Inventory R 43: (Alte) Reichskanzlei, I. Stammakten, Gr. 28: Parteien, 1. Politische Parteien, 1/5: Polen, 8 vols. (1900-1918), vol. 8 (1916-1918), f. 136-140.

37 Jerzy Kozłowski, Wielkopolska pod pruskim zaborem w latach 1815-1918, Poznań 2004, 281.

tives of the "Polish nation" and claimed the provinces of Posen, West Prussia, (Upper[38]) Silesia and other territories for the envisaged Polish state.[39] At the same time, they urged Polish members of the dissolving German Army to keep their arms and bring them to their home regions. Essentially, the Polish activists did not then plan an armed uprising but put their hopes on Western powers to help them achieve their goals. One reason for this was that up until then, the majority of Prussian Poles had not yet developed a clear political attitude and could not be relied upon to participate in any military action. Thus, the armed soldiers were at this point mainly regarded as an instrument to secure control upon the expected withdrawal of German troops.

However, to the surprise of the Polish leaders in Posen and Paris, the armistice of 11th November 1918 left the entire Prussian east under German control, and postponed the issue of possible territorial changes until the upcoming peace conference. Apart from the Allies' interest in keeping the German Army as a shield against the Bolsheviks, the British and Americans had growing doubts regarding the Polish claims to German territory, and were in no hurry to invest the Poles with sensitive areas.[40] In this situation, the National Democrats in Posen maintained close contact with Piłsudski in Warsaw as well as with Dmowski in Paris, and sought advice regarding their behaviour. While Piłsudski was at that time interfering in the Russian Civil War with the aim of territorial gains, and thus unwilling to open another front in the west, the Polish National Committee in Paris was encouraged by the French government to initiate an armed rebellion and create facts before the peace conference started.[41]

---

38 At the time, Lower and Upper Silesia formed one province that was divided on 14th October 1919 as preparation for the plebiscite on the adherence of Upper Silesia to Germany or Poland, Walther Hubatsch (ed.) Grundriß zur deutschen Verwaltungsgeschichte 1815-1945, Reihe A: Preußen, Bd. 4: Schlesien, Marburg/Lahn 1976, 8.
39 Speech made by the Polish Reichstag deputy Count Stychel on 23 October 1918, in: Stenographische Berichte des Reichstags, Vol. 214, 6196-6197.
40 MacMillan, 93-106. Michael Schwarz, "Ethnische Säuberungen" in der Moderne. Globale Wechselwirkungen nationalistischer und rassistischer Gewaltpolitik im 19. und 20. Jahrhundert, München 2013, 509.
41 Antoni Czubiński, Rola Wielkopolski i Poznania w kształtowaniu zachodnich i północnych granic odrodzonego państwa polskiego (1918-1921) [The role of Greater Poland and Poznań in the shaping of the western and northern borders of the reborn Polish state (1918-1921)], in: Andrzej Kwilecki (ed.), Polska myśl zachodnia w Poznaniu i Wielkopolsce. Jej rozwój i realizacja w wiekach XIX i XX, Warszawa etc. 1980, 63-127, here 95/96.

The main force that came into play here was a group of ethnic Polish soldiers of the Prussian Fifth Army Corps stationed in Posen and other garrison towns, as well as reservists and wounded soldiers that had been sent home, often with false attests issued by ethnic Polish military doctors.[42] In the summer of 1918, these soldiers began to collect and hide arms, gather information about the strategic situation of the Prussian Army, and sought to put themselves in important positions within the territorial units. By doing so, they wanted to make sure that no action could be taken by the army against the possible establishment of a Polish administration.

Later, during the interwar era, it was disputed whether these conspirators belonged to Pilsudski's or Dmowski's camp.[43] From today's point of view, it appears most appropriate to assign them a mixed political allegiance and a regional perspective. Eventually, the political cover for their actions was provided largely by the National Democrats who were believed to benefit most from this political change. In any case, for a long time the conspirators remained a small clandestine group with little contact with the civilian population.

At the same time, the Polish leaders in Posen sought a negotiating position vis-à-vis the new Republican government in Berlin: On 10th November, in Posen, a *Workers' and Soldiers' Council* was founded as part of the all-German arrangement for revolutionary structures. The same day, the *Central Citizens' Committee* in Posen renamed itself the *Supreme People's Council* (Naczelna Rada Ludowa), and claimed the status of local representative of the Polish nation next to the ethnically neutral *Workers' and Soldiers' Council*. The Polish usage of the term „People's Council " (Rada Ludowa) expressed a claim to democratic (not socialist) legitimation and so drew on the post-1917 *zeitgeist* that made practically everyone, including liberal and even certain right-wing circles, talk about some kind of "Socialism" as the new political order after the war.[44] In Posen, the term "People's Council", while lexically related to "Workers' Council", did not share the latter term's class-related meaning, but mainly expressed the National Democrats' idea of a classless, unified ethnic nation whose political goals would be predefined by the 'natural' leaders, i.e. the national-conservative elites.[45] When some more insightful groups among the Germans and Jews came

---

42 Karwat, 307-309.

43 For a summary that remains relevant today, see Dietrich Vogt, Der Großpolnische Aufstand 1918/1919. Bericht-Erinnerungen-Dokumente, Marburg 1980, 1-5.

44 For example, see Walther Rathenau's reflections on Germany's "socialist" future in his Von kommenden Dingen, Berlin 1917.

45 On the allegedly "national" attitude of all Poles, see Witold Łukaszewicz, Ogólna charakterystyka Rad Robotniczo-Żołnierskich i Chłopskich w Wielkopolsce i na Po-

to understand this national(ist) approach, they created their own "People's Councils"[46] however, these were quickly neutralised by their Polish counterparts who had already seized the crucial positions in public life. Likewise, they managed to take control – at least in the province of Posen – of the *Citizens' Militias* (*Bürgerwehren*) that were set up in autumn 1918 upon orders by the Reich government to maintain public order. The military equivalent to this development was the establishment by the Prussian military command of *Security Companies* (*Sicherheitskompanien*) within the garrisons in the border area; here, the Polish military conspirators saw to it that 'their' men occupied the pivotal positions in these companies.[47]

The readiness of the German *Council of People's Representatives* in November 1918 to talk on an equal level to the Polish bodies in Posen whose members were after all still German and Prussian citizens had several reasons: the Western powers demanded it, the Poles promised to adhere to the law and preserve order, and a priority for the upcoming winter was to secure the food supply from the agrarian east for Berlin and the industrial centres.[48] Moreover, the German left wing parties had in the past opposed the anti-Polish policies and where now ready to make certain concessions, even if not territorial ones. A special governmental envoy of known Polish sympathies, Hellmut von Gerlach, went to

---

morzu Gdańskim 1918-1920 [General characteristics of the Workers', Soldiers' and Peasants' Councils in Greater Poland and West Prussia, 1918-1920], in: Witold Łukaszewicz/Jacek Staszewski/Mieczysław Wojciechowski (eds.), Z dziejów rad robotniczo-żołnierskich w Wielkopolsce i na Pomorzu Gdańskim, Poznań-Bydgoszcz-Gdańsk-Toruń 1918-1920, Poznań 1962, 15-59, here 33 and 41.

46 On the German example, see Mike Schmeitzner, Deutsche Polenpolitik am Ende? Alfred Herrmann, der Deutsche Volksrat und die Nationalitätenkämpfe in Posen 1918/19, in: Johannes Frackowiak (ed.), Nationalistische Politik und Ressentiments. Deutsche und Polen von 1871 bis zur Gegenwart (Berichte und Studien 64), Göttingen 2013, 63-103. It should be mentioned here that People's Councils (Volksräte) were founded as well in purely German areas such as Lower Silesia. These bodies served to secure a smooth transition from the old to the new regime in the face of military insecurity. Jun Nakata, Der Grenz- und Landesschutz in der Weimarer Republik 1918-1933, Freiburg 2002, 55-58.

47 Vogt, Großpolnische Aufstand, 25-26, and Bogusław Polak, Walki powstańcze w Poznaniu (17 XII 1918 – 6 I 1919) [The battles of the rebellion in Posen (17.12.1918-06.01.1919)], in: Kronika Miasta Poznania 54 (1986), Nr. 4, 33-51, here 35.

48 Roland Baier, Der deutsche Osten als soziale Frage. Eine Studie zur preußischen und deutschen Siedlungs- und Polenpolitik in den Ostprovinzen während des Kaiserreiches und der Weimarer Republik, Köln etc. 1980, 192.

Posen on 18th November and received assuring statements about the "calm" situation there not only from the Polish representatives but as well from the civilian and military authorities. As a result, he agreed to use only "local" troops in the province of Posen, which meant – with a view to *Landwehr, Landsturm* and reserve troops – a predominance of ethnic Poles.[49]

Another important motive of the new Republican government was that in the face of revolution and counterrevolution at home, as well as the civil war in the Baltics and Russia, any additional problem that could endanger political stability had to be avoided. They had to find a balance between radical left-wing forces and the old conservative elites with whom they cooperated to avoid the breakdown of public order, but whom they did not fully trust. Especially complicated was their relationship with the *Workers' and Soldiers' Councils* that had sprung up everywhere after 9th November. As the actual source of revolutionary power, until December 1918 they often hesitated to pass that power on to the *Council of People's Representatives* as the institutionalised form of democratic reorganisation, and thus rendered political stabilisation more difficult.[50]

Here, one can identify a crucial difference between the German and the Polish perspective on the events of 1918/19. The revolution in Germany was a process of social reorganisation defined by the relations between classes, societal groups and political parties. Ironically, the national framework had been so reaffirmed by the World War that it was now not reflected upon much at all. As a consequence, the *Workers' and Soldiers' Councils* thought in terms of the classical "right-left" pattern, and were little receptive to the impact of other reference systems such as nationalism. However, the (elites of the) Poles and other stateless nations had just lived through that very stage of (political) national formation.[51]

---

49 Hellmut von Gerlach, Von rechts nach links, Reprint Frankfurt 1987, 232; and Baier, 193.
50 Cf. Ulrich Kluge, Die deutsche Revolution 1918/1919. Staat, Politik und Gesellschaft zwischen Weltkrieg und Kapp-Putsch, Frankfurt 1985, 54-69.
51 Cf. Miroslav Hroch, From National Movement to the Fully-Formed Nation: The Nation-Building Process in Europe, in: Gopal Balakrishnan (ed.), Mapping the Nation. London etc. 2012, 78-97.

6. THE DYNAMICS OF NON-UNIFORM REVOLUTION AND THE POLISH INCREMENTAL TAKEOVER IN POSEN

As a result, the German revolution had an accelerating effect on political processes in the province of Posen by undermining the existing public order, and its replacement by revolutionary bodies. While in the ethnic German core regions, the installation of revolutionary bodies did not change the national German nature of the body politic, in the ethnically mixed areas of the Prussian east it should rather trigger – in the view of Polish nationalists – a process of national differentiation leading up to secession. This 'simultaneity of the un-simultaneous' was not or too late realised by the German side. The Polish National Democrats who were both nationalist and highly conservative, regarded the social revolution in Germany as the result of defeat and inner breakdown. In their opinion, this could not concern the Poles as an Allied nation and thus "victors". This was in tune with the Western Allies' 'bourgeois' – anti-Bolshevist and anti-Socialist – position on the developments in Eastern Europe. Accordingly, the National Democrats made it clear at an early on that they were aiming to exploit the social upheavals in Germany for their own national revolution (which meant replacing a conservative German by a conservative Polish order).[52] In spite of this, left and liberal forces in Germany failed to register that crucial difference and erroneously regarded the Poles as allies in their battle against "Prussian authoritarianism".[53] This made them tolerate not only the *Citizens' Committees* (from mid-November 1918 renamed *People's Councils*) as local representations only of the Polish population, but in addition, the *Citizens' Guards* to be quickly dominated by the Poles even though they had been conceived by the Prussian Ministry of the Interior as nationally balanced bodies to secure public order.

This remained the principal Polish approach in the disputed areas. Formally, the Polish bodies assured the new Prussian and Reich authorities of their loyal cooperation for the sake of maintaining law and order, and of their support for "revolutionary achievements". In fact, however, they exploited the general state of confusion to execute a systematic outnumbering of the Germans in both the "revolutionary-democratic" and the traditional structures of public administration. The objective of this strategy was to politically Polonise the province, and

---

52 See, e.g., the main National Democratic journal *Kurjer Poznański* on 13th November 1918, quoted by Georg Cleinow, Der Verlust der Ostmark, Berlin 1934, 81. Similarly, this was uttered by the Endecja politician Władysław Seyda in early December 1918, Cf.Vogt, 22.

53 Cf. von Gerlach, 230.

isolate it from the German state – so pre-empting the expected peace settlement. In this context, existing German majorities at local or regional level were considered to be merely a technical problem that was to be resolved using all available means.[54] This implied a readiness to consider exerting pressure on the German population to leave what would become Polish territory, as later indeed happened.

Still, it needs to be emphasised that initially the National Democrats hoped to achieve these goals without any use of force, notably since they did not see any real chance of success given the still (at least outwardly) intact posture of the Prussian army in this area where during the war no fighting had taken place.

A particularly cunning tool used to mislead the German revolutionary authorities was to denounce as "reactionary" any local German criticism or resistance against the described changes,[55] which was rather bizarre given their own arch-conservative positions.

Indeed, the German members of the Posen *Workers' and Soldiers' Council* unknowingly played into the National Democrats' hands. They undermined the incumbent Prussian authorities whom they regarded as representatives of the old regime. At the same time, they accepted on 13th November 1918 formal parity between Germans and Poles but failed to realise that those Poles were delegates of the Polish *Supreme People's Council*. In fact, the Polish members were largely from aristocratic or middle-class backgrounds. When they came to dominate the provincial and local *Workers' and Soldiers' Councils,* they effectively became tools for Polish national reorganisation.[56]

Another crucial element here was the social and occupational structure in the province of Posen. With the exception of the city of Posen and a few other towns, it was a rural region inhabited by peasants, a few labourers and landowners.[57] . The nature of the revolution in industrial relations and class-based metropolitan society did not translate easily to the rural east. In any case, the assumptions by which the *Workers' and Soldiers' Councils* sought to drive revolution foundered in the east because the real cleavage there was national.[58]

---

54 Kozłowski, Wielkopolska, 286.
55 Vogt, Großpolnischer Aufstand, 31.
56 Ibidem, 18-19.
57 The cities and larger towns of West Prussia were predominantly German, while the industrial region of Upper Silesia, as mentioned, had a wholly different character.
58 In the more urbanised province of West Prussia, where the social structure of the Polish population was a bit more differentiated and 'modern' than in Posen, at least parts of the Polish workers did take an interest in the social agenda of the revolution, Czubiński, Rola Wielkopolski i Poznania, 88-89.

Altogether, one must admit a fundamental lack of critical awareness of Polish ambitions on part of the responsible German and Prussian institutions. Arguably, that was an outcome of the authoritarian governance style, a (too) trustful attitude towards formal legality and of the four-year self-deception (fuelled notably by the Supreme Army Command) over Germany's actual strategic situation. When the authorities failed to live up to their task of protecting the existing order, this led, together with the described bias on part of the *Workers' and Soldiers' Councils*, to a situation in which the German population was widely unable to produce an appropriate counterforce based on the same "national democratic" principles as the Poles.

After October 1918, the ethnically Polish masses that had so far showed a wait-and-see attitude, became more politicised and attracted to the national Polish idea. For them, this was a psychological way out of the otherwise bleak war experience. Within the context of the Western Allies' claim to lead the war for the liberation of the stateless nations, the Poles were granted the status of an independent and democratic nation that was supposed to play a role in securing the national-democratic reorganisation of the European landscape. In this way, while the ethnic German population, notably persons in public office, had to face a tremendous loss of position, the ethnic Poles could tear themselves out from this context by defining themselves as a victorious and 'morally unencumbered' nation.[59] But even now, there was no popular tendency towards any use of force; the conspirators kept pondering how to stage an uprising in such a way as to gain spontaneous mass support.

The Poles' *national revolution* went through similar stages of institutionalisation as did the social revolution in Germany, and was supported in this by the Polish authorities in Warsaw, which meant a violation of German sovereignty. De facto ruler Józef Piłsudski had on 30th October assured the German Envoy Harry Graf Kessler that he would not use force against Germany's eastern border, but on 26th November he included the provinces of Posen, West Prussia and Upper Silesia in the electoral scheme for the all-Polish *Constitutional Assembly* (*Sejm Konstytucyjny*). As a subsequent, equally illegal step, the *Supreme People's Council* in Posen organised the meeting of a *Partition Area Assembly* (*Sejm Dzielniczy*)[60] for Prussia from 3rd to 5th December. This was on the one hand, a measure to align the steps taken in Germany with the policies of the Polish government in Warsaw while National Democrat leader Wojciech Korfanty called

---

59 Roman Wapiński, Świadomość polityczna w Drugiej Rzeczypospolitej [Political Consciousness in the Second Republic], Łódź 1989, 195.

60 This referred to the partitions of Poland among Russia, Prussia and Austria in the late 18th century.

for unity among the Polish "estates" from the three areas.[61] On the other hand, it served to provide the up to then self-empowered *Supreme People's Council* with "parliamentary" legitimation, and thus end the revolutionary phase and enter into a 'regular' state-like phase of regime-building.

Still, as the entire Prussian east remained under German sovereignty, only German law applied in Posen. Moreover, as things stood, the Western Allies would have the final say about the future border. A such, after the meeting of the *Partition Area Assembly*, the Polish politico-military conspiracy was driven further, while the Prussian authorities were held by the Reich government and the Western Powers to rely on the stipulations of the armistice of 11th November. An occasion to strike offered itself to the Polish conspirators when Ignacy Paderewski, the famous pianist and mouthpiece of Polish nationalist ambitions in the west, announced his visit to Posen on 27th December. Although after debarking in Danzig he was bound to go to Warsaw, since he was escorted by British officers, the Germans could not prevent him from making his way to Posen. His arrival there created an emotional atmosphere in which the conspirators could hope to get support from the masses. In a deliberate move to provoke the German authorities, they hoisted the flags of the Allies next to the Polish flag. When German soldiers began to tear down the Allied flags, this was the signal for the conspiracy to strike. Using the moment of surprise, they came to control the city of Posen within a few days, and by January 1919 the bulk of the province. After that, the Germans managed to stop a further Polish advance to the south of the city of Bromberg; thus the rising could not spread to West Prussia and Danzig. When in early 1919, the German *Supreme Military Command* (OHL) prepared to reconquer the lost territory before the peace treaty was signed, the French pushed through that the prolongation of the armistice between Germany and the Western Allies of 16th February 1919 included the prohibition of any German military action against the Polish rebels. In this way, the *fait accompli* remained in place and was used by the Poles in Paris as evidence for their justified claim to these territories based on alleged popular will. However, in a certain contradiction to this logic, the Versailles Treaty would provide as well for the addition to Poland – without any referendum – of West Prussia as a predominantly German-inhabited region, which decision would lead to a massive forcible change of centuries-long grown population structures notably in the cities.

---

61 Document Nr. 2: Przemówienie Wojciecha Korfantego na zakończenie obrad Polskiego Sejmu Dzielnicowego [Speech by Wojciech Korfanty during the closing debate of the Polish Regional Diet], Poznań, 05.12.1918, in: W stronę Odry i Bałtyku. Wybór źródeł 1795-1950, vol. II (1918-1939), Wrocław 1991, 17/18.

As became visible here, Polish geostrategic interests and French protection granted to its new ally superseded the idea of national self-determination and facilitated the initiation of processes of de facto expulsion. Here, as in other areas of "reordered" Europe, the – at least claimed – Allied idea of a peace order built on the creation of 'pure' national spaces, and the allegedly 'natural' state of peace among democracies would founder on three contradictions. The newly created states were by majority neither nation states nor democracies, and they were anything but peaceful in the 'Darwinist' pursuit of their national egoisms. Moreover, their embracement of ethnic nationalism and military force as means of domestic and foreign policy avoided any thorough stabilisation of the region, and thus helped prepare the return, after 20 years, of the big players, Germany and Russia, in their worst possible versions, and their easy overthrowing of the Versailles Order.

7. FINALE: THE ESTABLISHMENT OF OFFICIAL POLISH RULE IN POSEN

A special *Ministry for the formerly Prussian Partition Area* (*Ministerstwo byłej Dzielnicy Pruskiej*) was established on 1st August 1919 in the Imperial Castle at Posen. Its task was to prepare the integration of these territories into the Polish state, and its first head was the National Democrat Władysław Seyda.[62] To be sure, in terms of international law, this territory (Posen and West Prussia) became part of Poland only through Versailles Treaty on 10th January 1920. Still, this step marked the de facto integration of this area into the new Polish state, and at the same time, mirrored the local Polish political elites' wish to exploit the still 'incomplete' status of "Prussian Poland" to gain a specific regional power base with as little dependence as possible on the national government in Warsaw. The policies run by the National Democrats and other right-wing parties in the region were guided, apart from anti-Germanism, by the "anti-revolutionary" agenda of keeping down any socialist or other left-wing forces and making "Western Poland" a conservative nationalist stronghold against the "red" Piłsudski regime in Warsaw.

Even though there was not much genuinely "red" content in the "socialism" of Piłsudski's *Polish Socialist Party* (PPS), it sufficed in the eyes of the *Endecy* that Piłsudski was less conservative than they were, was popular with the working class population in the more industrialised former Russian Poland, and most of all, enjoyed vast admiration as the (seeming) 'military founder' of the new

---

62 Cf. Andrzej Gulczyński, Ministerstwo byłej Dzielnicy Pruskiej, Poznań 1995.

Poland.[63] Notably on this latter point, in the face of widespread romantic militarism, the National Democrats' leader Roman Dmowski, despite his political experience and international contacts, could never hope to compete successfully with his rival at the national level.[64] As such, he and his followers would aim to have at least their own 'share' of the "national rebirth", emphasising two virtues as unique to Western Poland. It was – indeed – the historical cradle of Poland, with Posen and Gnesen having been the first political centres of the country in the Piast era. And *therefore* had been – much less credibly – a major centre of resistance against the partitions, and for striving for renewed independence.

8. CONCLUSION

When looking for transnational dimensions in the German revolution of 1918, its ties to the Polish national revolution in Prussia represents a particular point. Not only did this 'neighbourhood' confront two different perceptions of "revolution" at the end of the First World War, but the described process initiated a partial territorial and political break-up of the German Reich. The consequences were manifold. The Polish secessionist activities, too long ignored by the German side, triggered an irreconcilable national conflict much worse than anything seen before 1914. The loss of Posen and West Prussia added to the negative image with the political right of the November Revolution as "high treason", and helped undermine the Weimar Republic. On the Polish side, the "national revolution" did not entail much social progress but rather helped establish a nationalist and expansionist *raison d'état*, which in turn called in question the Allied claim of being able to create a better and more peaceful Europe.

---

63 Cf. Heidi Hein-Kircher, Political Cults as a Core Element of Political Culture. The Piłsudski-Cult during the Second Polish Republic as an Example, in: Magdalena Hułas/Jaroslav Pánek (eds.), Political Culture in Central Europe (10th-20th Century). Part II: 19th and 20th Centuries, Warsaw 2005, 181-201.

64 On their rivalry, Roman Wapiński, Rola Piłsudskiego i Dmowskiego w odbudowie państwowości [On Piłsudski's und Dmowski's roles in the rebuilding of statehood], in: Życie polityczne w Polsce 1918-1939, Wrocław 1985 (Najnowsze Osiągnięcia Nauki), 7-30.

Commentary

STEFAN BERGER

The contributions in this volume are a powerful call to de-emphasise the word 'German' in the term 'German revolution' of 1918/19. Indeed, the revolution was, in many senses, an intensely regional and an intensely transnational affair, even if it also had serious repercussions on the national imaginary. Ever since the boom years on the 'German revolution' in the 1960s and 1970s we can observe a steady stream, at times perhaps more of a trickle, of books and articles dealing with the revolution, often in regional perspective. Much of this research points to many differences in diverse parts of the German Reich and therefore to a need to localise the revolution in order to arrive at a less unilinear view of the many political and societal processes accompanying the revolution. At the same time, the 'German revolution' took place against a background of a European and even global revolutionary period lasting from around 1905 to around the mid-1920s. During this period we see a range of revolutionary upheavals, some successful, some unsuccessful, in different parts of the world, which need to be analysed together in order to understand both the specificities of these different revolutionary moments and to answer the question whether this period marks a universal moment in the global history of social protest. Of course, the recent explosion of studies in global history has found it much easier to arrive at a radical pluralisation of movements, protests and social processes, and it has been rightly cautious of formulating universals that are often steeped in western-centric logics. And the new global history has also chosen to focus more on global connectivities and interactions, thereby favouring the transnational over the comparative. However, a self-reflexive universalism should not shy away from asking the question whether we can identify universal moments, structures and problems in different realms of history, and combine such comparative investigations with an examination of interconnections between different revolutionary moments in diverse parts of the world. In the history of social protest, it could usefully be explored whether the period from around 1905 to around the mid-1920s forms a period of universal protest against a particular political, social and economic order that, for lack of a better word, we may call 'liberal capitalism'.

Opposition against and resistance towards the liberal capitalist order had been growing for a long time during the nineteenth century. It had, occasionally, erupted in violence and upheavals. The socialist and anarchist movements became the focal points of such opposition and protest. These movements were strongly transnational and even international in character, even if they were also subjected to intense nationalisation processes before 1914. The support of most socialist movements for the war efforts of their respective countries in 1914 powerfully underlines the extent to which these movements had been integrated into their respective nation states. Labour historians by and large, and with few exceptions, followed their protagonists and nationalised their histories, thereby contributing to the forms of methodological nationalism that ruled supreme over vast areas of historiography until fairly recently. Hence the question whether the 'German revolution' of 1918/19 can be contextualised as one spatial variant in a broader moment of global instability of capitalism is still looking for a convincing answer. The historiography of the revolution needs transnational perspectives in order to assess the question to what extent it forms part and parcel of a wider transnational moment of possibility for transformative change.

In some respects the 'German revolution' can be said to be well researched, especially when we come to the narrow politics of the revolution, i.e. the key political protagonists and the most important events during the revolutionary years of 1918/19. The groundwork was laid during the 1960s and the 1970s, at a time when there was a widespread societal feeling that the Federal Republic was in need of renewal and change, maybe even revolution. Protesting students, the beginnings of a coming-to-terms with the National Socialist past, widespread ambitions for societal reforms in many areas, reaching from education to a liberalisation of the law in diverse areas (abortion, homosexuality, family law) – all of this also meant that historians were keen to explore topics that seemed to raise the spectre of democratisation in the past. Sebastian Haffner's history of the 'German revolution' amounted to a fundamental re-interpretation of the revolution by an outsider. No longer was it seen as a Bolshevik threat that had been successfully averted by the forces of democracy – an interpretation upheld by leading post-war historians such as Karl-Dietrich Erdmann – instead it was now seen as a missed opportunity thoroughly to democratise Germany. The heroes of yesterday, such as Friedrich Ebert, became more problematical figures and the villains of yesterday, such as the Workers' and Soldiers' Councils now appeared in a more positive light. In a period, in which the democratisation of West-German society was high on the public agenda, historians also asked about the potential of the 'German revolution' to democratise German society at the end of the First World War. The seminal and pioneering works of Eberhard Kolb, Peter von Oertzen and Peter Brandt are prime examples of such research. From the 1980s onwards it became much quieter around the 'German revolution', although there has been some work, especially of a regional nature. What, one might ask, may be a contemporary incentive for researching the revolution today? One context is the current financial and economic crisis of capitalism, which has opened up spaces for discussing capitalism again. Far gone seems the triumphalism of a Francis Fukuyama, for whom the downfall of capitalism signalled the 'end of history' and the final victory of a liberal capitalist world order. This seems an appropriate moment to re-assess other moments of crisis of capitalism and to ask for potentials and past utopias that imagined alternatives to such liberal capitalist world orders. In other words, the global crisis of capitalism allows us to ask in which political and societal order we wish to live and what 'others' to capitalism are again imaginable. A look back into history might offer a range of interesting perspectives. Another possible context in which to re-assess the history of the German revolution is the global political threat from terrorism. Although terrorist violence is, of course, different from revolutionary violence, both provoke existing states and their monopoly on violence. Hence they threaten states and provoke harsh state reactions. How far, one might ask, has the state been prepared to go in the past and under which conditions?

Whilst historical research is always being carried out against the background of contemporary political and societal concerns, it cannot be reduced to the latter; it also follows its own 'scientific' logics, and it should even seek to protect the historicity of the past against all-too-facile instrumentalisations of the past by contemporary agendas and concerns. However, the development of research agendas and concerns within the field of history are often intimately connected to the development of wider self-understandings of the societies in which historians are working. Thus we witness, from the 1970s onwards, a re-definition of the political which goes far beyond party politics and formal political processes and comprises all spheres of human life and is captured by slogans such as 'the personal is the political' or Rainer Langhans' infamous statement 'what do I care about Vietnam; I have problems reaching orgasm'. In that sense, as can also be seen by several contributions to this volume, there is an increasing trend in the historiography of the German revolution to see the narrow political events of 1918/19 in a wider context of circles of revolution that comprise not only formal politics but also social, economic and cultural developments, including a pronounced gender politics. The concrete revolutionary upheaval of 1918/19 is thus connected to longer-term questions of societal change. Another example is the rise of media history in the midst of a media revolution associated with the rise of the internet and a digital revolution. The intense interest in media history makes it possible to re-assess the history of the revolution also from this perspective and to ask to what extent the media had the power to create and construct the 'realities' of the revolution and its subsequent perception. This leads us to the field of representations of the revolution and the diverse ways in which the revolution has been memorialised. The field of memory history has been an extremely prominent one over recent years, for reasons mostly associated with changing regimes of historicity and changing relationships in our perception of the interrelationship between past, present and future. We can indeed ask the question to what extent the revolution of 1918/19 has become part of the German realm of memory, and by extension, we might also ask, to what extent the wider revolutionary period between 1905 and the mid-1920s has become part of a European or global realms of memory. Whilst the answer to the former question is possibly no, the answer to the latter is definitely no. And yet we stand at the very beginning of explorations of memory cultures associated with the revolution. It remains very much a task for the future to explore the memory of the revolution as a palimpsest and to reveal the different layers of meaning that are part and parcel of this palimpsestic memory of the revolution.

I have so far pointed to three different ways of recontextualising and resituating the 'German revolution' of 1918/19 – first, the context of global challenges to liberal capitalism, secondly, the context of challenges to state order, thirdly, the context of representations and memory. In all three areas violence and the containment of violence are important features to be examined, and the concern with violence is also to the fore in many contributions to this volume. The revolution unleashed powerful energies to unhinge existing societal rules and borders and it called for a rebordering that produced manifold conflicts in the course of the Weimar Republic. The widespread call for 'calm and order' during the revolution was undoubtedly reflecting the desire of wide sections of the German population to channel the revolutionary energies into calmer waters and restabilise a society that had been, in the eyes of many, unhinged. Ironically, that desire was powerful also among many revolutionaries. After all, German socialists had been famous for their discipline and their self-control long before 1914, and whilst some, like the French socialist leader, Jean Jaures, or the British socialist Bruce Glasier ridiculed them for their concern with order and control, the socialist German subculture of order and discipline came to haunt them in the 'German revolution'. Lenin therefore surely had a point when he famously remarked that a German revolutionary would first buy a ticket to the station platform before occupying the train station. Large parts of German society, including German socialists, came to identify Bolshevism with disorder, whereas they longed for order, even if their vision of order was still substantially different from the order that had existed in Imperial Germany. The powerful discourse of 'calm and order' was indeed one reason why there was such a powerful urge of a return to 'normality' and an unwillingness to consider a more substantial reform of diverse sectors of society. The revolution had unleashed a new liberal regime with unprecedented lack of censorship and freedom of speech. This gave space for new social movements, including the homosexual emancipation movement. The revolution thus was also a movement of citizens and a moment for citizens in which they could feel both a new sense of empowerment and a sense of disillusionment with high hopes associated with revolutionary fervour.

The prominence of street politics and of unruly crowds in the revolution of 1918/19 seemed a sign that emotions, passions and irrational behaviour had gripped the populace, which many socialists were as afraid of as those intent on maintaining bourgeois order or aristocratic privilege. Ever since the brilliant work of Klaus Theweleit we are very much aware that the revolutionary, and even more so, the counterrevolutionary turmoil was associated with a perceived threat to the existing gender order. Yet the actual role of women in the revolution remains as underexplored as the detailed exploration of representations of manliness inherent in gender discourses during the revolution. There had been a mass mobilisation of women in the war, in which the governance of sexuality had become a key concern. This formed the background of fears about a changing gender order in the revolution, despite the fact that most of the key actors in the revolution, on all sides of the conflict, were men. Yet, as we have known for a long time, women were not mere victims of violence in the revolution. They had important roles on all sides of the conflict and were agents in that conflict, even if that agency remains to be fully explored and understood.

Let me, at the end of those brief reflections, return to the beginning and re-emphasize the benefits that can be derived from transnationalising the 'German revolution'. It is well-known that Friedrich Ebert was afraid of becoming the German Kerenskii in the revolution. The successful Bolshevik revolution in Russia was a major stimulans for actors in the German revolution. A global anti-Bolshevism in liberal capitalist regimes also meant that representations of the enemy were changing after 1917 – the Soviet Union rather than a militarist Germany now became the main enemy, so much so that, by the mid-1930s, only twenty years after the outbreak of the First World War, serious political forces in western liberal capitalist regimes considered allying themselves to fascist Germany in the struggle against the Communist Soviet Union. The strength of that anti-Bolshevism, I would argue, can only be understood if one takes into account the impact of the whole revolutionary moment from 1905 to the mid-1920s. It made the challenge to liberal capitalist orders real and it triggered a powerful defence of the order that was exacerbated by the ongoing economic and political crises in the interwar period, in which it could appear as though liberal capitalism was squeezed between Communism on the left and Fascism on the right. Ultimately liberal capitalism mustered a strong enough response to emerge resilient and powerful enough to form one of two possible world orders in the bipolar world of the Cold War. After the end of the Cold War, followed by a brief spell of capitalist triumphalism, liberal capitalism is again under pressure to justify itself. This, as this book demonstrates, is a good moment for studying revolutions.

Commentary

DIRK SCHUMANN

The revolution that ended the war for Germany and created the "Weimar Republic" – however we may define its duration –has been an understudied subject for a long time and remains so at present. It is to be hoped that the illuminating essays of this volume will help change this situation and trigger new research with the novel perspectives and questions they suggest. A commentary on the multifaceted work presented in this volume cannot be expected to discuss each of the contributions in detail. I will instead address some general issues that are brought up by them, primarily by those focusing directly on developments in Germany.

Moving away from older approaches to the revolution that focused on socio-political movements, political events, and institutions, the volume integrates more recent theoretical and methodological perspective, most notably the "cultural turn" with its many facets and also the "spatial turn". Rightly so and in line with recent scholarship on the Weimar Republic, it also distances itself from interpretations that posit a causal relationship between the revolution – in this older view typically seen as somehow "thwarted" – and the Nazi take-over in 1933. Instead, it places the revolution in a broader and earlier historical context, emphasizing the contrast between the fairly stable and peaceful prewar decades and the period of war and upheaval beginning in 1914. Thus, the revolution is to be seen first and foremost as an outcome of the war, not as the precursor of the later "German catastrophe".

In his monograph on Germany after the First World War, Richard Bessel characterized the Weimar Republic as a "post-war society". Defining the revolutionary period rather broadly, as lasting from 1916 to 1923, fits in with such a perspective. It may be helpful, though, to make this periodization more specific. From late 1916, given the dire food situation, given the split in the socialist movement, which resulted in the creation of the Independent Social Democrats (USPD) in 1917, and given the changing military odds following the entry of the USA into the war that same year, there was growing dissatisfaction among the German population, undermining the legitimacy of the Imperial government and, definitely since early 1918, taking on an explicit political character, as the continuation of the war itself was questioned and domestic reforms, such as the abolition of the Prussian three-tier suffrage system were demanded. However, these were still developments that only paved the way for the collapse of Imperial Germany, but not yet the concrete actions on the ground that brought about this downfall in November 1918 and the creation of a provisional government of the two Socialist parties.

Apart from these actions, contemporary perceptions do matter, as the editors point out in their introduction and as the contributions by Nadine Rossol and Mark Jones in particular demonstrate. For contemporary observers, the sight of overwhelming masses, marching peacefully through the streets, in combination with the perception of a "power vacuum" (Rossol), visually manifesting itself by the absence of uniformed policemen from the streets, left a profound and lasting impression, creating hopes or profound fears, certainly a sense of instability, depending on the social and political position of the observer. In this moment, what Reinhart Koselleck has termed the "horizon of expectations" ("Erwartungshorizont") was profoundly altered and opened up. From a culturalist perspective, the specificity of the historical moment that the revolutionary events of the fall and winter of 1918/19 created thus becomes evident. Hence, this suggests to take the revolutionary events seriously in their own right and to distinguish clearly between a preliminary stage of the revolution and the revolution itself as string of key events and impressions. It also suggests examining how perceptions of politics changed or were reinforced among Germans as a result of the impressions of the crucial days from November till January. This would include studying coverage of events in Berlin and other capitals, especially Munich, in the press and other media and the references that this produced in the years to come in the media. For this purpose, the typology of crowds provided by Mark Jones in his essay is helpful.

Taking 1916 as the starting point of the revolutionary process raises the question to what extent the actors in this process above all aimed at ending the war and to what extend (and from what point in time) they also wanted to put an end to Imperial Germany and set up a new democratic order, however defined. If the character of the revolutionary movement as a peace movement is stressed (e.g. by Michael Geyer), this would help explain why it lost momentum and size after the beginning of 1919 and became focused on and radical in specific regions. The argument of Oliver Haller's piece, however, complicates the picture. In his view, the collapse of morale on the Western front in 1918 was due not so much to a "covert military strike", as Wilhelm Deist has described it, but rather to overall exhaustion caused by an influenza epidemic that disproportionately weakened German soldiers. As these soldiers, according to Haller, otherwise would still have been willing to hold their own against the Allied onslaught, this then would suggest a bigger divide between the soldiers and the civilian population at home and would cast some doubt on the assumption of a gradually growing quest for peace on the front and at home. From this perspective, the revolution would seem to have been largely an affair of Germans on the home front. The argument also sheds new light on Friedrich Ebert's well-known, fateful, and somehow misinterpreted remark, when addressing troops returning to Berlin, that no enemy had defeated them on the battlefield. How this revisionism will hold up, remains to be seen. It will certainly require more research on how frontline troops reacted to the revolutionary momentum building up in Germany in the fall of 1918 and to the actions of their navy comrades that eventually triggered the overthrow of the monarchies.

A focus on space is among the research perspectives in the history of the revolution that the volume seeks to strengthen. This applies to the occupation of space, which is discussed or alluded to in the essays by Jones, Rossol, and Canning, and also to contests over space and its borders, which is a topic in Jens Boysen's contribution. It seems that here is a field that holds quite a bit of potential for research not only on the history of the revolution but also on the history of the Weimar Republic on the whole, based obviously on a concept of space not as a container but as a social and cultural construct, associated with different meanings and, not least, emotions by the various actors defining space. Hence, in addition to describing the presence of crowds in certain parts of urban space, their profile and behavior, the actions - or inaction - of security forces, and the reactions of observers to it, it would also be important to examine how in the course of revolutionary events crowds (and individuals) moved through urban space, how they used streets, buildings, neighborhoods, to what extent and how they ventured beyond paths usually taken and how urban space became endowed with new meaning in the process. This is relevant because the months since November 1918 were a time of intense mobilization, definitely in the cities, as not only crowds primarily drawn from the working classes made their appearance but as the middle classes soon also formed councils, staged demonstrations and their form of "strike" during the conflicts in a number of cities in the spring of 1919.

The deployment of security forces during these violent confrontations adds another element to this reordering of space. Whether or not those forces were familiar with the urban areas to which they were sent may have influenced their behavior there, in particular their readiness to use military force in a civilian environment not resembling the previous war zones in Western or Eastern Europe. There are good reasons to assume, as earlier studies have found, that the increasingly violent confrontations in many cities since the beginning of 1919 left a legacy of mutual enmity between middle and working classes. However, the novel perspective on space, combined with the history of everyday life, would promise a more nuanced picture of social relationships and imaginations connected with urban space in the revolutionary months of 1918/19. It would also be helpful in understanding the effects of the massive reoccupation of public space by supporters of the republic from various stripes in the demonstrations that were triggered in many places by the assassinations of Matthias Erzberger in 1921 and Walther Rathenau in 1922.

While space in German cities became contested in the course of the revolution, a similar development occurred with respect to Germany's borders, primarily, but not exclusively in the East. In his essay, Boysen emphasizes the contrast between an unsuspecting provisional government, led by an SPD that was bound by a legalistic mindset, and a Polish national movement that shrewdly used its chances to seize territory formally still belonging to the Germany for the newly established Polish state. Whatever the options of any German government may have been in this situation, placing these findings in a broader context with a culturally informed perspective on space helps clarifying the framework, within which the revolution unfolded in Germany. Following the armistice and the subsequent return of German soldiers from the vast occupied territory in Eastern Europe, holding the Eastern German boundary became a difficult task and remained so for several years, until in 1921 Upper Silesia finally was partitioned, following a plebiscite, and heavy fighting with Polish insurgents. Here in particular, national and ethnic identities were far from clear-cut, as many inhabitants in the region were bilingual, while sharing the same – Catholic – faith. This created a specifically harsh – and violent – contest between the German and the Polish camp. This violence and the overall insecurity of the Eastern border contributed to what Rüdiger Bergien has described as a "bellicist" consensus ranging from Social Democrats to German Nationals, manifesting itself in covert efforts to organize paramilitary forces that were to protect the borders. German sovereignty over space was marred in different form in the West, as Allied forces occupied the Rhineland following the armistice and stayed there through the 1920s. Here, perceived German weakness found one powerful expression –

again, displaying a consensus from the right to the moderate left – in the form of organized women's protests (by the Rhenish Women's League) against the deployment of soldiers from African colonies who allegedly transgressed norms of sexual behavior and thus posed a threat to the integrity of German women and the whole "national body". In sum, the perceived inability of Germans to control 'their' space properly prompted intense fears, created new demands for a militarized masculinity, and gave women a new public role, albeit in defense of traditional female tasks and virtues. These were aspects of the imaginary of masculinity and femininity that have to be taken into account in addition to the contrasting features of providing women with the right to vote, while dismissing them from many wartime jobs that Kathleen Canning describes in her essay.

The contributions to this volume explicitly place the German revolution in a transnational context. The war and its aftermath fostered social and political upheaval in many countries, even in those, as Florian Grafl shows for Spain, which were not among the belligerents. As far as the imaginary is concerned, the revolution in Germany right from the beginning was a transnational affair. While US President Woodrow Wilson's Fourteen Points triggered hopes for a fairly mild peace, the Bolshevik revolution and the civil war violence in its wake created both intense fears and great hopes, depending on the political position of the observer. In contrast, transnational networks of actors apparently were of lesser importance, at least at the heyday of revolutionary events in the fall and winter of 1918/19. Hence, while the papers on Spain and the USA in particular provide us with a comparative perspective, helping us not to see hysterical anti-Bolshevism as a German specificity and confirming that the breakdown of the state monopoly of violence tended to exacerbate political and social violence, it remains up to further research to determine the impact of developments in other countries on the revolution in Germany. For this purpose, it would be necessary to systematically study the media coverage of the revolutionary upheaval abroad and examine the imaginary of fear and hope used there as well as potential lessons articulated by German media with respect to domestic affairs.

The revolution, also given the inter- and transnational context in which it was unfolding, mobilized people and captured their attention with particular intensity, including writers and artists, as Ian Grimmer shows, who under other circumstances would have remained on the sidelines of politics. Still, and here the consequences of the war come into play again, not everybody participated and became interested in the political developments to the same degree. As the war came to an end, many returning soldiers as well as civilians sought to return to 'normality', meaning, above all, enjoying oneself and taking opportunity of a culture of leisure that now began emerging with full swing. The new eight-hour day, along with high employment, after an initial upsurge of the unemployment rate in the wake of demobilization, paved the way, as had, especially for those males too young to be sent to the military, the erosion of traditional authority during the war, due to the absence of schoolteachers and policemen who had served as soldiers. Especially for young people, the revolutionary months and immediate postwar years until the catastrophe of hyperinflation in 1923 therefore provided chances to take part in a blossoming mass culture in an unprecedented way. This is a dimension of everyday life that must not be overlooked but which usually gets lost when the revolution as a political event and process is discussed. It would probably be a mistake to draw a clear line between those engaged in politics and those interested in leisure, but political mobilization in the revolution could not be taken for granted. How it occurred would require, among others, analyzing how media and the various forms of publics operated and, again, taking a closer look at spatial settings.

About the Authors

Gleb J. Albert, postdoctoral researcher at the University of Zurich. His PhD thesis (Bielefeld 2014), is titled "The Charisma of World Revolution: Revolutionary Internationalism in Early Soviet Society, 1917-1927".
Among his most recent publications are: 'To help the Republicans not just by donations and rallies, but with the rifle': Militant Solidarity with the Spanish Republic in the Soviet Union, 1936–1937, in: European Review of History 2014/4, 501-518; 'Verehrte Komintern!'. Die Dritte Internationale als politisches Symbol und charismatische Institution im frühen Sowjetstaat, in: Jahrbuch für Historische Kommunismusforschung (2013), 17–38; 'German October is Approaching'. Internationalism, Activists, and the Soviet State in 1923, in: Revolutionary Russia (2011/2), 111-142.

Stefan Berger, Professor of Social History and the History of Social Movements at Ruhr-University Bochum, Director of the Institute of Social Movements and Executive Chair of the Foundation Library of the Ruhr. Among his most recent publications are: with Christoph Conrad, The Past as History. National History Writing in Modern Europe (Basingstoke, 2015), edited with Joana Seiffert, Erinnerungsorte: Historisierung eines Erfolgskonzepts in den Kulturwisssenschaften (Essen, 2014), edited with Bill Niven, Writing the History of Memory (London, 2013).

Jens Boysen, historian and political scientist, since December 2010 research fellow at the German Historical Institute in Warsaw.
Among his most recent publications are: Zwischen Nationalismus und Internationalismus. Zivil-militärische Beziehungen in den preußischen Ostprovinzen Posen und Westpreußen während des Ersten Weltkriegs, in: Alfred Eisfeld/ Guido Hausmann/Dietmar Neutatz (eds.), Besetzt, interniert, deportiert. Der Erste Weltkrieg und die deutsche, jüdische, polnische und ukrainische Zivilbe-

völkerung im östlichen Europa, Essen 2013, 127-151; A Denied Part of Modernity and a Denied Driver of Modernisation. Armed Forces and Civil-Military Relations in the Twentieth and Twenty-First Centuries, in: Ralph Schattkowsky/Adam Jarosz (eds.), Questions of Civil Society. Category-Position-Functionality, Cambridge 2013, 97-110; Die Polnische (Volks-) Armee in der (Volks-)Republik Polen (1943/44-1989/90), in: Heiner Möllers/ Rudolf J. Schlaffer (eds.), Sonderfall Bundeswehr? Streitkräfte in nationalen Perspektiven und im internationalen Vergleich, Munich 2014, 149-164.

Kathleen Canning, Sonya O. Rose Collegiate Professor and Arthur F. Thurnau Professor of History, Women's Studies and German at the University of Michigan.
She is author of "Languages of Labor and Gender (1996) and Gender History in Practice (2006)" and coeditor with Kerstin Barndt and Kristin McGuire of Weimar Publics/ Weimar Subjects: Rethinking the Political Culture of Germany in the 1920s (Berghahn 2010). She is also editor of the book series, "Social History, Popular Culture and Politics in Germany," published by the University of Michigan Press. Her current book project is entitled "Citizenship Effects. Gender and Sexual Crisis in the Aftermath of War and Revolution in Germany, 1916-1930."

Norma Lisa Flores, Visiting Assistant Professor of Modern European History at Grand Valley State University in Allendale, Michigan.
She completed her dissertation in 2012 entitled "When Fear is Substituted for Reason: European and Western Government Policies Regarding National Security 1789-1919."

Florian Grafl, PhD candidate, Giessen University.
Recent publications: A blueprint for successfully fighting anarchist terror? Counter-terrorist communities of violence in Barcelona during the pistolerismo, in: Jussi M. Hanhimäki/Bernhard Blumenau (eds.), An International History of Terrorism. Western and Non-western experiences, London etc. 2013, 51-64; "¡Deú nos en guardi, quins lladres!" - Urbane Gewalt in Barcelona zur Zeit der zweiten Republik, staatliche Interventionsversuche und die Reaktion der städtischen Akteure, in: Informationen zur Modernen Stadtgeschichte 2/2013, 31-42; Witzfiguren in der „Stadt der Bomben"? Charles Arrow und Joan Rull in den öffentlichen Diskursen Barcelonas zu Beginn des 20. Jahrhunderts, in: Christian Hoffstadt/Melanie Möller/Sabine Müller (eds.), Mord und Totlach, Bochum etc. 2014, 101-112.

Ian Grimmer, Senior Lecturer in Modern European Intellectual and Cultural History, University of Vermont.
He completed his Ph.D. at the University of Chicago with a dissertation titled "The Politics of Geist: German Intellectuals and Cultural Socialism, 1890-1920." His current research focuses on the group of intellectuals in German-speaking Central Europe associated with the idea of "Aktivismus".

Oliver Haller, Adjunct Lecturer at University of Waterloo. Among his most recent publications are: Germany's Western Front. Translations from the German Official History of the Great War, 1916 (forthcoming); Destroying Hitler's Berghof. The Bomber Command Raid of 25 April 1945, in: Canadian Military History 20 (2011), 5-20; German Industry, the Cold War, and the Bundeswehr, in: James S. Corum (ed.), Rearming Germany, Boston 2011, 145-176.

Kirsten Heinsohn, Associate Professor of German History at the University of Copenhagen (Department of English, German and Roman Studies).
Among her publications are: Konservative Parteien in Deutschland 1912 bis 1933. Demokratisierung und Partizipation in geschlechterhistorischer Perspektive (2010); Diaspora Identities. Exile, Nationalism and Cosmopolitanism in Past and Present (ed. with Susanne Lachenicht 2009).

Mark Jones, PhD, currently holds an Irish Research Council International Career Development Fellowship at University College Dublin and at the Free University of Berlin (IRC Elevate Fellowship supported by Marie Curie Actions).
His first book upon the German Revolution of 1918-19 will be published by Cambridge University Press. He was educated at Cambridge University, the University of Tübingen, and at Trinity College Dublin, where he graduated with a first class honours degree in History and Political Science placed first in his class. He completed his PhD at the European University Institute in Florence in 2011.

Anthony McElligott, Professor of History and Head of the Department of History, University of Limerick, Ireland. Elected a fellow of the Royal Historical Society in 1999 and Member of the Royal Irish Academy.
He has published widely on the Weimar Republic and the Third Reich. His most recent book is Rethinking the Weimar Republic: Authority and Authoritarianism, 1916-1936 (Bloomsbury Academic 2014). He is now working on a study of the Holocaust in the Eastern Aegean.

Nadine Rossol, PhD, Lecturer in Modern European History at the History Department of the University of Essex and Fellow of the Higher Education Academy.
Her current research project focuses on the German police from the 1920s to the 1950s. Among her publications are the book Performing the Nation in Interwar Germany 1926-1926 (Palgrave 2010), journal articles and chapters on political culture and festive staging in the Weimar Republic as well as the journal article Building Ideological Bridges and Inventing Institutional Traditions. Festivities and Commemorative Rituals in the Fascist and Nazi Police, with Jonathan Dunnage, in: Crime, History and Societies (forthcoming 2015).

Dirk Schumann, Professor of Modern and Contemporary History at Georg-August-University Göttingen.
Among his most recent publications are: edited with Cornelia Rauh, Ausnahmezustände. Entgrenzungen und Regulierungen in Europa während des Kalten Krieges (in press, Göttingen 2015); Post-war Societies (Germany), in: 1914-1918, online. International Encyclopedia of the First World War, ed. by Ute Daniel et al. (Berlin 2014); with Eberhard Kolb, Die Weimarer Republik (Munich 2013).

Klaus Weinhauer, Professor of Modern History at Bielefeld University.
Among his most recent publications are: Freedom of Choice? Drug Consumption in Germany and England from the 1960s to the 1980s (forthcoming, Palgrave Mcmillan); edited with Sylvia Schraut, Terrorism, Gender, and History since the 19th century (special issue of: Historical Social Research 39 (2014), No. 3); edited with Dagmar Ellerbrock, Stadt, Raum und Gewalt (Informationen zur modernen Stadtgeschichte 2/2013).